Bold as a Lion

The life of Bendigo - Champion of England

J.P. BEAN

D&D Publications

First published 2002 by
D&D Publications
PO Box 225
Sheffield S11 7DD

ISBN 0-9507645-2-3

Layout by Steve France

Printed by Hi-Tec Print,
Dinnington, South Yorkshire

Contents

Cover picture:-
Ben Caunt tries to strangle Bendigo in their third fight, 1845.

(From *Famous Fights Past and Present*
Police Budget Edition)

Acknowledgements

Thanks to:

Ken Campbell, Dave Hill and Andy Andrews, whose musical *Bendigo – the Little Known Facts* sowed a seed that took more than twenty-five years to germinate.

Mary Croft, for her invaluable assistance in researching Bendigo's family background.

Brendan Ingle, who trains boxers in a way that Bendigo would have approved, for insight and inspiration.

Dick Johnson, ex-boxer and author of two books on the prize ring.

Graham Rooksby, Secretary of Nottingham Ex-boxers Association.

Cyril Gibbons, for the fight records of Bendigo's opponents.

James Morton, author and lawyer, for advice and encouragement.

Christopher Roden of the Arthur Conan Doyle Society, Canada

The staff of Nottingham Local Studies Library; Nottingham University Hallwood Library; Nottinghamshire Archives; Liverpool Local Studies Library; Sheffield City Reference, Lending and Local Studies Libraries; Sheffield City Archives; Leicestershire Record Office and the British Newspaper Library at Colindale.

As always, my family and friends.

J.P.Bean
Sheffield, 2002

Bold Bendigo - Champion of England

Prologue - Hats in the Ring

At twenty minutes past three on a sweltering afternoon in July 1845, two men faced each other in a field at Lillingstone Level, on the Oxfordshire and Buckinghamshire border. William Thompson, known to all as Bendigo, was a jocular fellow of thirty-four. If his round, mischievous face bore little evidence of thirteen years in the prize ring, his muscular body suggested he possessed considerable strength. But standing five feet ten inches and weighing slightly over twelve stones, at the side of the giant before him he looked small. Ben Caunt, aged thirty, was six feet three inches tall. To get down to a fighting weight of fourteen stones he had sweated and trained like no mortal man should. His face wore the scars of earlier battles and, while Bendigo was relaxed and cheerful, Caunt was tense and surly.

Bendigo and Caunt were about to fight for the championship of England, a contest long awaited by both men and their followers. Twice before they had met, with each claiming one victory, but the outcome of both those fights had been contentious - and the results hotly disputed. There was no love lost between the fighters. Caunt resented Bendigo's cocky attitude, his shifty way of fighting and the presence at the ringside of his supporters - a lawless gang of cudgel-wielding thugs known as the Nottingham Lambs. Bendigo, the superior boxer despite his height and weight disadvantages, dismissed Caunt as a "big, chuckle-headed navvy" who was fortunate to be sharing the same ring.

Fifteen thousand spectators were packed around the roped-off, twenty-four foot square of turf on which Bendigo and Caunt would do battle. From all over England they had come to see the fight; many by excursion trains on the newly-built railways. The wealthy arrived by horse and carriage, now parked in prime positions to afford a good view. These were the Corinthians of the prize ring, the nobility and gentry and the men directly associated with pugilism – collectively known as the Fancy. Others came by gig, trap and cart. The rest, the ordinary fans, there to support their hometown man, arrived on foot, trudging long miles over several days, sleeping in barns or under hedges along the dusty country roads. No one could doubt their commitment.

The illegality of prize fighting meant that the location had been kept secret until as late as possible. Thus the assembled thousands gathered in the morning at the village of Wolverton, the nearest railway station, and tramped ten miles to Whaddon where a ring was set up. Once there, they heard that a constable had warned Bendigo and Caunt that they could not fight in the county of Buckinghamshire, and so the whole crowd had been obliged to walk or ride another eight miles over the border into Oxfordshire, to this field at Lillingstone Level.

At the ringside were swell coves in toppers, cravats and Newgate knockers;[1] frock-coated young bloods from the universities; pot-bellied publicans in their finest waistcoats; truculent butchers; stockingmen and hosiers come down from Nottingham to cheer Bendigo; farmhands and blacksmiths who had laid their last pound on Caunt. It was as colourful a gathering of Victorian society as was ever seen in one place, with the underworld, always close to the sporting world, widely represented. The crush and confusion of a major prize fight brought golden opportunities for the gonoph and dipper,[2] whose long, dextrous fingers would relieve many a wealthy spectator of his pocket watch or wallet before the day was done.

The noise of the crowd was deafening. Odds were offered and bets laid; Bendigo's followers yelled encouragement at him and abuse at Ben Caunt, whose partisans responded in like manner. As the crowd surged and heaved, everyone struggled to be better placed to see the action when it began. There was pushing and shoving and frayed tempers under the blazing sun. Arguments broke out and blows were exchanged. In the inner ring, a twelve-yard area around the twenty four-foot roped square, where only privileged spectators and the two umpires and referee were permitted, the Nottingham Lambs had taken over. Disciplined in their disorderliness, they had already established their own enclosure for those willing to buy a ticket at between one and five shillings, depending on the customer's purse. Now the ring officials – ex-pugilists and London bruisers themselves, and armed with horse-whips – were powerless to stop them moving closer. Bludgeons swinging, the Lambs were at the ropes of the prize ring itself, to be on hand to cheer their man Bendigo, and to lend assistance should he require it during the fight.

---

[1] Pronounced whiskers, sideburns
[2] Pickpockets

Bendigo and Caunt brought huge cheers from the crowd when they announced their arrival in the ring in the time-honoured manner, by hurling their hats into the air as they climbed through the ropes. They tossed a coin to choose corners and their respective colours – orange for Caunt, blue with a white spot for Bendigo– were tied to their corner posts, where their seconds stood with the water, buckets, towels and brandy that might be necessary to revive the men in between rounds. Bendigo raised laughs all round when he pulled a wad of banknotes from his pocket and offered a £50 side bet to Caunt, who grimly declined. All seemed ready for the fight to commence but then an argument broke out between the rival corners over the choice of referee and there was further delay until a sporting squire whose carriage was parked close by could be reluctantly pressed into action.

At last the fighters removed the greatcoats that had protected them from the sun. The moment had finally come for them to walk to the scratched line in the centre of the ring and to begin the battle. Tensions that had risen relentlessly during the preceding hours finally crackled and snapped in the afternoon heat as, stripped to the waist and wearing knee-breeches, long stockings and spiked boots, the two fighters came together in combat. On the ropes was a banner with the inscription "Caunt and Bendigo, for £200 and the Championship of England. 9th September 1845. May the best man win."

1] The Boy Bendigo

Bendigo always claimed he was a triplet, the last in a family of twenty-one children and born on the 11th of October 1811 in Nottingham. His father, Benjamin Thompson, was - he said - one of the most celebrated mechanics in the Midland counties, a man who could tap and screw an egg and the inventor of the modern nut-cracker. His mother possessed more earthy talents. Known for her singing in taverns as well as her fine moustache and her stomach powders, Mary Thompson, according to legend, smoked a pipe and had a powerful right hand. She passed on this gift to her youngest son at an early age, teaching him to fight in the southpaw style. If he came home and said he'd been beaten in a fight she made him go out and beat the other boy, or if he did not he would get a thrashing from her. She encouraged him throughout his career in the prize ring and it was her goading that brought him out of retirement at the age of thirty-eight, to fight for the championship one last time.

Born William Thompson, his real name featured rarely in report or conversation. As champion of England, hero of the infamous Nottingham Lambs and – much later - as a hellfire-and-damnation evangelist, he was known simply as Bendigo. Even in court, where he was hauled up for fighting and drunkenness a reputed twenty-eight times, magistrates addressed him by the nickname that he had borne since childhood. When he died *The Times* printed an obituary headed "Death of Bendigo" without mention of William Thompson. And as to how he came to be called Bendigo, like so many aspects of his life, explanations range from the exotic to the erratic.

In the most popular version, Bendigo is derived from Abednego - as in Shadrach, Mesach and Abednego - who, in the Old Testament, were thrown into the fiery furnace by King Nebuchadnezzar. Being a triplet, the young William Thompson is said to have identified with the third of this unfortunate trio.

The first documented reference to the nickname was in *Bell's Life in London*, the chronicle of the prize ring, on 12th January 1834, when it was reported that a Liverpool man, Bill Looney, was prepared to make a match with "Abednego" for £50 or £100 a side, to fight half way between Liverpool and Nottingham. Nothing came of this particular challenge, nor one made the following month in the same pages, which stated "William Thompson, alias Bendigo, is open to fight George Weston of Fazely". A year later, when he fought Ben Caunt for the first time, *Bell's Life* referred to him as "Abednego of Nottingham", but by the time of his next contest Abednego was corrupted to Bendigo, as it would remain for the rest of his life.

Much later, a more prosaic explanation was offered in a publication by a Nottingham printer, Ishmael Wilson. In a booklet that claims to be autobiographical, *Life, Battles, Conversion and Death of Bendigo, Champion of England*, first published in 1889 and priced at one penny, Bendigo is quoted:

> "The reason of my going in the name of 'Bendigo' was, when I was a boy, and was sent on errands by my parents, I used to stay out for hours and sometimes all day and night, and when my father came to find me, he would see me either fighting or playing in the streets, and when my pals used to see my father coming to fetch me they would say, Bendy, go, your father is coming; thus my name, Bendigo, originated from those circumstances."

Hardly illuminating, but whatever the truth – and the language of this account is unlikely for a rough and ready, illiterate prize fighter – Bendigo, or on occasion Bendy, it would be.

But if there is little conclusive evidence as to his nickname, there is none at all to confirm that he was a triplet. He begins the above account "According to the Register of St Mary's Church I was born on the 11th October, 1811 . . ." In fact, the register gives no date of birth, only the date on which Richard and William Thompson, twin sons of Benjamin and Mary Thompson, were baptised – the 16th October. While Bendigo maintained that he was a triplet and that the third child died soon after birth, he never explained what became of the second brother, Richard – but the St Mary's register reveals that he too died in infancy, on 28th October 1811, only twelve days after being baptised.[3] Whether Bendigo

[3] If there was a third child, he or she clearly died before baptism and would thus not have been buried according to the rites of the Church of England. As Bendigo's birth date was prior to the Parochial Registers Act, 1812, there would be no other registration of the third child's death.

was a triplet or a twin, his life would be one of individual achievement, for nowhere was a man more the master of his own destiny than in the prize ring.

Nottingham town centre, where Bendigo was born and grew up in New Yard, off Parliament Street, was a turbulent place to live in the early years of the 19th Century. Once one of the most pleasant towns in England, industrialisation had turned it into a slum. The population rose from 11,000 in 1750 to 29,000 in 1800 and it continued to rise until by 1830 there were 50,000 people, half of them on poor relief. The town had a reputation for radical politics and a populace that expressed itself through mob violence at little or no provocation, especially at election times. Meetings held in the Market Place, only a few hundred yards from Bendigo's childhood home, provided excellent opportunities for those inclined towards mayhem, in particular a large and violent band of thugs known as the Nottingham Lambs. Their later presence at Bendigo's fights was guaranteed to enliven events outside – and sometimes inside –the ring.

The Nottingham Lambs were a force to be reckoned with, wherever they went. Their origins are believed to lie in the Second Battalion of the 45th Regiment of Foot of the Sherwood Foresters. Why they were called Lambs is unclear – possibly the name refers to the hosiery trade in which many of the original members were employed in civilian life. Or maybe it derived from their propensity for violence and the slang word 'lamb', meaning to beat or thrash.

According to the recollections of elderly townspeople as published in local papers much later,[4] in wartime the Lambs were a great asset to the British Army. They were said to be trusted and admired by the Duke of Wellington, who, according to Lamb lore, on one occasion owed his escape from capture to some of their number. In peacetime, they were the terror of Nottingham and far beyond. Ruffians, scoundrels, brawlers and boozers, they were the archetypal 'unruly element'. The Lace City was their home ground, but they colonised the ringside at prize fights and were despised and feared in equal measures by all whom they fell upon.

Bendigo became the Lambs' unofficial leader, their hero whom they followed to battle and gave their undying support. To him they were firm friends and fellow spirits. He could depend on the Lambs to intimidate opponents and rival supporters; they bet on him to win and, with one

---

[4] See Scrapbook xlll page 83 in Nottinghamshire Local Studies Library, cuttings dated ca 1920

exception when he was disqualified, went home in profit. That their support reflected badly on him with the prize ring authorities and the press did not trouble him. Bendigo never criticised the Lambs' behaviour no matter what their depredations. They were his people.

Generations of Nottingham Lambs could always be guaranteed to stir up trouble at election times. They did not follow any individual political leader or party; they were available for hire by whoever offered the most cash or ale. Seventeen riots took place in Nottingham between 1780 and 1799 and the Lambs were usually in the thick. People were seriously assaulted, windows smashed and property wrecked. So lawless was the town that, as the British government took precautions against the spread of possible unrest following the French Revolution, the first barracks to be located in the provinces was built in Nottingham Park, in 1793. Three years later an election candidate was chased out of the town and along the Derby road by a mob. On other occasions candidates were jostled, had their pockets picked and were prevented from entering the Exchange Hall to attend their nominations. Every election until 1812, the year after Bendigo was born, had some element of violent conflict. Later, in 1831, parliamentary reform riots led to the burning of Nottingham Castle, an event regarded by many in the town as one of the great moments in Nottingham reactionary history.

To add to the unrest around the time of Bendigo's arrival in the world, Luddite riots had erupted in the town only a few months earlier, as workers in the hosiery industry – along with lace making, the main source of employment in Nottingham - protested at the new machinery that had laid them off. Thousands of red coated troops were mobilised to the town and a contingent of Bow Street Runners was sent from London. Food riots broke out, too, as the price of flour and bread soared.

But despite the turmoil, the unemployment and the desperate lack of money, Nottingham's publicans were doing good business; in 1799 there were 156 public houses in the town, a figure that had risen to 182 by 1815. On just one side of Long Row, a town centre thoroughfare, there were seventeen inns and taverns. Drink was an escape, albeit a temporary one, from the harsh demands of exploitative labour and the crowded discomfort of the slums.

Number 20, New Yard, was a three-storey brick tenement in a cobbled alley, barely five yards wide and fifty yards long. Three steps led from narrow pavement to the door. At other houses in the street, since re-named Trinity Walk, lived chimney-sweeps, saw-sharpeners, and a cane chair-mender. The building where Bendigo first saw the light of day was redeveloped in the 1970s. Today an estate agent's office stands on the site and the only reminder of its history is a plaque on the wall:

"Bendigo"
William Abednego
Thompson
was born here
1811

Life was hard. Poverty and squalor were the fate of the working classes and they could do little about it. Education was the privilege of the wealthy and boys like Bendigo did not go school. Instead he roamed the neighbourhood, a ragged street urchin who ran wild with juvenile gangs from nearby York Street, Coalpit Lane and Meadow Place. They fought in the yards and back alleys, preyed on weaker children sent by their mothers to buy bread, begged on the pavements and stayed out of their overcrowded, uncomfortable homes for as long as possible. Need brought about a curious morality, as he would later explain: "When I was a boy and up to the time when I was a young fellow, my life was a rough 'un, and if I saw any chap eating and I was hungry I'd take his grub away from him. . . but I never would what you might call steal anything."[5]

For Bendigo, a lively, spirited boy, it was a life without complaint. Naturally athletic, he could run, jump, scuffle and fight with the best. On fine days he went fishing in the River Trent, a pastime he would follow with great enthusiasm all his life. The poverty of his family doubtless did not trouble him, for he had never known anything different. Most of all he enjoyed a great degree of freedom. That freedom was to end suddenly. In October, 1827, a week before Bendigo's sixteenth birthday, his father died suddenly in the Kings Head public house on Chapel Bar, just a few hundred yards from home.

In the Bendigo legend, details of Benjamin Thompson's life are sketchy. Bendigo said that his father moved to Nottingham from London, where he had served an apprenticeship as a cabinet-maker, that he married his mother soon after arriving in the town and that they had twenty-one children, of which he was the youngest. In old age he would recall how his father "had a bit of a turn for science, and he had a big telescope. He used sometimes to let me look through it and I liked it. He used to talk

[5] See, James Greenwood, *Low Life Deeps*. Chatto & Windus, 1881

Bendigo's birthplace – New Yard, off Parliament Street, Nottingham

about the starry heavens to me, and point out Wenus and the Great Bear and Jupiter . . . they looked so beautiful through the telescope."[6]

Bendigo probably never knew the full extent of his father's "turn for science". A man of exceptional skills, he achieved nation-wide recognition as a toolmaker and is credited with inventing the bobbin-and-carriage used on the lace-making machines developed by John Levers, a seminal figure in the history of the Nottingham lace industry. Benjamin Thompson was born at Groby, a hamlet in Leicestershire and was apprenticed to a chemist in London by a wealthy uncle.[7] Later he became acquainted with the celebrated optician John Dolland and learned from him how to make telescopes and microscopes.

Benjamin left London in mysterious circumstances, which caused his uncle to disown him, arriving in Nottingham in the late 1780s or early 90s. There he quickly found employment. According to William Felkin, Benjamin Thompson was renowned for his skills as "a brass turner, an optician, a maker of prismatic division lathes and of various curious and useful instruments."[8] He was said to be able to make a complete optical instrument single-handedly - smelting, fusing and purifying the metals; turning in wood, iron, brass and ivory; grinding the object glasses, making the slides and assembling the parts. When a flute was required by the Prince Regent for presentation to a foreign visitor, the musical instrument maker who was given the order enlisted Benjamin Thompson, who went to London to complete the work.

Ingenious craftsman as he was, Bendigo's father did not reap financial reward for his work. Others gave their names to machines and innovations and obtained the patents. Unfortunately, Benjamin Thompson had a fondness for ale and low company and his independent nature caused him to be seen as unreliable. In the words of William Felkin, "He had great but misdirected talents, and his careless habits were manifestly inconsistent with the comforts of home and well-being of his family."

When Benjamin Thompson died, he left his widow, Mary, destitute. The only child remaining at home was Bendigo and they had moved from New Yard to Cross Street. Without even the meagre earnings that

---

[6] ibid.

[7] See William Felkin, *History of the Machine-Wrought Hosiery and Lace Manufactures*. David & Charles 1967 (Centenary Edition). Felkin makes no reference of Benjamin Thompson being a cabinet maker and does not appear to have been aware that he was the father of Bendigo. The date of Benjamin's birth is unclear: his burial certificate in 1827 states he died aged 67, which means he was born in 1760. At that time no church existed at Groby, Benjamin's birthplace, but a Benjamin, son of John and Rebeccah Thompson, was baptised on the 26th September 1770 in the adjoining parish of Glenfield.

[8] Ibid.

Benjamin brought home when he deemed to work, rather than drink, they were forced out of their home and into the Nottingham Union – better known as the workhouse. The twenty-one weeks that Bendigo spent there had a profound effect on him, one that he would never forget.

Grim, squalid, insanitary and verminous, the workhouse was the last stop for people who had nothing. More overcrowded than even the homes they had been forced to leave, the inmates lived huddled together and were kept alive on basic rations, working long hours for their shelter. Bendigo hated this wretched existence but his natural spirit and the sly cunning that would serve him well in the Prize Ring soon came to the fore. He was put to work grinding corn in a hand mill. The corn was poured into a hopper at the top and he was expected to grind it by turning the handle all day, but he soon worked out that it was much easier to turn the wheel backwards and let the corn drop through, whole and unground. The ploy was soon detected and he was punished by further deprivation of the already meagre rations. After just over five months Bendigo and his mother somehow managed to secure their discharge from the workhouse and he vowed that neither of them would ever return.

When he was older, Bendigo often said that he took up pugilism to keep his mother out of the workhouse. The close relationship she had with him appears to have been irrevocably strengthened by their joint experience at this time, but a question that cannot be answered is: why was he admitted to the workhouse at the age of sixteen. In later years, while making no mistake about his age at the time his father died, he implied that until then he had never worked – unusual when children hardly out of infancy were being exploited and subjected to all manner of inhumanity for a few pence a day. No records for the Nottingham Union have survived and we have only his word – which has been proven in other respects to be unreliable - that he and his mother were admitted. It is odd that such a strong, fit sixteen-year old was not able to work to provide for his mother and himself.

Another puzzle is what had happened to his older brothers and sisters and why did none of them take in their mother and younger brother? Bendigo only ever made reference to one of his brothers, John, two years older, who later became a successful optician and businessman in Nottingham. For many years after Bendigo's death, the Nottingham newspapers printed occasional anecdotes by people who had known him in his lifetime, but none gave any clues as to any other brothers or sisters.

The registers of births, marriages and deaths in the parish of St Mary's, Nottingham provide some details of Bendigo's family history and it is more complicated than the hitherto accepted story. In that account, his father, Benjamin, moved from London, met and married his mother, Mary, they had twenty-one children of whom Bendigo was the youngest and Mary Thompson died aged eighty-two or eighty-four. In fact Benjamin and Mary did not marry until 1805 and if, when she died she really was eighty-two as stated on her burial certificate,[9] then she married at the age of thirty-three.

Mary was not Benjamin Thompson's first wife. On 10th December 1792 he had married Sarah Wheldon at St Mary's Church and their first child, Rebecca, born at an address stated as "Accdy Court" was baptised on 25th August the following year. Four more children – John, Benjamin, Sarah and Patty - were baptised at two-year intervals and at least three of them died before their second birthday. In early 1803 Benjamin was left a widower, when his wife Sarah died. She was buried on 3rd February 1803.

Two years later Benjamin married again. His bride was Mary Levers, said to be the niece of John Levers, for whom he had worked on developing the lace-making machine. Mary was six months pregnant as she walked down the aisle at St Mary's on 12th July 1805. Their first child was baptised on 11th October, the parents' address stated as New Street – probably New Yard - where his first wife, Sarah had died. Like the first child born to his late wife, Mary's first was also named Rebecca, followed again at two year intervals by Thomas, another John and then the twins, Richard and William. Although Bendigo always claimed to be the "youngest of twenty-one children", a younger sister, Mary, was born in January 1815. He was nearly seven years old when she died in July 1818.

The sum total of the children of John Thompson's two marriages who were baptised is eleven, a figure far short of that which Bendigo so often quoted. Of course, it is feasible that in an age of high infant mortality rates ten babies died at birth or before they could be baptised. Alternatively, either or both parent might have had children by previous but untraceable marriages. However many survived beyond childhood, only John, born two years before him, was to figure in Bendigo's adult life.

---

[9] At this time – 1854 - there were no documents, i.e. birth certificates, that would confirm the age of deceased. The age stated would have been that given by relatives. Bendigo referred to his mother being "nearly eighty" in 1850 but the Census of 1841 shows her living with his brother John Thompson at Pelham Street, Nottingham and her age is given as 60. According to the Census of 1851 she was lodging in Milk Square, aged 70. Her address at the time of death was stated to be Milk Street. By this reckoning she was twenty four when she married Bendigo's father in 1805.

According to Bendigo's own account, he went into the workhouse a boy and came out a man. To earn money for himself and his mother, he took up hawking oysters on the pavements and in the town pubs. Soon, his brother John found him a job with his own employer, a local iron turner. He moved on from there, out of the town centre to nearby Radford, where he worked for a spell at Smith's Machinists. His life was starting to take the same direction of any typical young man in the developing industrial towns of the 1820s. But Bendigo's destiny was not to be typical in any way. He never rose above the class to which he was born – he probably would not have wished to – but he escaped the clinging, claustrophobic demands of humdrum work and became famous and feted throughout the land.

Bendigo was a natural sportsman. In Ishmael Wilson's booklet, he says:

> "In my juvenile days I was constantly engaged in all sorts of athletic sports; I was also passionately attached to Fishing, for which I was considered a first rate hand. I have also been noted for Cock fighting, Badger Baiting, Running, Somersaulting, Cricket & c. I have lobbed a stone 200 yards and a cricket ball, 5 ½ oz, I have lobbed 115 yards."

He goes on to detail some of his more celebrated achievements with fishing rod and cricket ball, before stating "When I was a youth I became a boxer of notoriety . . . " His use of the word "notoriety" is interesting, reflecting society's attitude towards illegal prize fighting.

At the time that Bendigo was growing up, Nottingham was a stronghold of bare knuckle fighting. Sparring with the 'muffs' – large padded gloves - went on at several public houses patronised by the local Fancy. They held meetings at the Lion and Unicorn, where the landlord, a man named Jephson, had furnished and decorated his parlour to resemble that in the London hostelry of the great former champion, Tom Cribb. At the Foresters Arms, St Ann Street, ex-pugilist Ned Maltby kept house, while the landlord of the Butcher's Arms on Newcastle Street was Bill Broadhead, who became known as 'The Father of Nottingham Boxing'.

Bouts were fought on Nottingham Racecourse, Bagthorpe Common, Breaston Fields, Bluebell Hill and sometimes at the annual Goose Fair. In Bendigo's early days one of the best local fighters was the middleweight, Sam Turner, who became his mentor, trainer and friend. Born in 1802 and, unlike many pugilists, a man who had a trade – he was a glove maker - Turner began his ring career in 1820. In his early days he was known as the Bluecoat Boy Champion on account of his education at the local Bluecoat School. Sam Turner retired in 1830 but ten years later made a comeback at the age of thirty-eight. When he was almost fifty, on a trip to London with Bendigo, he offered to fight any man in the world for a purse of £100. There were no takers.

Another popular Nottingham middleweight was Dick Hill. He was eighteen when he got the sack from his job in an engineering forge for taking a day off to attend the boxing booth at the Goose Fair. A year later, 1826, saw his first appearance in the prize ring and he beat all before him until he fell victim to consumption at the age of twenty-two. During his illness he had two more bouts – one of sixty-six rounds lasting one and three quarter hours and the second of sixty-nine rounds. He lost both and died at the age of thirty.

There were other Nottingham men before Bendigo whose exploits in and out of the ring made them local celebrities in an age when celebrity was rare. Of John Shaw, a Life Guardsman, it was said that he would surely have become champion of England had he not been killed at Waterloo in 1815. His bravery was commemorated in verse by Sir Walter Scott.[10] Bill Atkinson, who lost to Dick Hill in a sixty-four round fight that lasted two and a quarter hours, was known as the Nottingham Pet on account of his snappy dress and reputation as a ladies' man. He married the daughter of a clergyman, but the marriage was ill-fated and his wife died in a lunatic asylum after less than two years of wedlock.

Bendigo learned from watching these men as they trained and sparred in the pub gyms and did battle in the neighbourhood against other fighters – coal miners, gypsies, soldiers, blacksmiths, anyone with backers who would put up the money. When the fairs came to town he made for the boxing booth where his speed and natural punching power proved too much for the resident bruisers. He fought youths and men in the streets and at the age of sixteen, soon after leaving the workhouse, he had his first fight for money. "That was my first set-to," he recalled, years later. "It was for a purse, a collection made amongst the crowds on Selston-common and offered, for the sport of the thing, to any two lads who would fight for it. I fought and won it."[11]

He continued to spar with experienced fighters, all the time honing his skills and developing the style that would excite crowds and frustrate

---

[10] *Paul's Letters to his Kinfolk*

[11] James Greenwood, *Low Life Deeps*. Chatto&Windus, 1876

every opponent who faced him. He was keen, fast and cunning. His name was being spoken in the inns and taverns as a young man to look out for. The pugilists and publicans of the Fancy, the gonophs and pickpockets who hung around fairgrounds and prize fights, the cockfighters and badger-baiters and that ruffianly band known as the Nottingham Lambs – they liked the look of young William Thompson. He was one of their own.

And so in 1832, Bendigo gave up his job at Smith's Machinists in Radford. He turned his back on the debilitating daily grind of exploitative labour. It was time to strike out in the world on his own account, time to carve out a career. He made his debut in the prize ring.

2] The Prize Ring

By the time Bendigo began to make his name as a pugilist in the mid-1830s, the prize ring had lost much of the glamour it had enjoyed in earlier decades. Many of the wealthy aristocrats and fashionable men about town, known in sporting circles at the time as Corinthians, had found other pastimes. Deterred by deaths in the ring and – of more concern to them as betting men - by allegations of fixed fights, they sought new ways to gamble away their family fortunes. The lustre had faded from a sport that only two decades earlier was patronised by the future King George IV and his brothers. Now the ring was in slow but steady decline, with the ruffianly element more in evidence and the magistrates and new police force becoming increasingly reluctant to turn a blind eye, as they had so often in the past.

The history of English prize ring begins in the early 18th Century with James Figg, who in 1719 claimed the title of Champion Bare-Knuckle Fighter of England. Figg originated from Thame in Oxfordshire and was an expert in the martial arts of his time. Boxing with bare knuckles was but one of his talents; he was known equally for his prowess with the cudgel, quarter-staff and short stave, as well as his swordsmanship and fencing. Prize fighting in Figg's day bore little resemblance to modern boxing; wrestling and throwing were allowed, as was gouging an opponent's eyes, kicking him and attempting to strangle him. In James Figg's most famous contest, which was held in a tiled booth on the bowling green at Southwark, he fought Ned Sutton, a pipe maker from Gravesend. Sutton picked Figg up and threw him from the ring. Figg replied by slamming Sutton to the floor, kneeing him in the stomach and forcing him to yield with an armlock.

James Figg defeated a queue of challengers "for money, love or a bellyfull" during his eleven years reign as champion, which ended with his retirement in 1731. He began his fighting career in the fairgrounds around London, but his reputation in what was an up-and-coming sport soon brought him friends among the gentry, who backed him when he opened the first indoor boxing arena on Tottenham Court Road. Figg's 'amphitheatre', as it was known, was a cross between a fairground booth and a theatre. Here, he taught "the noble science of defence" to wealthy Corinthians. He was patronised by an exclusive clientele. His friend William Hogarth engraved a business card for him and the price of admission for fights in which Figg was involved was fixed at a level way beyond the ordinary working man - two shillings and sixpence,[12] compared to the three pence they would have paid to watch a day's cricket.

James Figg

Figg's finest pupil was Jack Broughton, who, on the champion's retirement, beat all other aspirants to claim the title. Broughton was no Corinthian, he was a waterman who rowed people on the Thames before making a name for himself as a fighter. In 1743, he opened his own amphitheatre in what is now Oxford Street. It was a spacious venue with private boxes, a gallery and a pit for the less well-heeled. Broughton concentrated on pugilism, rather than cudgelling or the other fighting sports which his predecessor had favoured. He was a fine wrestler and

[12] Twelve-and-a-half pence in decimal currency – at that time more than a day's wages for a working man.

more than ready to indulge in gouging or throttling, but he realised that striking with the clenched fist was a potent weapon, especially in the damage it could cause to the face.

Two years before he opened his academy, Broughton fought a tough battle against George Stevenson, a coachman from Yorkshire. Stevenson had beaten all before him up north. He was persuaded to travel to London to challenge Broughton and was backed by the Prince of Wales – whose brother the Duke of Cumberland was Broughton's backer. They fought in a booth at the fairground on Tottenham Court Road, but Broughton had not prepared as well he might due to illness. Nevertheless he won the bout after trapping his foe in an armlock and giving him a terrible beating which left the coachman unconscious and with broken ribs. Stevenson never made it back to Yorkshire; he died a month later.

Jack Broughton was troubled by the death of George Stevenson, caused by injuries he had inflicted. In an attempt to try to avoid such a tragedy happening again, soon after opening his amphitheatre he resolved to bring some semblance of order to the sport of pugilism by drawing up a set of rules of combat for fights within his establishment.

The Rules - "for the better regulation of the Amphitheatre; approved of by the Gentlemen, and agreed by the Pugilists, August 10, 1743" - read:

1. That a square of a yard be chalked in the middle of the stage; and every fresh set-to after a fall, or being parted from the rails, each second is to bring his man to the side of the square, and place him opposite to the other, and till they are fairly set to at the lines, it shall be not be lawful for the one to strike the other.
2. That in order to prevent any disputes, the time a man lies after a fall, if the second does not bring his man to the side of the square within the space of half a minute, he shall be deemed a beaten man.
3. That in every main battle, no person whatever shall be upon the stage, except the principals and their seconds; the same rule to be observed in by-battles, except that in the latter, Mr Broughton is allowed to be upon the stage to keep decorum, and to assist gentlemen to get their places; provided always, he does not interfere in the battle; and whoever pretends to

infringe these rules, to be turned immediately out of the house. Everybody is to quit the stage as soon as the champions are stripped, before they set-to.

4. That no champion be deemed beaten unless he fails coming up to the line in the limited time; or, that his own second declares him beaten. No second is to be allowed to ask his man's adversary any questions, or advise him to give out.
5. That in by-battles, the winning man to have two thirds of the money given, which shall be publicly divided upon the stage, notwithstanding any private agreements to the contrary.
6. That to prevent disputes, in every main battle, the principals shall, on the coming on the stage, choose from among the gentlemen present, two umpires, who shall absolutely decide all disputes that may arise about the battle; and if the two umpires cannot agree, the said umpires to choose a third, who is to determine it.
7. That no person is to hit his adversary when he is down, or seize him by the ham, the breeches, or any part below the waist; a man on his knees to be reckoned down.

The rules were intended primarily for the fights within Jack Broughton's establishment, but they soon became adopted universally by the prize ring. The rules were a basic attempt to impose regularity and fair play, although there was no mention of gouging, kicking or attempting to strangle. They stood unchallenged and without revision for the next ninety-five years. When they were eventually replaced in 1838, the first championship fight to be held under the new London Prize Ring Rules was that between Bendigo and Deaf Burke.

Jack Broughton became known as the 'Father of Boxing'. He developed a range of punches at a time when pugilists slugged at each other with little technique. He taught "persons of quality" to box at his house in the Haymarket, where he introduced padded mufflers to protect the hands and facial features of his pupils. Stuffed with wool and padding, these early examples of what would become modern boxing gloves widened the appeal of the sport in London society. Broughton enjoyed the patronage of the Duke of Cumberland, who, two years after backing him in his amphitheatre venture, wrote his own name in the history books by defeating the army of Bonny Prince Charlie at Culloden in 1745.

Jack Broughton

Broughton's reign as champion ended in 1750 at the hands of Jack Slack, a Norwich butcher who first insulted and then challenged him after a dispute at Hounslow Races. With an excess of confidence brought about by his status as champion, Broughton did not prepare as he should have done, believing his opponent would back out. The night before the fight he sent Slack ten sovereigns to ensure he turned up. Slack did turn up and, despite being 10-1 underdog, beat Broughton after only fourteen minutes with a punch between the eyes that temporarily blinded him. The Duke of Cumberland, who had wagered £10,000 on the champion winning, declared at ringside, "What are you about, Broughton? You can't fight, you're beat." The stricken fighter replied, " I can't see my man, your Highness. I am blind but not beat. Only let me be placed before my antagonist and he shall not gain the day yet." Slack did gain the day, to the disgust of the Duke of Cumberland, who was convinced – albeit wrongly - that Broughton had sold the fight. Within weeks his amphitheatre was closed and Broughton never fought again.

It was to be over thirty years before the prize ring had another outstanding champion. Broughton's conqueror Jack Slack, although a hard hitter, was an unattractive character who, when his reign as champion ended, became a trainer with a reputation for fixing fights. The closure of Broughton's premises, through pressure exerted on the magistracy by the Duke of Cumberland, meant the prize ring was driven outdoors. No longer was there a school or academy where up-and-coming young men could be coached by a tutor with the skills of a Figg or a Broughton. In London, fights were now held at places like Tothill Fields, Moorfields and The Hollow at Islington – long associated with low class sports like cock throwing.[13] Even here the magistrates exerted a new-found vigilance, with the effect that locations in the provinces became more and more popular. On the heaths and open spaces around Birmingham and Bath, and on racecourses at Ascot Heath, Maidenhead and Doncaster, local magistrates were less inclined to interfere.

Law enforcement at this time was still in the hands of the magistracy. It would be some years before police forces were introduced to the cities and towns. The usual method of attempting to suppress organised fights was for the local justice to arrive at the scene, often accompanied by the parish constable, and to read the Riot Act to the assembled throng. The respect for authority prevalent at the time, which seems remarkable by modern standards, meant that the crowd would almost always comply with the order and move on. For this reason many fights were located close to county boundaries, where it was easy to slip onto new ground, out of the jurisdiction of the hostile "beak".

Despite the law's antagonism to the prize ring, as far as is known no spectator was ever prosecuted for attending a fight. Courts and the press frequently issued warnings that those present were aiding and abetting, but when prosecutions occurred it was usually only the fighters and seconds who found themselves in the dock. The death of a fighter in the ring could lead to his opponent being charged with manslaughter but the authorities' antagonism to prize fighting was more concerned with breaches of public order and keeping people away from their work than protecting fighters from injury. A typical charge levelled at fighters who were arrested was causing a breach of the peace, or sometimes unlawful or riotous assembly. Occasionally it could be more serious; in 1803 Jem Belcher and Joseph Bourke were accused of conspiracy to fight a duel but, although the judge uttered stern words, he merely bound them over to keep the peace.

---

[13] Hurling stones at a tethered cock.

The emergence of Tom Johnson as champion in 1783 brought about a reversal in the decline that had set in after the great days of Figg and Broughton. Johnson, whose real name was Jackling, moved from Yorkshire to London, where his enormous strength meant he soon found work as a corn porter. He was 14 stones but stood only 5 ft. 9in. tall and gave height to most of his opponents. Fast on his feet, he brought a new mobility to the ring, moving round opponents to confuse them and throw punches from different angles. In 1789, on a turf stage at Banbury he beat Isaac Perrins of Birmingham, giving away six inches and three stones. The fight lasted sixty two rounds over an hour and a quarter and Johnson left the ring wealthier by £533, his share of the purse, and £1000 given to him by a backer who won £20,000 on the result – phenomenal amounts for the times.

A Londoner, Daniel Mendoza, was the next significant champion and the first in a long line of Jewish boxers. Mendoza improved on Jack Broughton's technique of picking punches and on Tom Johnson's innovative footwork. He too was not a big man; he stood only 5 ft. 7 in. and weighed 11½ stone but he was a scientific boxer who made his style fashionable by holding exhibitions. Mendoza won two out of three fights with Richard Humphries, considered by the Fancy to be the best man in England at the time. He toured England and Ireland with a boxing booth, was no stranger to prison cells and was so quick on his feet that on more than one occasion beat a horse in a race from London to Croydon.

Known as the 'Star of the East', Mendoza shunned the shaven head favoured by most fighters and wore his dark hair long and curly. This proved to be his downfall - in 1795 he lost his title as champion when beaten in nine rounds by Gentleman John Jackson, whose sobriquet did not prevent him from gripping Mendoza's locks with his left hand while severely punishing him about the face and head with his right. Mendoza, who was twenty-nine, retired from the ring. Years later, living in extreme poverty, he had two more fights, losing the second at the age of fifty-two.

Gentleman Jackson's victory over Mendoza was the third and last fight of his career. He opened an academy at 13 Old Bond Street, London. Intelligent, articulate and of fine physique, he set the fashion by his dress sense and had the style and manners to become accepted by the gentry. It was said that he taught over a third of the peerage to box and those who attended his academy included the Dukes of York, Clarence and Norfolk; the Marquis of Waterford; Lord Chesterfield; Captain Wellesley, the future Duke of Wellington and Lord Byron, who called Jackson "The Emperor of Pugilism" and for a time sparred with him every morning.

Despite his short career as a fighter, in retirement John Jackson was able to exert a great influence on the prize ring. His advice was sought by dukes and commoners alike and in 1814, along with other well-connected members of the Fancy, he founded the Pugilistic Club, whose motto was "a fair ring and no favours and may the best man win." The first governing body in boxing, it imposed some order on the sport by arranging locations, holding stake money and actively working to eliminate fixed fights. The crowds started to return but prize fighting remained illegal.

Daniel Mendoza

Almost all contests were by now held in fields, on grass rather than wooden platforms, within a roped, twenty-four foot square held up by eight posts. Fighters' colours, in the form of large, bright handkerchiefs, were tied to the posts, which were unpadded and offered no protection to a fighter whose back could be broken by being slammed against one. It was still acceptable, and would be much later, in Bendigo's day, to grab an opponent by the waist, turn him upside down and pile drive his head into the ground, or to drop on him when he had fallen and smash an elbow in his face. Purring - kicking with spiked boots - was allowed and, while Broughton's Rules were observed, arguments arose frequently regarding their interpretation by umpires and referees. As a result, when matches were made, a form of contract, known as the 'articles of agreement', was drawn up, specifying what would and would not be allowed, as well as the financial arrangements.

Fights could - and did - last for several hours, with each man attended by a second and bottle-holder, on whose knees he sat in the thirty second breaks between rounds. A round ended when one man went down.[14] While falling without being hit was a foul, a man could easily gain a brief rest by falling to a soft punch, a tactic which would later be employed by - and cause much criticism of - Bendigo.

The emphasis was to aim blows at the face, from long range. Fighters hardened the skin on their hands by pickling them, but long before the end of a bout they would be swollen and slashed by the repeated impact on an opponent's head. Blows to the body were more dangerous to achieve; it meant getting inside the other man's guard with the risk of being wrestled to the ground and crushed beneath the opponent's full, descending weight.

Gentleman John Jackson was instrumental in reviving the prize ring and reviving interest that had lain dormant since Broughton's championship reign came to its sudden end. Jackson was succeeded by some notable fighters: Jem Belcher, Henry Pearce –known as the Game Chicken, John Gully – who went on to become a Member of Parliament - and Tom Cribb. Cribb held the title from 1805 to 1820, a period known as the Golden Age of prize fighting. The glamour returned to the sport and the nobility returned to the ringside. Cribb's most famous battles were against two black American fighters, Bill Richmond and Tom Molyneux. Richmond, a former slave, was beaten over ninety minutes at Hailsham in Sussex, but Molyneux came close to dethroning Cribb.

In 1810 Molyneux, recently arrived in England, challenged Tom Cribb, saying that if Cribb would not fight him then he, Molyneux, would be the champion of England. His claim caused outrage throughout the Fancy. That an American - and a black American - could even have designs on the title was unthinkable. It was only five years since the Battle of Trafalgar when Admiral Lord Nelson had decreed "England expects every man to do his duty". The Fancy was in no doubt: Tom Cribb was expected to do his duty and dispatch this upstart.

Cribb was not so enthusiastic. Eventually, under pressure from the nobility, who were adamant that only an Englishman could be champion of England, Tom Cribb met Molyneux at Copthall Common, near

[14] The longest round recorded lasted 77 minutes, in the fight between Peter Morris and Jack Hartley, August 1860.

Grinstead in Sussex, in December 1810. The day was bitterly cold, rain was falling and 20,000 people gathered to watch what history has recorded as the first international boxing match. After twenty-eight rounds Molyneux punished Cribb with a series of body blows then knocked him down with a right to the face. Cribb could not reach the line marked in the centre of the ring within the thirty seconds allowed and the black American was about to be declared the winner - until Cribb's second dashed across the ring and accused Molyneux of carrying weights in his hands.

It was a cunning, underhand ruse, but it saved the day for Cribb. While the referee, Sir Thomas Apreece, ironically a man noted for his honesty and sense of fair-play, investigated the complaint, Cribb's seconds revived him by blowing brandy up his nostrils and he recovered sufficiently to continue fighting. In the meantime, Tom Molyneux had become severely affected by the cold as he was made to stand about waiting, so that he could not regain his concentration. Shaking and shivering, he was knocked unconscious six rounds later. Molyneux had been beaten by underhand trickery. For Cribb it had been a close call. To a man, the Fancy breathed a sigh of relief.

Tom Cribb wanted to retire from prize fighting but Molyneux was still around, still fighting and again threatening to claim the title if it became vacant. Once more Cribb was reluctantly pressed back into training, once more a huge crowd congregated – 25,000 strong with a large turnout of the nobility including the Marquis of Queensberry. The location this time was Thistleton Gap on the Rutland and Leicestershire border and Cribb ended the day a national hero having knocked the unfortunate Molyneux senseless for a second time.

In 1822 Cribb announced his retirement to become landlord of the Union Arms, Panton Street, Haymarket. A well known haunt of the Fancy, on the bar stood a stuffed dog, Billy, famed for killing fifty rats in less than a minute.[15] Ratting was a keen interest of betting men, along with cock fighting and other blood sports. Cribb now nominated his adopted son Tom Spring as successor to the championship and Spring, whose real name was Winter, proved a worthy champion, winning two epic battles with Jack Langan. In the first, at Worcester Racecourse, the fight had to be temporarily halted when a specially-built grandstand collapsed, killing and injuring spectators. The second bout, in 1825, for a stake of 500 guineas was Spring's last appearance in the prize ring, brittle

[15] The pub has survived to the present time. Now named Tom Cribb, its walls are decorated with Prize Ring memorabilia.

hands forcing him into retirement. Like his mentor, Spring took a public house, the Castle Tavern, Holborn.

The Golden Age of the prize ring was coming to an end. Perhaps its finest moment in terms of general recognition occurred on 19 July 1821 in the unlikely setting of Westminster Abbey, when John Jackson was commissioned to provide a team of pugilists to keep order at the coronation of King George IV. The new king had been a firm follower of the ring as Prince of Wales and Prince Regent but it was an odd situation, the bestowal of royal approval on an illegal sport. Tom Cribb, Tom Spring and the black American Bill Richmond were among the eighteen pugilists, resplendent in liveried uniforms. Jackson's ushers ensured the event passed without mishap.

But the crooks and swindlers were returning to the fight game. Several scandals over fixed matches emerged in the early '20s and the influence and membership of the Pugilistic Club declined so much that in 1825 the club folded for good. John Jackson, its founder and mainstay, who had worked tirelessly to promote honesty in the sport, was so disillusioned that he closed his academy at Old Bond Street. His enthusiasm took another blow in 1830 when he refereed a fight between an Irishman, Simon Byrne and Alexander McKay, a giant Scot known as the Highland Hercules. McKay was knocked unconscious and died a few hours later. No one placed any blame on Jackson,[16] but he lost much of his old interest in the prize ring. His last appearance between the ropes would be as a second to Deaf Burke when he fought Bendigo in 1839.

Cribb and Spring were respected champions and honest men, but the same could not be said of some who came after. Jem Ward, who claimed the championship in 1825 by beating Tom Cannon, was mistrusted by the Fancy after throwing an earlier fight for a £100 bribe. His opponent in that contest, Bill Abbott, was no match for him, and Ward urged him on, shouting "Hit me, hit me", before falling to a soft blow to ensure a result that satisfied his friends who had placed bets at long odds on Abbott. This scandal was still fresh in many minds when Jem Ward declared himself champion. It proved to be the final straw for the Pugilistic Club, which was dissolved soon afterwards.

In January 1827, Ward made a straightforward defence against Peter Crawley, a butcher. Crawley knocked him out and he was unconscious for

[16] Simon Byrne was charged with manslaughter at Buckinghamshire Assizes in July 1830. The jury took only five minutes to find him not guilty.

several hours. But three days after his victory, Crawley, who was known as 'Young Rumpsteak', retired from the ring to concentrate on his butchery business, and Ward soon claimed his title back. Two years later he was at the centre of another outrage when he accepted £50 in advance to fight the Irish champion Simon Byrne and then cried off on the day of the fight, as thousands waited for his arrival at the ringside. The bribe this time was said to be £500, Ward having become caught up once more in a dilemma between his backers and his betting friends. Ward and Byrne eventually met in 1831, Ward emerging an easy winner after thirty-three rounds. It was his last fight, but he held on to the title of champion by the simple means of demanding stakes too high for the backers of prospective opponents. For the next seven years he continued to wear the championship belt at benefits and exhibitions, without venturing into the prize ring to defend it. In 1838, in a letter to *Bell's Life*, he hinted, rather than announced, that he had retired. By then he was trainer to a new man, a leading contender for the championship and the talk of the Fancy - William Thompson of Nottingham, better known as Bendigo.

3] The Duke of Limbs & Big Ben Caunt

As he reached the age of twenty-one, Bendigo was strong, fit and possessed of a natural cunning honed in the slum streets and pub gyms of Nottingham. For five years he had sparred with and learned from experienced local fighters like Sam Turner and Bill Atkinson. Occasionally he had earned a few pounds from small-scale fights – he claimed his first paid fight was at the age of sixteen. Now he was set to embark on a career in pugilism, to 'enter the lists proper', as the Fancy termed it. But he needed a money man, someone to put up sidestakes that would attract opponents.[17] All fighters needed backers and Bendigo found his in Joseph Whitaker, landowner and squire of Ramsdale House, known to all as the Duke of Limbs.

Whitaker's estate at Arnold, just outside Nottingham, ran to 1800 acres. Born in 1798, he was a true sporting squire of the times, an accomplished horseman who rode to hounds and a dedicated breeder of fighting cocks. He developed a new strain of duckwing birds that fought an historic contest against Lord Derby's finest at the Cockpit in Tufton Street, Westminster. The 'main', as such events were known in cockfighting circles, was attended by the cream of the prize ring, including John Jackson, Tom Cribb and Tom Molyneux, as well as such famous names as Beau Brummel and the Prince Regent.[18] The latter lost heavily by backing Lord Derby's birds, which were soundly defeated by those of Whitaker.

The Duke of Limbs' nickname came from his powerful build. Wide-shouldered and possessed of extraordinarily well-developed arms and legs, he cut a fine figure at the ropes of the prize ring. He stood over six feet tall, wore side-whiskers and dressed in the fashion of the day - grey

---

[17] Each fighter's backers put up a sum of money as a sidestake, which was the prize for the winning fighter. The backers, men of substance, hoped to profit by betting on their man. Bets were made on who would be first to draw blood, first to knock down his opponent and on who would emerge as winner of the fight. Bets were laid in advance of the day and at the ropes, with odds changing throughout as the fight progressed.

[18] Later, George IV

beaver hat, a green coat with silver buttons, a flowered waistcoat, leather riding breeches and shining top boots. His malacca cane and monocle gave him a foppish air but he had true Corinthian manners. It was said of him, "He had a strong vein of eccentricity and some considered him as mad as a hatter."[19] He was reputed to carry a bag of guineas in one pocket and a brace of pistols in the other, and he was not averse to putting on the muffs and sparring – if he could find anybody willing to take him on.

Joseph Whitaker - the Duke of Limbs

Although his background was one of wealth and class, Joseph Whitaker had the common touch. A prodigious drinker, he was equally at home in the fighting pubs of Nottingham as on his country estate. He was a stalwart of the Nottingham Fancy and had a great appreciation of boxing skills. So, when one day in 1832 he came across Bendigo sparring with Sam Turner, the Duke of Limbs liked what he saw. He agreed to put up stakes for Bendigo's fights. It was a partnership that would last eighteen years, from Bendigo's early "bye" fights to the championship of England.

Although Bendigo's first paid fight was as a sixteen year old against an unnamed opponent for a few pounds, it was not for another five years that he had his first recorded bout in the prize ring. That came in 1832, against

[19] P.H.Ditchfield in *The Old English Country Squire* (Methuen 1912)

Joe Healey, a man described as "a local notoriety". He beat him in sixteen rounds, but no other details have survived. As prize fighting was illegal, there was no coverage in local newspapers and the mainstream press would only report the major fights, or if some disaster, like the death of a combatant, had occurred in a lesser event. The one paper to show much interest in prize ring matters was *Bell's Life in London and Sporting Chronicle*, but even then a fighter rarely came to notice until he had met established 'names'.

This early success was followed by another a few months later, when he defeated Bill Faulkner in eleven rounds. The following year, 1833, fighting every month from March to November, he won nine times. His first three opponents were never heard of before or since. Ned Smith, Charlie Martin and Lew Jackson each failed to meet the scratch in under five rounds. Next up was the more experienced Tom Cox, who had earlier fought Sam Merryman, a well-known Notts. man, but Cox only lasted to the ninth. Charles Skelton went in three, Bob Burton from Leicester,[20] in nine and Bill Mason also in three.

He was doing well, but needed testing with better, more experienced opponents, ones who would could take punishment and hit hard in return. Bill Moulds, known as Winterflood,[21] was chosen. He had been in with the best men around Nottingham, losing to Bendigo's mentor Sam Turner and to Dick Hill, but winning four more fights, including an eighty-seven minute battle of 140 rounds against Bill Broadhead, a leading light in Bendigo's early career. Moulds fared even worse than the others. When they met in Bulwell Forest in October 1833, the up-and-coming Bendigo knocked him out in the first round and Winterflood never fought again. Bendigo finished off the year with another win over eleven rounds against a man whose ring career went no further, Bill Keyworth.

It had been an impressive start and Bendigo's reputation began to spread beyond the Nottingham Fancy. Eleven wins in eleven fights was an enviable record and his crafty style of leading with the right hand and foot, bending low to avoid being hit, was different from the way anyone else fought at the time. Most of all, Bendigo was a popular character, with his penchant for doing somersaults and other acrobatics. Nor was the prize ring his only arena. Like his patron the Duke of Limbs, he was an enthusiast for cock fighting, while on a spring evening he liked nothing better than a spot of badger baiting. He played cricket, took part in running races for bets and, in quieter moments, fished the River Trent.

[20] Sometimes referred to as Tom Burton

[21] A Notts man, born 1806. Often confused with a fighter from Bath, also called Bill Moulds and known as Winterflood

And when he wasn't engaged in these activities, he was out on the town with his friends, the Nottingham Lambs.

Sport, both of the athletic and the 'blood' varieties, had a strong tradition in Nottingham. Open spaces such as The Meadows were ideal for disorderly games of football and cricket matches, with dog-fights another popular pastime. Cockpits were situated at most of the main inns, including the White Lion, the Lion Inn and the Peacock. The Bull Ring in the Market Place had been the scene of much gore and blood-letting in earlier times - such was its importance to town culture that a by-law existed to fine anyone who killed a bull without it having been first baited by dogs. This barbaric practice was thought to make the beef more tender.

The Nottingham people were also partial to eccentrics. A crowd of fifteen thousand gathered in the town in 1773 for a ten mile race between two noted runners of the day – both athletes running completely naked. In 1821 several hundred assembled to watch an unemployed baker gather a hundred stones placed a yard apart, with his mouth, and put them in a basket. While the enthusiasm for blood sports reflected the brutality of human life at the time, the affection for oddball entertainers was based on an admiration for those who had risen out of the mire. Such people were different, they did not conform. Bendigo, with his showmanship and irreverent attitude to most things in life, was part of that heritage.

New Year 1834 brought the first indication that the editor of *Bell's Life*, was aware of Bendigo. On 12 January the paper announced:

> "Bill Looney of Liverpool is tired of doing nothing and, rather than stand still, he is prepared to make a match with Abednego for £50 or £100 a side, to fight halfway between Liverpool and Nottingham. His 'tin' will be ready any time at Peter Taylor's, The Grapes, Peter Street, Whitechapel. Liverpool."

Bill Looney, of Irish parents, was a tough and rugged fighter, the same age, height and weight as Bendigo. He had made a name for himself as the champion of Liverpool docks before his first 'bye', against a bricklayer for £1 a side. He had the backing of the powerful Liverpool Fancy and had beaten some of the best fighters around. Maybe the Duke of Limbs felt that Bendigo was not ready for such an aggressive opponent yet, but the challenge was not taken up. Instead, five weeks later on 16 February came the first reference in the newspaper to Bendigo by his actual nickname –

> "William Thompson, alias Bendigo, is open to fight George Weston of Fazely in one or two months for £10 to £50 a side. His money is ready at the Bell Inn, Burton-on-Trent."

Nothing was heard again of Weston, but Bill Looney would eventually be accommodated, three years later.

Bell's Life, which had now recognised the existence of Bendigo, chronicled the prize ring each week in a small section of its four broadsheet pages. The rest of the paper was made up of general and other sporting news, the latter covering horse racing, cricket, hunting and such esoteric delights as cockfighting, dog fighting (known as the canine fancy), a regular section on Cumberland and Westmoreland wrestling, trotting, skittles, angling, pigeon and sparrow shooting, pedestrianism, rackets, nurr and spell, archery and chess. For those with needs beyond sporting information there were advertisements for cures for gonorrhoea – "the original and only Remedy ever discovered - Ayling's Specific Extract", cures for corns, advertisements for "Best Beaver Hats, 17/6d", for prints of horses and much more.

For the whole of Bendigo's fighting career, the paper was edited by Vincent George Dowling, who had taken over in 1824. Dowling was a remarkable man. In 1812 he had enjoyed the sort of 'scoop' every journalist dreams of when he was first to seize John Bellingham after he shot the Prime Minister, Spencer Perceval, in the lobby of the House of Commons. As *Bell's Life* editor he covered many prize fights, turning out in all weathers in his tweed suit, travelling by coach and trap on long journeys over several days at a time, then clambering fences and trudging through muddy ditches to reach the ringside. In time, Dowling would be critical of Bendigo's ploys in the ring and even more critical of the behaviour of his supporters, but for now he was giving the Nottingham newcomer valuable exposure.

Bendigo's record between 1832 and 1834 is based on a list of his early fights included in newspaper reports at the time of his death.[22] Some of his first eleven fights are verifiable, such as the one with Bill Moulds, alias

---

[22] See *Notts and Midland Counties Daily Express*, 28 August 1880

Winterflood, although ironically this one has occasionally been discounted by ring historians who confused the Nottingham Bill Moulds with the fighter of the same name from Bristol. In Bendigo's account, he had only one fight in 1834, that being a victory against an otherwise anonymous "Bingham Champion" in January. A small village on the road between Nottingham and Grantham, Bingham was not a big enough place to boast a champion, but if this fight did take place in an organised ring, *Bell's Life*, who mentioned Bendigo in the same month, made no reference to it. As with other early opponents, the "Bingham Champion" never threw his hat in the prize ring again.

As Bendigo took things easy for most of 1834, his friends the Nottingham Lambs were displaying the sort of outrageous behaviour that was to make them such integral players in his own later career. In March they had a day out, following one of their older favourites, Bill Atkinson, to Newport Pagnell. The man known as the Nottingham Pet was a twenty-six year old tailor by trade and had been a prize-fighter since he was eighteen. Only five feet four inches tall, he was as cocky and aggressive out of the ring as he was in it. He was matched against a hard puncher, Owen Swift, a man recognised as the best at nine and a half stone in England.[23] But during the fight's preliminaries Atkinson became impatient, insulting the commissary – the man responsible for fight arrangements - and threatening to punch him in the mouth.

Corinthian behaviour this was not, but the Nottingham Pet's followers were not monocled swells or tweeded squires. They were ale-swigging, twig-wielding Lambs. And for Pet and Lambs the day was to get worse. When, after thirty minutes of hard fighting, Owen Swift got the upper hand and Atkinson's brother called upon the Nottingham mob to "break in the ring and save the day", they were beaten back by the staves and bull whips of the ring officials. It was rare defeat for the Nottingham Lambs and one that would not happen again. In just a few years Bendigo would become their number one favourite, the financial stakes would be much higher and the Lambs would make no mistake as to who was in command at the ropes.

Later in the year, the Lambs turned out in force again when Bill Atkinson fought Ned Murphy. *Bell's Life* had condemned their efforts to rescue their man against Swift, saying "Such conduct is as unmanly as it is

---

[23] Two of Owen Swift's later fights ended in the death of his opponents. He was convicted of the manslaughter of Anthony Noone in 1834 and served six months hard labour. In 1838 he fled to France following the death of Bill Phelps, known as 'Brighton Bill'. On his return he was arrested but acquitted, despite one of his seconds having been convicted and sentenced to three months while he was away. The death of 'Brighton Bill' led to the New Rules of 1838 being introduced.

disgraceful". This time they reported "His Nottingham friends stood by to ensure fair play." In Lamb terminology that meant ensuring a victory for Atkinson.

Bendigo returned to the ring in July 1835. He had been absent for eighteen months. Now, articles were entered into by his backers, principally Joe Whitaker, the Duke of Limbs, for him to fight a man who, over the next ten years would become his great and, at times, bitter rival. Benjamin Caunt hailed from Hucknall Torkard, a village five miles from Nottingham, and was the son of a gamekeeper in the employ of the poet and prize ring patron, Lord Byron. At twenty-one, Caunt was three years younger than Bendigo and, although he had a reputation as a fighting man in his neighbourhood, this was to be his first appearance in the prize ring. By comparison with Bendigo's height of five feet nine inches and weight of eleven and a half stones, Caunt was of Herculean proportions. He stood six feet two and weighed over fifteen stones. It would be, in the parlance of the ring, "a horse to a hen".

Caunt watched with scorn and envy as Bendigo made a name for himself. The gamekeeper's son had no experience in the professional ring, but he was the scourge of poachers on his master's estate and no one had come close to beating him in a set-to or brawl. He had grown up in a lively environment, encouraged towards combat sports by his uncle, Ben Butler, a well-known wrestler and breeder of fighting cocks. Butler's birds, which he allowed to wander over the roads and gardens of the village in the daytime, were a source of annoyance to his neighbours but in great demand by the Fancy of several counties. He was a popular figure at important cock fights and a good friend of the Duke of Limbs.

Ben Butler told the Duke about his nephew's growing talents as a pugilist and took him to watch young Caunt beat a local man in a wrestling match. The Duke was impressed and set about arranging for him to spar with Bendigo. When they did, Caunt looked the better man with the gloves on, but such impressions were deceptive. A battle of words and bad temper then ensued as Caunt insulted his smaller opponent whenever opportunity arose and tried to goad him into agreeing to fight. To add to the seething atmosphere between the two men, bitter arguments and scuffles broke out between their supporters, the rural ruffians of Hucknall who supported Caunt and the more organised and ruthless Nottingham Lambs.

After all the talk and challenging, Bendigo finally agreed to meet Caunt. The decisive factor was said to be his mother telling him, as mothers do, to "fight the hulking lout and shut his rat-trap mouth."

Agreements were entered into for stakes of £25 a side and Bendigo promptly left the dirt and distractions of the town to train in the countryside. With £10 provided by Whitaker he set up base at the Green Dragon Inn, in the village of Chilwell, under the supervision of his friend and mentor, Sam Turner. He knew that he would need greater fitness and strength to meet Caunt than he had needed for any of his previous opponents and he spent the first days working in fields adjoining the inn, scything and mowing grass from dawn until dusk, exercise intended to strengthen the muscles in his back and shoulders.

The villagers were surprised to find a prize fighter in their midst and even more surprised that he did the work of three men in a day. He and Turner did their roadwork along the country lanes and footpaths and across open fields, leaping styles and gates as they went, filling their lungs with fresh country air. Each day he sparred with Sam Turner and any of the Nottingham Fancy who came out and wanted to put the mufflers on. Every morning the Duke of Limbs drove over to the Green Dragon in his horse-drawn gig to check on progress.

Throughout his fighting career Bendigo was diligent in his training. Between fights he made merry in the inns and taverns, but when preparing for a bout he submitted to the harshest rigours. In the prize ring, just as in modern boxing, the fighter's commitment to preparation and the skill and experience of his trainer were vital to the outcome of a fight.

Even in the mid 1800s, training methods followed the rituals of an esoteric science. Developed and refined by professors of pugilism from the ring's earliest days onwards, they were designed to increase strength, lung-power and both hand and body speed. Another important aspect of training was the development of what the Fancy called "bottom" – the stamina to endure prolonged exertion and brutal punishment. Bendigo, faster with his hands and on his feet than anyone around at the time, would avoid serious punishment throughout his career. But even possessed of his rare natural agility, he needed to sharpen his reflexes and hone his punching power through dedicated training.

Bendigo and Ben Caunt fought on 21st July 1835 in a meadow behind Appleby House, a secluded old roadside inn in a dip on the road from Nottingham to Ashbourne. Bendigo was seconded by his trainer Sam Turner and Sam Merryman. In Caunt's corner were his uncle and backer, Ben Butler, and his trainer, Harry Bamford. The day was fine and the Nottingham and Birmingham Fancies turned out in large numbers.

When Bendigo slipped through the ropes and into the ring a great cheer went up from his supporters. The weeks of training had left him in fine condition, his muscles rippled in the sun and he exuded confidence as he joked at the ropes with his friends the Lambs. But the admiring glances he received turned to gasps and murmured oaths as Ben Caunt disrobed to reveal his huge chest, arms and finely conditioned stomach.

It looked as if Bendigo might have been wiser to ignore his mother all these months and to continue avoiding Caunt. The physical advantage that Caunt was blessed with seemed too much for his smaller opponent. But those who doubted the man described by one writer of the day as "deadly and poisonous as a rattlesnake with about the same ethics" reckoned without his cunning tactics and superior boxing skills.

Early in the fight Bendigo discovered to his cost that he would be punished and seriously injured if he allowed Caunt to get close. Superior in the clinches, several times Big Ben grabbed him, threw him to the ground and fell upon him, letting an elbow dig into Bendigo's throat or stomach. Even with his remarkable agility, once those long, heavily muscled arms wrestled him, Bendigo was trapped. Four times he was slammed to the ground and four times winded. It was enough to make him adopt more evasive tactics. From then on he kept at a safe distance and proceeded to pepper shots at his less mobile opponent. Using his southpaw stance to cause confusion, he connected with bruising punches to Caunt's head and body, then pretended to slip and dropped to one knee, bringing the round to an end.

Round after round this went on, Bendigo combining trickery with verbal warfare as he insulted Caunt between rounds, pulling faces at him and calling him a "chuckle head", a "dirty toad" and much worse. Whenever the big man charged forward, Bendigo hit him a clean shot, danced away and slipped with dramatic emphasis on some unseen object. Caunt's face and head were showing the marks of battle but his own punches could not find Bendigo. Each time he went back to his corner for the thirty-second break, Caunt was more and more frustrated.

By the end of the twenty-second round, Big Ben could control his anger no more. Before time could be called to bring the fighters to the scratch, he rushed across the ring and demanded "Wilt thou stand up and fight fair, thou damned hound?" Resting nonchalantly on his second's knee, Bendigo's response was brief and pithy. Caunt was so enraged that he hit him with a full force, foul blow that knocked both fighter and second head over heels backwards. Not even Bendigo had seen that one coming. The fight was over. Caunt was disqualified and the referee, Arthur Matthewson, declared Bendigo the winner.

Controversial decisions in the prize ring were usually followed by disorderly scenes. This time was no different to those that would follow when Bendigo and Caunt met again. Caunt's backers were livid at losing their money on a foul. They felt Bendigo's shifty tactics should have been penalised by the referee. The navvies and farmhands who had bet on the big man fell into instant dispute with the Nottingham Lambs and, in their haste to set about each other, the ring was broken down.

In more considered circles, opinion was divided as to who should have emerged victor. One contemporary report stated "It was the expressed opinion of the spectators that, had Caunt kept his temper and husbanded his strength, the issue would have gone the other way, as he proved himself game to the backbone, while his opponent was made up of dodges from heel to headpiece."[24] Dodges from heel to headpiece indeed, but *Bell's Life* took a different view. Describing Ben Caunt as "a fine, promising yokel of twenty one", the oracle of the Fancy pointed out that he was "desperately punished" and that "courage, weight and perseverance were completely served by science". The reporter left no doubt that Bendigo was a worthy winner.

Bendigo's fight with Caunt brought him a great deal more recognition within the Fancy than he had enjoyed so far. It was his first bout to be reported in a national newspaper, albeit a short article and not the detailed round-by-round account that his later bouts would merit. His victory over a man so much taller, heavier and stronger brought him to the attention of new backers, while other fighters – "all the big 'uns of the North Countrie" as they were popularly known – were keen to take on the cocky fellow who had beaten Big Ben Caunt.

First to challenge was a Bradford man, John Leechman, who fought under the name Brassey. He informed Bendigo in November, via the pages of *Bell's Life*, that he was prepared to meet him halfway between Nottingham and Bradford for £25 or £50 a side. But Bendigo did not respond – he had taken up with a travelling boxing booth and his whereabouts were unknown.

Most fairgrounds or race meetings had a boxing booth. Local youths and men were encouraged to take on the resident pugilist over a few rounds and if they got the better of him – a rare event - they won a pound or two. Such booths were very popular attractions and drew big crowds of paying spectators. In his mid teens, Bendigo had been a young challenger

[24] Quoted in *Pugilistica*, Henry Downes Miles, 1906

when the boxing booth came to the Goose Fair in Nottingham. Now he was part of the show run by an occasional prize fighter, Levi Eckersley, gaining experience and a regular income, while sharpening up his skills by taking on all-comers.

He joined Eckersley after the Caunt fight in July, travelling from Nottingham by mail coach to meet up in Sheffield. He took with him only a change of clothes, a pair of mufflers and some money given to him by the Duke of Limbs. The booth rolled round England on its horse-drawn wagon, taking in all the town and county fairs, spending St Leger week in Doncaster and trundling up and down endless byways.

He spent the summer and autumn trading blows with the best that rural England could muster. His days and evenings were spent outwitting burly navvies who were egged on by their drunken pals, slipping the Sunday punches of well-muscled blacksmiths and dodging the low blows and crafty digs of yokels who fancied their chances. And as the season's changed and cold chill of winter approached, Bendigo returned home to Nottingham.

Sparring, performing somersaults and generally enjoying himself, he had learned much on his travels – from the unpredictable challengers and also from fighting men he had met along the way. The owner of the booth, Levi Eckersley was himself an experienced, although limited, campaigner in the prize ring, while Peter Taylor, who travelled with him, was a leading light of the Liverpool Fancy.

Later, Bendigo would enlist Taylor as his trainer, but for now he was back in the Lace City. And just to let everyone know, he celebrated his homecoming by throwing half a brick 115 yards across the Trent with his left hand.

4] Bendigo, Brassey and Looney

While Bendigo was roaming the land with Levi Eckersley's boxing booth, several would-be opponents stepped forward and announced their wish to meet him within the ropes of the prize ring. Brassey of Bradford and Looney of Liverpool had already issued challenges, yet to be taken up, and two more Liverpool men, Bob Hampson and Charley Langan, who fought as Young Langan, were eager for action.

Bendigo had an easier target in mind – another Liverpool man, Tom Britton. He was a strong but limited fighter who could absorb severe punishment. In February 1836 he lost a gruelling fight with Young Molyneux, a Moroccan ex-seaman whose real name was James Wharton, over 201 rounds lasting four hours and seven minutes. By the end of the fight Britton's head had swollen to twice its normal size and he was bleeding profusely, but when the verdict went against him he chased the referee round the ring, followed by four or five of his friends, all wielding cudgels.

In Britton, Bendigo's backers recognised a possible opponent who would put up a good fight, but would be too slow to seriously trouble their man. They lost no time in issuing a challenge: *Bell's Life* of 21st February 1836 announced:

> "Bendigo of Nottingham is prepared to make a match with Tom Britton for £50 a side. His weight does not exceed 12st."

But Tom Britton was not interested. He could still feel the bruises and cuts from the Molyneux fight and he was not keen to go in with Bendigo, who had proved against Ben Caunt that he was a clever boxer and a tricky customer all round. Doubtless calculating that the Nottingham Fancy would be reluctant to lay out twice the £50 they were offering, he replied that he would not fight for less than £100. There were doubts that Britton could raise such a sum and for the time being he dropped out of Bendigo's plans.

Bendigo now began to spread his wings away from Nottingham and to spend time in Sheffield, using the Rose and Crown, Blind Lane as a base. There was a great interest in prize fighting in the Sheffield area, with some up-and-coming fighters. In April, six thousand people trekked eight miles out of town to Killamarsh Meadows to see a Sheffield man, James Markham, face one of Bendigo's Nottingham friends, John Potts, for £20 a side. Bendigo acted as Potts' second and after twenty- eight rounds, seeing his man had no chance of winning, gave in for him. Not for him the long, cruel round after round to unconsciousness. A century before his time, Bendigo realised that fights were won with skill and science and it is a mark of his humanity that he prevented Potts suffering injuries that many other cornermen would have seen as obligatory.

In May, he made his own return to the ring, taking on Brassey of Bradford, who had wanted to fight him since the Ben Caunt victory. Otherwise known as John Leechman, Brassey took his ring name from his time working in a brass foundry. He was six feet tall, two stones heavier than Bendigo and, at twenty-one, four years younger. Well-known in his hometown, he had won his first six fights and considered himself the Yorkshire champion. Out of the ring, he led a gang of thugs who were available for hire by politicians at elections.

Bendigo and Brassey met on Tuesday 24th May 1836 at Deepcar, a hamlet nine miles from Sheffield, on the Manchester road. The match was made for £50 a side and both men had trained well, Bendigo at Woodhouse Mill where he sparred with Sam Merryman, who acted as his second on the day. The fight began at a pace – no sooner did they shake hands than Brassey let fly with a vicious punch which Bendigo neatly stopped before replying with a right hook to the mouth. At ringside the Nottingham Lambs encouraged him with shouts of "The fight's your own" while the crowd, estimated at between two and three thousand, was excited to see blood drawn so early. It was a furious pace for an opening round and it ended with Brassey rushing in for a throw, but Bendigo stopping him in his tracks with a punch to the head.

In the second round Brassey tried to hurt Bendigo with punches to the body but the man they called Bold `Un parried and responded with punches to the face and head. They grappled and fell, Bendigo on top. In the third, Brassey staggered him with a hard blow to the body, but

Bendigo closed in and threw the bigger man with what an observer described as "one of the cleanest cross-buttocks we ever saw."[25]

By the end of the fifth round it was clear that Bendigo was looking the better of the pair. He was 6 to 4 on with the bookies at the ropes and his blows to Brassey's head were finding their mark, while Brassey's best shots were parried away. Bendigo, noted *Bell's Life*, "was quick as a cat and he could get away from a hit like a first rate professor."

After fifty-two rounds of throwing punches at a target that moved faster than he could blink, swinging at thin air as the Lambs mocked and derided him, Brassey's frustration reached boiling point. He had been out-punched and out-wrestled by a smaller and lighter man. He did what Ben Caunt had done before him - he lost his temper. Grabbing Bendigo by a thigh, he tried to throw him backwards in a somersault. One of the umpires declared it a foul and he was disqualified. Amidst much dispute and argument on the part of Brassey's followers, the referee James Hutchins, whose more conventional role in life was that of editor and proprietor of the *Newark Times*, declared Bendigo the winner.

His victory over Brassey impressed the northern Fancy. He had fought a tactical and skilful battle against a man who had never before been beaten. Brassey was most annoyed at having been disqualified and immediately demanded a re-match but it did not come about. Bendigo was willing to fight him again, but Brassey's backers must have foreseen such a contest as throwing good money after bad, for it never materialised. The following year, while leading his band of ruffians on behalf of Tory candidates during the general election that followed the accession of Queen Victoria to the throne, the Bradford man suffered a different sort of reversal. He and his thuggish friends were beaten by a rival gang and the two Tories who had hired them failed to get elected.

Meanwhile, Bendigo's name was very much on the lips of the Fancy. Throughout the summer of 1836 opponents were proposed, challenges issued and stakes offered. One fight looked like coming off when deposits were laid with Jem Bailey, a Yorkshireman who had earlier fallen to Brassey. Bailey's backers then had second thoughts and decided to cut their losses, thus forfeiting their money.

In July, Bendigo caught the mail coach to London, where he put up at a well-known sporting house, the Queen's Head in Haymarket, kept by an

---

[25] By taking his opponent in a neck hold, a fighter could throw him over his hip or buttock, known as the 'cross-buttock', onto his back. When well executed, the opponent landed head-first on the ground, the thrower fell on his abdomen and the felled man was often rendered insensible and incapable.

ex-fighter Jem Burn. The Cockneys took to Bendigo's quaint Nottingham ways and his agile tricks and he was soon sparring in the back room of the pub with anyone who fancied pulling on the muffs. The Queen's Head was a stronghold of the London Fancy and a regular meeting place where fight arrangements and deposits were made. Burn, the landlord, took a keen interest in all matters of a sporting nature. He owned a celebrated bitch, Nettle, who weighed 22lbs and was unbeaten in fights with other dogs - when the dog died of yellow jaundice in 1837, *Bell's Life* commented on the sad event "she always won her matches in gallant style." [26]

Jem Burn was keen to back Bendigo but he stayed loyal to the betting men of Nottingham who had supported him from the start. The Duke of Limbs was still keen for him to face Tom Britton - he of the terribly swollen head against his last opponent, Young Molyneux. As before, Britton did not respond to the bait, but his conqueror Molyneux jumped at it. He had wanted to fight the Nottingham hero for over a year and showed his keenness by offering £100 as a stake, but he stipulated that Bendigo must weigh no more than 11st 6lb on the day.

The autumn brought more talk but still no action. A Coventry man, Jack Flint, known as Wopper, was all but lined up, but he took another fight in which the bridge of his nose was broken and he was knocked senseless. Young Molyneux came back into the reckoning and Bendigo, who had returned to Nottingham from London with only a sovereign in his pocket, needed the money. "I'm not particular about a few pounds in weight as I want a customer and mean fighting," he said. Now he was spending time with the Liverpool Fancy, having been introduced by his friend from the travelling boxing booth, Peter Taylor, who kept a pub in the town. Taylor, a disciple and associate of the ex-champion Jem Ward, was carving out a reputation as a trainer.

As it had been in London, there was plenty of interest in Liverpool among would-be backers. Peter Taylor was well-connected and stakes of £100 to £80 were quickly offered for Bendigo to fight Young Molyneux. Before this could happen Molyneaux took a fight in December at Woore, in Staffordshire, against an unbeaten but out-of-condition Birmingham publican, Harry Preston. On the day, Bendigo assisted Peter Taylor in Preston's corner. They were out of luck – Preston suffered his first loss

---

[26] Dog-fighting was a popular 'sport' in London at the time. Great care was taken in their training, feeding and exercising and promising dogs were carefully matched in just the same way as pugilists. Dogs were also backed to kill a given number of rats in a set period. A vivid account of a ratting evening can be found in Henry Mayhew's *London Labour and the London Poor*.

when Young Molyneux tossed him out of the ring and he landed on his head. Bendigo dragged him to his corner but no amount of brandy being forced down the senseless Preston's throat or blown up his nostrils could revive him. Word went round the ring that he was dead, as Bendigo and Peter Taylor bundled him into a carriage and sped to Woore, hoping to find a doctor. On the way Preston recovered consciousness and lived to fight another day.

It was a close call for Bendigo; had Harry Preston died, he as second would almost certainly have been charged with manslaughter. As it was, he was left with the knowledge that Preston's conqueror, Young Molyneux, was keen to fight him next. Molyneux was shaping up as an extremely dangerous fighter. Bendigo stated his willingness to accommodate him, but, despite his challenges, Molyneux must have been wary because he insisted the fight be at eleven and a half stones, a weight he knew the Nottingham man could not achieve.

Bendigo's trip to Woore had been eventful and the place made an impression on him. The ring for the Molyneux - Preston fight was formed in a field surrounded by hedges outside the small village, which lay eight miles from Newcastle-under-Lyme. The Falcon Inn, with its thatched roof provided a warm welcome and Bendigo needed no persuasion to enter into an agreement to fight there the following month against Young Langan, said to be a "promising plant from the Emerald Isle" and backed by "a gentleman from the Sod". Langan's previous planned fight had been cancelled at the last minute when he got himself arrested for assaulting a policeman. In all the speculation and rumour of the previous months his name had not figured as an opponent for Bendigo, although he had issued a challenge eighteen months earlier, immediately after the defeat of Ben Caunt. Now the fight was on and the New Year found Bendigo once more in close training.

The morning of 24th January 1837 was wet and misty in Woore. Rain had poured down through the night and the village street was more suited to ducks than the horse-drawn wagons and gigs covered with umbrellas that carried the betting men and fight fans towards the site of the ring. Inside the Falcon Inn, where he had spent the night, Bendigo gloomily received the news that the inner ring was a quagmire, even before the crowd began to arrive. It was too wet even for the Nottingham Lambs to cause trouble. The prevailing mood was one of disappointment.

All morning the downpour continued, as more and more people arrived by horse and on foot. The landlord of the Falcon was doing marvellous business, but at the same time becoming anxious as to how

Bendigo vs Young Langan,
as illustrated in *Famous Fights, Past and Present*

the day might be resolved. Five hundred men were now congregated – the joint Fancies of Nottingham and Liverpool, where Young Langan was based. If such a large number of rough, tough and worse-for-wear types turned nasty, Woore was going to have a problem. Then, around noon, after hours of gloom, the rain suddenly held off, the sky cleared and the Lambs and their Merseyside counterparts put down their tankards and made their way to the field.

Both Bendigo and Young Langan wanted to fight. They had trained hard and were fully prepared. But both were dismayed at the state of the turf, sodden and uneven, giving way to the foot. After some debate between seconds and backers it was agreed that they would wear spiked boots, with the condition that if either wilfully spiked the other he would lose the fight on a foul. Langan's colours of Irish green and Bendigo's bird's eye blue were tied to the posts. The crowd shouted and cheered their relief at not having had a wasted journey after all. The two men stripped for action.

Young Langan's record in the prize ring was inferior to that of Bendigo, who was favourite with the bookmakers at 6-4 on. The Irishman's previous contests had been in his home country, with opponents of lesser class, but at more than thirteen stone to Bendigo's 11st10lb he had a distinct weight advantage. He tried to rush in and wrestle as Bendigo showed superior science, planting heavy blows on the ribs of the "Long `Un", as his friends at the ropes called him. For many of the Liverpool men, who had heard about Bendigo but not previously seen him fight, it was a disappointment to find that their man was not in the same class. Every time he tried to force the fight Bendigo picked him off, drawing first blood, although sometimes coming off worst when they both fell.

After twenty-eight rounds had passed, Bendigo, although hurting the Irishman with punches, began to look tired. Several times Langan had fallen heavily upon him and the Lambs were getting agitated as he came out for the 29th seeming to lack his normal enthusiasm. Langan, seeing that his opponent was unsteady on his legs, bustled in for the kill . . . but to the Lambs' relief the Bold `Un was "fibbing". Instead of finding a spent force, Langan found he had "caught a tartar" as the ring men called it. As he stormed forward, Bendigo planted an uppercut on his chin, followed by a throw to the ground.

Four painful rounds later, "blind as a pup" with both eyes closed, Langan's seconds saved him from further punishment. In the bitter afternoon, stumbling and falling in freezing mud, the two men had fought for an hour and thirty-three minutes. Bendigo, while a clear winner, had nonetheless taken some punishment, in particular from Young Langan's elbows and knees during the falls. Said *Bell's Life*: "Both men received so much pepper that they will not want to spice their chops for some time to come."

In fact, Bendigo did want to spice his chops – and as soon as possible. He had come up trumps again and knew that soon he might get a chance to fight for the title of Champion of England. Two weeks after disposing of Young Langan he again put out a challenge to Tom Britton, but while the fighter was willing, his backers were not. Bendigo returned to Nottingham, from where he offered via the pages of *Bell's Life* "to fight any man in England who happens to have £10 for 50 a side."[27] The £10 was to be a first deposit. He said he was "to be heard of at any sporting house in Nottingham" and as he was in want of a job he would not refuse any 12 stone man. He got one in Bill Looney.

Looney of Liverpool had wanted to fight Bendigo since January 1834, when he stated his intentions in *Bell's Life*, giving "Abednego", as he called him, a first mention in that paper. At the time Looney was backed by betting men based at Peter Taylor's public house, The Grapes Inn, Liverpool. Now, Taylor was Bendigo's trainer and Looney had just been released from a three month prison sentence.

Keen to get back into the ring, Bill Looney offered to fight any man in the world for £100 or £200. His offer was instantly taken up by Jem Ward, the Black Diamond, who, despite not having fought for six years, continued to claim the championship. Ward, aged thirty six and now also based in Liverpool, issued a response to Looney, who was ten years younger, saying "I will accommodate this great and mighty hero for his own sum of £200 a side." Looney's bluff was called. He could not raise the £200 and anyway did not wish to fight Ward, who was – when not engaged in fixed contests – a top class man. He got out of his difficulties by saying, not unreasonably, that he thought Ward to be in retirement when he made the challenge. Instead, Looney and his backers quickly entered into articles with the Duke of Limbs to fight Bendigo for £50 a side, "and as much more as he could get", a sum which was later settled at £100.

This arrangement was to everyone's satisfaction. Looney had found a customer and Bendigo was to meet a man who was a formidable - but sooner or later inevitable - opponent. At the same time, Jem Ward could continue to call himself champion because nobody was able to raise the stakes he demanded. There also another benefit for the crafty Ward, through his associate Peter Taylor, Bendigo's, new trainer. With the fight fixed for 13th June 1837, halfway between Nottingham and Liverpool, Bendigo left the distractions of his hometown to train at Crosby in Lancashire under the direction of Jem Ward and the watchful eye of Peter Taylor.

Bendigo knew that Bill Looney would be the hardest opponent he had faced. Ben Caunt had been huge and powerful, but his lack of mobility and short temper made him vulnerable to the faster, wise-cracking

---

[27] £10 as a first deposit on a sidestake of £50

southpaw who, so long as he could avoid being thrown, had an advantage. Looney was a hard nut as well as a good fighter with a great deal of ring experience. He, too, was unbeaten - a fact which caught the wholehearted attention of the Fancy. This would be an evenly-matched contest, who would emerge the victor? Would the cocky Nottingham man get his come-uppance? Would the rough, tough ex-jailbird Looney put him in his place once and for all? On Merseyside, the dockers and sailor boys were counting the days; in Nottingham, the Lambs dusted off their twigs. When the day dawned, a fine summer morning, many of them had already arrived in the village of Chapel-en-le Frith, a village in the Derbyshire Peaks, miles from anywhere meaningful, on the road from Manchester to Buxton.

As with most prize fights, Bendigo v. Looney was held on a Tuesday and many of those attending began to arrive on the Monday. Tuesday was a popular day to hold fights because it avoided the necessity of large numbers of people travelling on the Sabbath for the purpose of an illegal activity. The Fancy might have been less than squeamish when it came to sport, but it was traditional in its observances.

On the Monday morning, Bendigo arrived at Chapel-en-le-Frith with Peter Taylor, from their training quarters at Crosby, while Looney came from Aintree. Bendigo met up with the Duke of Limbs at the Old Pack Horse Inn, where his fighting colours, the blue bird's eye, already covered the inn's sign. By the afternoon, into the evening and throughout the Tuesday morning, every sort of conveyance known to follow a horse could be seen rolling and trundling along the narrow stone-walled lanes, up the hills and down the dales of Derbyshire. Swells in drags, tilburys and barouches; butchers and publicans in gigs and traps; farmers and gamekeepers in dog carts – all were on their way to see the biggest prize fight to have ever taken place in the county. By nightfall there was not a stable to be found where a tired nag could rest, nor a bit of hay for it to eat.

The following morning, soon after 11am, the fighters left their lodgings and proceeded to the summit of a nearby hill, closely followed by around two thousand people. The Nottingham Lambs met Bendigo's new friends of the Liverpool Fancy, but, apart from the Jem Ward and Peter Taylor camps, their loyalties were split because Looney was of course one of their own. Ben Caunt, desperately keen for a re-match with Bendigo, was in attendance, while Sheffield and Birmingham were well represented in the multitude. As ever, the Lambs bet heavily on their hero, but many of the Liverpool and Birmingham men backed Looney. They had been impressed by his past wins, especially against the redoubtable Bob Hampson, whom he had beaten three times, and they did not foresee Bendigo having the stamina or strength to out-fight him. The bookmakers agreed: Looney was favourite at 5 to 4 on.

A few minutes after noon, Bendigo entered the ring, its stakes painted sky blue, with the letters LPR, signifying Liverpool Prize Ring, encircled in a wreath of gold. His arrival was greeted with loud cheers. He was quickly followed by Looney and they shook hands. Bendigo's seconds were his trainer Peter Taylor and – curiously - his last opponent, Young Langan; Bill Looney was attended by a pugilist named Joe Birchall and Young Molyneux, the dangerous black fighter who still wanted to meet Bendigo. The fight, which lasted ninety-nine rounds, was reported in full by *Bell's Life,* whose account, in the unique language of the prize ring, can be summarised:

> "Round 1. - The appearance of Bendigo, on coming to the scratch, was of the first order, and as fair as a lily, whilst Looney displayed a scorbutic eruption on his back. Both seeming confident of victory put up their fives, caution and 'stock-taking' for a few moments being the order of the day. Looney made a half-round right-hander, which told slightly on the ear. He then made three hits at the head and body, which Bendigo stepped away from, and dropped a little left 'un on the chin. Bendigo was not idle, but on the defensive, and succeeded in putting in two left-handers on the canister, and blood, the first, made its appearance from the mouth and under the left eye of Looney. This was a long round; in the close, Bendigo was thrown.
>
> 2. – Looney, all anxious, made play left and right; one told on the ear, a scramble, both fighting; Bendigo thrown, but fell cat fashion.
>
> 3. – Bendigo put the staggers on Looney with a left hand poke on the head; closed, and both down on their sides.
>
> 4. - Both came up smiling. Bendigo made two short hits, had his left intended for the 'attic' stopped, but put in a straight one on the breast, and the round finished by both men hammering away right and left in splendid style until Looney was sent down.
>
> 7. – Looney made two short hits with the left; Bendigo stopped his right at the ear; some capital in-

fighting took place, in which Looney got his right eye cut, and Bendigo slipped down.

8. – This was another good round, but in the end Bendigo got his man on the ropes in such a position as to operate pretty freely on his face, and showers of 'claret' were the consequence. Looney fell through the ropes, Bendigo over him.

9. – Looney came up as gay as possible, with two to one against him, and a slashing round ended in favour of Bendigo; Looney down.

10. – Bendigo sent home a tremendous whack on the left eye, which drew claret. Looney seemed amazed and put up his hand to 'wipe away the tear.' Looney thrown.

11. – Up to this round there was not a visible mark of punishment on Bendigo. Looney put in two hits on the left ear, but was thrown through the ropes, Bendigo over him.

13. – Looney hit short with his right on the body, but was more successful in the next effort; planted it on the ribs, and staggered Bendigo to the ropes, where both struggled down.

14. – A capital round, in which some heavy hits were exchanged, and Looney fell.

15. – Looney staggered his man again with his right, and, in making another hit, Bendigo dropped on his nether end, throwing up his legs and laughing."

Bendigo's clowning did not go down well with the Liverpool men who had backed Bill Looney. For them, the fight had not been proceeding according to hopes, with Looney taking most of the punishment. Bendigo's trick of hitting and falling brought howls of angry protest. But for the next two rounds Looney came back with hard blows to the ribs and ear; now it was the turn of the Nottingham men to be worried that their man was not taking the fight as seriously as he should. . .

"18. – Bendigo pressed Looney on the ropes, held him for some time in a helpless position, and gave it him severely in the face, the claret flowing copiously. He was lowered to the earth by a little stratagem on the part of his seconds.

19. – Notwithstanding the loss of blood in the last round, Looney was lively to the call, went up to his man, and knocked him through the ropes with a body blow.

> 20. – Looney caught his man with a right; a struggle on the ropes in favour of Bendigo. Both down.
>
> 22. – A rallying round, which Looney finished by knocking his man through the ropes by a blow on the breast."

Although badly battered, Looney was far from beaten and Bendigo was not getting it all his own way. By the 26th, although he "popped in three very heavy hits on the face" as well as three hits to the body, he looked weak as he went down to gain a thirty-second rest. Whether he was deceiving or not, the Lambs roared him on and scuffles erupted in the outer ring as they tried to get close enough to lend physical assistance. It was the signal for a Bendigo revival.

> "27. – Looney hit short. Bendigo gave it him on the conk, and threw him a clever somersault.
>
> 28. - Looney put in his right heavily on the ribs, which compliment was returned by a stinger on the head, which staggered him down.
>
> 30. – A slashing round; give and take was 'the ticket' on the ribs and head, until both went down weak.
>
> 33. – Bendigo put in two facers and threw his man heavily.
>
> 35. – Bendigo got on the ropes and Looney dragged his man back
>
> 38. – Looney planted a nasty one on the ribs, followed his man up, and forced Bendigo through the ropes.
>
> 39. – Looney planted three tidy hits on the head and body, as did Bendigo on the mug, again tapping the claret; but in the end was whirled to the ground.
>
> 41. – Looney caught Bendigo's head, put in a smart uppercut, but was thrown clean."

Bendigo, despite catching blows from Looney's right hand, was still relatively unmarked. There was dark bruising on his left arm where he had parried the shots, and around his left ear, but he did not have so much as a scratch on his face. Looney's face, however, told a different story – his face was swollen and cut almost beyond recognition. His left eye was completely closed with terrible gashes both over and under it; his right eye was cut and blood ran from his nose and mouth. But Bill Looney possessed that characteristic much beloved of the Fancy - he was "game". As the 42nd round opened, he rushed in, put in two sharp hits on the head, and downed Bendigo in a heap on the grass.

So it went on, round after bloody, bruising round. Weariness gave way to near exhaustion and it was now that both men's hard training paid dividends. With his vision impaired, Looney tried to damage Bendigo by wrestling and throwing him, but the latter's speed and agility meant that most times he was able to get away.

> "54. – Looney missed a heavy uppercut and swung himself through the ropes.
>
> 55. - Bendigo got Looney's head in chancery,[28] peppered away and again the crimson stream flowed. Both down.
>
> 57. – A close, in which Looney threw Bendigo a burster, with his head doubled under.
>
> 58. – Bendigo, being doubled on the ropes, received a few heavy hits on the ribs, but on Looney striving for his head he got away and both went down.
>
> 59. – A close, Looney receiving a shattering blow. Looney had his man on the ropes, but was too weak to hold him, and received another burster for his pains.
>
> 61. – Looney, again on the ropes, caught pepper in the face until it assumed a frightful appearance, and the claret gushed freely; he escaped by the cords being pressed down."

Looney, although in big trouble, was no quitter. His right eye was almost closed but he still believed he could win. In the 62nd he rushed in wildly, grabbed Bendigo in his arms and threw him and the next five rounds went largely in his favour. In the 68th he hit Bendigo a blow in the chest that sent him flying backwards against one of the ring posts with such force that he rebounded and fell flat on his face. Yet the Bold `Un's resolve and his seconds' powers of revival in the thirty seconds they had, after dragging him back to the corner, meant that in the next round, as Looney rushed in, Bendigo grabbed him, punched him on the nose and threw him.

> "73. – Bendigo gave three facers, but was thrown.
>
> 74. – Looney bored his man to the ropes and sent him through them by a muzzler.
>
> 75. – Bendigo slipped his left at the call, but closed an eye and went down."

---

[28] Where a fighter has one arm round his opponent's neck, at his own waist level. The opponent's body being bent forward, the fighter is able to deliver an uppercut to the face, with his free hand.

Looney's followers did not like this. A few rounds earlier they had given Bendigo the benefit of the doubt when he had gone down after claiming to slip on a tuft of grass. Now they howled with rage, calling him a cheat and a "cur", to which the Lambs responded by swinging their twigs and hurling abuse. Bill Looney, for his part, did not complain – no doubt he was glad of the brief rest. In the 83rd he had Bendigo on the ropes and gave him a heavy blow to the ribs. He was about to repeat the dose, but stood back when the Nottingham Lambs cried "foul". Two rounds later Looney was floored by a clean blow to the jaw and for the next six rounds Bendigo threw him about the ring at will.

> "92. - Bendigo showed a good feeling in this round. In the struggle Looney got seated on the under rope, but Bendigo would not take advantage and walked away.
>
> 93,94 – Looney down in both these rounds.
>
> 95. – Looney rallied a little and made two hits tell with the right on the ear, and Bendigo went down rather shook.
>
> 96, 97. – Both down together. Bendigo gave a muzzler in the last, got his man on the ropes, but was too weak to hold him.
>
> 98. – Looney put in his right on the temple but was thrown very heavily.
>
> 99 and final round. – Looney came up as blind as a bat and rushed in with his right, when Bendigo mustered up all his strength and gave him another fall. Molyneaux, finding it useless to prolong the contest, gave the signal of defeat."

And so, after fighting relentlessly for two hours and twenty-four minutes, Bendigo emerged the winner. The final throw, in the 98th round had been a piledriver, where Looney had been picked up and dropped headfirst onto the ground. By the end he was in a terrible state - his eyes were badly cut, his lips and nose mangled, he had lost some teeth and a great deal of blood. He was conveyed to his bed and could not be moved for days.

Bendigo left the ring to great cheers. Throughout the fight the Nottingham Lambs had caused a great commotion at the ropes, especially when their man was hit or thrown. Although by no means as damaged as Looney – his only facial damage was a black eye - Bendigo had endured some hard punishment from Looney's right hand and could not bear to be touched on his left side. Yet he walked a quarter of a mile to the horse-drawn gig that was take him back to Manchester for the night. And just in case anyone did not understand why he was known as the Bold Bendigo, they found out the following morning when he turned up at Newton races.

His victory was well-deserved. *Bell's Life* was generous with praise for Bendigo who had won first blood, first knock down and the battle:

> "He stands with his right leg foremost, has a good knowledge of wrestling, steps nimbly backwards to avoid and hits out tremendously with his left. . . being much improved since he fought Young Langan he will no doubt prove a troublesome customer to any 12 stone man who will meet him."

Now accepted by the Liverpool Fancy as one of their own, even though he had beaten their local man, a fortnight later Bendigo enjoyed a bumper benefit night at the Queen's Theatre in the town centre. Benefits, where fighters sparred, wearing mufflers, were popular attractions; the fans paid to see their heroes at closer quarters than they often could at prize-fights and the pugilists earned good money without risk of serious injury. Such nights were noted also for the challenges issued and, as in all things, Bendigo did not disappoint. After the sparring was over he took the stage, loudly claimed the title of champion and announced that "for a cool hundred pounds" he would fight any man in the kingdom.

5] The Big Chucklehead

When Bendigo declared himself champion, his was just one more claim to a title that had fallen into confusion and disrepute. Not that many people outside Nottingham would consider him to be the champion anyway – his announcement at the Queen's Theatre, Liverpool was more a statement of intent than one which he could expect the Fancy to accept. In reality he was merely letting everyone know that he had arrived in the top division and meant business.

Jem Ward had been the last man to win the title in the ring, when he defeated Jack Carter in 1828. He defended it only once, in 1831 against Simon Byrne, after which he was presented with a championship belt at the Tennis Court, Windmill Street, London, a popular venue for many a benefit and exhibition. The presentation was attended by many Corinthians, swells and 'professors' of pugilism. Ward offered to fight any man in the world for a sum up to £500 but there were no takers.

A year later he moved to Liverpool to become landlord of the Star Tavern in Williamson Square and announced his intention to retire from the ring, saying he would hand over the belt to the first man who proved himself worthy of it. Several challenges were made but the Black Diamond, as he continued to style himself, avoided them, demanding side stakes too high for anyone to match.

The worthiest challenger of all, Deaf Burke, had claimed the championship on Jem Ward's announced retirement in 1833. He defeated the only other major contender around at the time, Harry Macone, but Ward continued to style himself champion and price himself out of reach. Deaf Burke toured the country doing exhibitions to try to raise the necessary backing, only for Ward to keep increasing his demands. Ward had no interest in going to the scratch with Burke, whose last fight had resulted in the death of his opponent, Simon Byrne - coincidentally also Ward's last opponent. When Burke realised he was being stalled and that Ward had no intention of fighting him, he set sail for America to pursue his fistic fortunes across the Atlantic.

Jem Ward – the Black Diamond – soon to be Bendigo's mentor

Jem Ward, while being highly rated as a scientific fighter, was disliked by the London Fancy, the self-appointed prize ring "establishment". He had been denounced after the earlier scandals of two fixed fights and, even in a sport where sharp practices abounded, many backers and betting men would not forgive him. The Pugilistic Club, of which John Jackson had been a founder and mainstay, no longer existed, but its spirit was kept alive by another ex-champion, Tom Spring. His Holborn pub, the Castle Tavern, was the unofficial headquarters of the London Fancy, and the meeting place of the Fair Play Club, which Spring and his friends formed in 1828 to attempt to maintain some regulation and order in prize fighting. The club bought new ropes and ring stakes, to be used at officially recognised fights, and these were held by an appointed commissary, an ex-fighter, Tom Oliver.

Every New Year, Spring held a dinner and in January 1835 the main subject of discussion was the problem of getting Jem Ward to either defend or abdicate his title to the championship. It seemed obvious to all present that no person should be able to hold on to the title by demanding side stakes beyond the reach of prospective opponents. It was said that Ward could, if he wished, ask for £1,000 or even £10,000 and thus retain a title to which other men might have stronger claim. What was needed, the company decided, was an upper figure at which all challenges should have to be accepted.

Although the Fair Play Club had no real standing, as prize fighting remained an illegal activity, Tom Spring was influential within the London Fancy - and in consequence throughout the land. He agreed wholeheartedly with the proposal, as did the other pugilists and Corinthians who were present. It was moved and seconded that the maximum stake at which the champion of England should be considered bound to accept a challenge should be £200, and that if Jem Ward refused to fight Deaf Burke for this sum "he shall no longer be considered champion of England, but that Burke shall assume the title until bound to yield to a man of greater merit." The resolution was carried unanimously.

Jem Ward, who was not at the dinner, was unimpressed by resolutions passed by anyone concerning his title to the championship. From his chair in the singing room at the Star Tavern, a hostelry which, according to the *Liverpool Citizen,* was "a drum largely frequented by the greatest blackguards in the country", he despatched a letter to *Bell's Life* denying the right of Spring or any of those assembled at the Castle Tavern dinner "to legislate in what shall or shall not be the maximum stake for which the championship of England ought to fight." The way he saw it, he was champion and would remain so until he decided otherwise. The Fair Play Club thought differently and declared Deaf Burke champion, but nothing was resolved as Burke could not find opponents with backing and at the same dinner declared his intention to go to America.

More than two years passed before Bendigo made his claim, which was angrily disputed by Bill Looney, Tom Britton and Bill Fisher, all of Liverpool, and by Young Molyneux who had made the city his base. Each thought he had a better right than Bendigo to call himself champion and demanded the right to prove it against him in the ring. But while Bendigo had loudly offered to fight any man in the world, he did not see any of them as realistic opponents. Looney, whom he had soundly beaten, wanted a return match but could raise only £50 a side – half the stake of the earlier bout. Tom Britton, who had been thrashed by Molyneux, now offered to put up £100 but his backers would have been unlikely to risk their money if the challenge came within sight of being taken up. Fisher was a durable opponent but beating him would attract little interest away from Merseyside, while Molyneux's offer was easy to dismiss. He was unbeaten and a match with him would have caused excitement within the Fancy, but he would only fight at 11st7lb, a weight he knew the Nottingham man could not make.

Amidst the confusion of claims and challenges, Bendigo decided on a change of scenery. Unlike the vast majority of ordinary working class people of the time, who were born, lived and died in the same town, often without ever leaving it, he had been able to spread his wings further afield. Prize fighting had given him opportunities to see places denied to his fellows, whose lives followed the conventional grind of hard, tedious labour in the factories and sweatshops of Nottingham. The months he spent travelling with Levi Eckersley's fairground booth were an education and since then he had spent periods in Sheffield and Liverpool, as well as making his first trip to London.

Now, as he waited for a meaningful opponent – in particular the "official" champion Deaf Burke, who was still in America - he decided to leave Nottingham for a while. He needed to earn a living and he decided upon a change of scenery and to make his entry into that traditional business of the prize fighter – inn-keeping. Why he did not take a house in his home town he never revealed, but on 15th October 1837, it was announced in *Bell's Life* that Bendigo had "cast anchor at the Manchester Arms Inn, Sheffield, where he will be glad to see and serve all friends with the best of things necessary to make them comfortable."[29] And just to remind prospective ring opponents that he was available if the price was right, the report continued: "He cannot fight Looney for less than £100 a side."

Bendigo was already known and admired by the Sheffield sportsmen, themselves strong allies of the Nottingham Lambs. He had spent time in the town earlier, staying at the Rose and Crown in Blind Lane, but his tenure of the Manchester Arms was the cause for great excitement. Sheffield had a few resident pugilists, but no one of the calibre of Nottingham men like Sam Turner, Sam Merryman or Bill Atkinson, let alone the Bold Bendigo. Soon after his arrival, Bendigo set about to improve matters and liven up the local prize-fighting scene.

One of the better Sheffield pugilists was Joseph Lowe, who kept a beer house on the next street, Trippet Lane. Within a week of Bendigo taking over the Manchester Arms, a match was made there and deposits laid for Lowe to fight a Manchester man, Thomas Rivitt, the following month, within twenty-five miles of Sheffield. Bendigo took Lowe under his wing, and he became known in the prize ring as Bendigo's Pupil. He was the

[29] According to the Sheffield Year Book 1842, the proprietor was Abraham Horsfield, who, as well as being described as a victualler, was licensed to hire out gigs and to saddle horses. The inn was later known as The Saddle.

best of the Sheffield men but not even Bendigo's teaching and inspiration could lift him beyond the level of mediocre.

Prize-fighting in Sheffield gained in popularity through Bendigo's presence, but he had by no means cut his ties with his old friends and associates. On 24th November 1837 he was in the parish of Willoughby-on-the-Wolds, fourteen miles from Nottingham, acting as second to Sam Merryman in his fight with his rival townsman Bill Atkinson. The fight had been eagerly anticipated by the Fancy for weeks and spectators travelled from far afield, including many from London. Their approach to the fight was summed up in *Bell's Life's* finest prose:

> "The road to the mill[30] presented the usual motley groups which are customary on these occasions. The sporting butcher mounted on his fast trotting bit of blood, going along by the side of the swell Corinthian who in vain attempted to shake off the knight of the marrow bones and cleaver – the clergyman mounted on his neddy with a pin in his shoe as the best substitute he could get for a spur, with which and by dint of sundry wax he got up the steam of his Jerusalem tit to the rate of six knots an hour, appeared quite as much at home, and more ready for a brush, than the scions of aristocracy dashing along in their chariots."

The Nottingham Lambs, that resolute bunch of roughs who stood firm against all and every outsider, were in a dilemma. Both the fighters were Nottingham men and both were their friends. That Merryman and Atkinson had harboured a rivalry since a long-ago teenage encounter in the ring caused much soul-searching for the hard-bitten Lambs on this frozen winter's morning. Ben Caunt, who arrived with his entourage at ringside, was in no doubt who to back. His money was on Sam Merryman, a surprising choice given the big man's dislike of Bendigo, seconding in the latter's corner. Caunt was in jaunty mood throughout the fight, asking "How do you like that one Bill?" when Atkinson fell to an uppercut. Later he suggested that the referee needed his eyeballs washing and accused him of backing Atkinson, who emerged the winner when Bendigo threw in the towel for Merryman to save him further punishment after thirty four rounds over two hours and ten minutes.

Maybe it was the confusion they felt over who to support, but the Lambs were on their best behaviour all day. There were no wild scenes at

---

[30] Slang term for fight. Pugilists were sometimes referred to as 'millers'

the ropes or wanton damage to local property, no assaults of rival followers. It was by no means unknown for them to fall out and fight among themselves when no one else was available, but on this occasion the peace was maintained and they conducted themselves like true sportsmen.

Caunt's attendance at the fight was not brought about through mere interest in the sport. Ever since his loss on a foul to Bendigo at Appleby House two and a half years earlier, he had been smarting and seeking a return. After the Atkinson/Merryman bout he issued a loud challenge to Bendigo, whom he scoffingly called "the professing champion of England" to fight for £50 a side. Bendigo dismissed the offer from "the yokel", saying he would meet him any time for £100 and no less. Refusing to be put off, Caunt said he would be in Sheffield in two weeks time and would meet Bendigo at the Barrel, an inn in Pond Street kept by a man named Bill Cook.

Caunt travelled to Sheffield but Bendigo did not bother to not turn up at the Barrel Inn. The following week Caunt returned and, after much argument, Bendigo, seeing Caunt was seventeen stones and out of training, said he would fight him for £50 at Christmas - only two weeks away. Caunt refused, but on Boxing Night they met again. Caunt now had backers willing to stake £100 and Bendigo declared "at that price or any other the big chuckle-headed navvy is as good as a gift of the money to me." Caunt resented his rival's barbs, but resolved to gain his revenge in the ring. The match was fixed for the first Monday in April, to be held in the neighbourhood of Doncaster.

Ben Caunt's earlier loss to Bendigo, in July 1835, marked his debut in the prize ring. He did not fight again for over two years. He returned to the ring with two fights against Nottinghamshire unknowns, William Butler and Bill Bamford – the latter known as Boneyford - both of whom he beat easily, more through strength than science. In the same period Bendigo's reputation had spread throughout the country, via the ring grapevine and the pages of *Bell's Life*. Caunt did not hide his envy and resentment. He wanted to soundly beat the "self-styled champion" as he decried him, and to claim the title for himself. It was ambitious and audacious after only three fights, but such was the disarray surrounding the championship.

While Caunt milked the publicity of the upcoming battle in a series of benefits and exhibitions around the northern counties, Bendigo immediately went into strict training. Just as he had done twelve months earlier when preparing for his fight with Bill Looney, he journeyed to Liverpool and put himself under the supervision of his friends Peter Taylor and Jem Ward, the ex-champion.

Mistrusted by the London Fancy he might have been, but the wily, cunning Ward was one of the top trainers of his time. Attention to detail in the preparation of a fighter was vital and Bendigo had always been fortunate in the men whose ring wisdom had guided his career. Without a doubt, his backers, and particularly Joseph Whitaker, the Duke of Limbs, had considerable influence in such matters, because prize-fighting was organised by and for the purposes of gambling men, who expected the trainer to provide regular progress reports throughout the preparation period.

Vincent Dowling, later editor of *Bell's Life*, outlined the work involved in training a pugilist in his 1841 book, *Fistiana.* He suggested that between two and three months' build-up was considered the best way of preparing for a fight and advised "all backers never to patronise and all sporting men never to bet on the man who will not submit to a regular course of training." The trainer, he said, should "talk of nothing but how the victory is to be obtained and show his man how. Lead the soul along and the body must follow. Yet guard him against blind confidence and tell him of his faults."

After a few days easing in, with potions taken to purge the system by causing vomiting, sweating was the main priority of the second week, the aim being to reduce weight. The day would begin with a run before breakfast and later a long walk, interspersed with bursts of speed. Hard exercise was taken wearing flannel clothing and, on retiring for the night, the fighter drank hot milk, curdled with ale and slept in warm clothes to keep his temperature up.

On road work, Dowling said: "While jogging along, the conversation should be of the pleasant sort; viz, concerning the coming battle, former encounters, how many battles are won and lost, and so on." Sparring took place once a day during training for no less than an hour at a time, with the trainer preparing his man for all the opponent's foibles and modes of fighting. On days when bad weather prevented outside activity, Dowling recommended: "Spar at home, grind the meal, rub down a horse, play at ninepins, leapfrog or any manly exercise."

Careful attention was paid to a fighter's diet while in training. One celebrated old pugilist, Dutch Sam, would not train without a daily - and liberal – intake of gin, but the consumption of spirits was generally avoided. However, Dowling recommended a pint of ale a day, brewed three bushels of hops to the barrel. Tea and coffee were considered to provide no useful function, while Dowling swore by water gruel - salt and oatmeal in water – as "the all-potent iron prince of health and strength".

He recommended two meals a day: breakfast at 8am and dinner at either 2pm or 5pm. Rump steaks - good for muscle nourishment – were served with all fat removed. Veal, lamb, game and poultry, soups, fish, pies and puddings were avoided at all costs. Butter and gravy were banned, as was anything spicy as it was thought spices reduced the volume of muscle by absorption. The only vegetables worthwhile, according to Dowling, were potatoes.

Potions known as 'physicks' were administered freely. They took the form of pills containing mercury or senna and powders to induce sweating. Likewise, bleeding, purging and induced vomiting were all part of the trainer's programme. Stiff joints were treated with farrier's oils and for ligaments and tendons a veterinary compound - opodeldoc made up of soap, spirits of wine and camphor.

Dowling prohibited all indulgences: "spirits, porter, gross feeding, stimulants, tobacco, onions, pepper and sexual intercourse must vanish and no more be heard of within the first week." On the latter prohibited activity he said: "Indulgence with women is every bit as bad as indulgence with wine. Indeed, the one leads to the other; both enfeeble, undermine and at last prostrate the constitution."

There were strict guidelines even for ablutions, fighters being advised to wash in soapy water until "the long-adhering dirt and grease can be got rid of." In a period when cleanliness was not a high priority for many people, Dowling admitted that men might be embarrassed to the point of repugnance at washing their bodies. Nevertheless, he felt it was an essential part of the preparation, with the body afterwards rubbed down with course linen, followed by a brisk walk.

After a hard day's privations, bedtime came early. Dowling advised it should be "gone about pleasantly in an airy chamber with a chimney, but without curtains of any sort, on a hard bed of coarse linen."

Thus the top trainer prepared his man as well as any thoroughbred racehorse - and Bendigo submitted to this kind of regime without complaint. In between fights he engaged in his pastimes of cock-fighting, badger-baiting, angling and all the rest. He drank and joked the nights away, whether in Nottingham with the Lambs or in Sheffield behind the bar of the Manchester Arms, but once a match was made he left his pals and his usual haunts and got down to the hard work necessary to maintain the strength, speed and timing to carry him through the longest fight.

Although 3rd April, a Monday, had been announced three months earlier as the date of Bendigo's second fight with Ben Caunt, the location was a closely guarded secret. All that was known by those who intended to be there was that it would be in the neighbourhood of Doncaster. Vincent Dowling, the editor of *Bell's Life*, left London at 7.30pm on the previous Saturday evening by mail coach in order to report the fight for his paper. His account of the journey gives an insight into the lengths he and many others went to in order to follow the prize ring around the country.

All that Dowling knew was that the fight would take place between Doncaster and Selby, a town to the north. He boarded the Glasgow mail in the yard of the Bull and Mouth, close to the Post Office at St Martin-le-Grand. After calling at Islington the coach, with three other passengers aboard and coachman and guard up front, headed north, along what is now the A1. The night was frosty and the travellers, although well wrapped, were cold. By breakfast time they reached Grantham in Lincolnshire, and on they went, into the Dukeries and on into Yorkshire. Dowling, having confessed to his fellow passengers that he was editor of *Bell's Life in London*, became suspicious that one of the party might be a magistrate and was concerned in case the man had any inkling as to the purpose of his journey. On arrival in Doncaster, when the man was greeted as "My Lord" it transpired that he was a judge, on his way to the Pontefract Quarter Sessions.

At Doncaster, Vincent Dowling put up at the Angel, a coaching inn. *Bell's Life* had touts around the country who kept their ears open for prize ring information, but when the local man came to meet the editor he had no good news to impart as to location. Rather than being disappointed, Dowling found this heartening, for it proved that the necessary secrecy had been observed, which meant there was less likelihood of the fight being interrupted by "beaks".

That afternoon all was quiet in Doncaster, the locals being blissfully unaware of what lay ahead. Meanwhile, from Nottingham and the surrounding towns, from Sheffield, Manchester and Liverpool, in high spirits and with great anticipation, the Fancy had already set out. By the evening every road into Doncaster was thronged with carriages – "flies, phaetons, gigs and fish-carts, all laden to dangerous excess, and with a perfect disregard to the qualities of the horses engaged in the service." And as the better off sportsmen were hauled along by horse-power, as always, hundreds more, those known as "hard-ups", simply walked. Some had tramped the highway for several days, sleeping wherever they could find a barn or stable, eating whatever they could buy, steal or kill. No distance was too great to travel for the supporters of Bendigo and Ben Caunt.

By the time the cavalcade disturbed the Sunday peace of Doncaster, the locals had discovered what was afoot. In the Angel inn, Dowling lay in his bed as "The whole night long the rattle of wheels, the pattering of horses feet and the shouts of the anxious throng, proclaimed the interest which was felt and the wild spirit which was abroad." Pontefract was believed to be the favoured location for the fight, the town having been once represented by John Gully MP, a top prize fighter who had retired from the ring with his faculties intact and taken up politics.

By early morning the invaders who had congregated in and around the market square, were encouraged to proceed along the Selby road. Vincent Dowling took breakfast and followed the trail for seven miles until he reached Askern, a small village known for the healing qualities of its pond water. Here, he found a large crowd of sporting coves gathered outside the White Swan, where Bendigo had taken quarters with Peter Taylor. Ben Caunt was billeted at the Hawke Arms, only two miles up the road. Already the ring was formed, in a field off the main road, between the two hostelries.

Vincent Dowling – editor of *Bell's Life in London*

Dowling's arrival in a post-chaise at first aroused suspicion among the crowd gathered at the White Swan. He was met, "the scowling looks of some of the hard-ups, with whose private signs we were unacquainted, with more fear than affection." There was loud speculation that he was a "beak" but Izzy Lazarus, a Sheffield publican and occasional fighter, recognised him as "T'editor o' Bell's Life in Lunnon" and hostility quickly turned to admiration and excitement at the presence of such a great man. Even those who could not read – and there were many, including Bendigo - recognised the importance of *Bell's Life*, the weekly bible of the prize ring.

Dowling did not linger with "the unwashed from the hardware Country" as he disparagingly termed those from the industrial towns. He entered the White Swan to meet Bendigo, who was still in bed - " like a bacon sandwich, comfortably encased between two slices of flannel, vulgarly called blankets." It was the first time the editor had met the Bold `Un, whom he found in high spirits and expecting a victory. Dowling was impressed with Bendigo's very healthy appearance – "a rough, handy-looking fellow, very muscular.".

Having discussed prospects with Bendigo, Dowling returned to his waiting post-chaise and proceeded up the road to the Hawke Arms, where he met Ben Caunt. The man himself was dressing for battle. His father sat beside him "and if having a gigantic son is a source of pride he has sufficient to render him doubly so." Comparing Caunt, who was fifteen and a half stone to Bendigo, who weighed 11st10lbs., was, said Dowling, a "camelopard to a nylghau"[31] – yet the bookmakers had Bendigo favourite at five to four.

At the chosen site a large crowd was gathered. The Lambs patrolled the inner ring, ready and eager to crack heads with their long, heavy twigs. Bendigo and Caunt were expected at any moment, but the air of anticipation quickly changed to one of annoyance with the arrival of two magistrates and several constables on horseback, who announced their intention to keep the peace. It was suggested that the fighters, their attendants and the crowd should "mizzle out of the West Riding" if they wanted to avoid the force of the law.

The crowd, disappointed at being moved on, voiced their resentment and unwillingness to co-operate. Many of the Nottingham Lambs swung their cudgels threateningly in the air, growling that the "beaks and

---

[31] Roughly translated, a giraffe to an antelope

bluecoats" would not be able to do much about it if they chose to stay put. Why should they move on - many of them had walked many miles from their homes in Nottingham and Sheffield, just to get here? But Jem Ward, who had arrived in advance of the fighters, forced his way to the front and settled the unrest. Shouting to the crowd to calm down, he assured the lawmen that they would do as instructed and all would be well.

At this point, Ward assumed the role of director of the event. He took advice from people present who had local knowledge and decided that the fight would have to be moved to Hatfield, about seven miles away. The new location was within a short dash of the Lincolnshire border, should another move be necessary. The Liverpool commissary, who was responsible for setting up the ring, was informed and Ward set off, together with one of Caunt's seconds and Young Langan, who had been entrusted with Bendigo's spiked fighting shoes.

A scene of great confusion now ensued, with some of the Fancy following Jem Ward and others hanging about to follow Bendigo and Caunt, who had recently arrived and were waiting on the main road in their carriages. Neither of the fighters knew that Ward had declared Hatfield as the next stop and so when a local chimney sweep by name of Grear took it upon himself to lead the larger crowd, including the commissary with his ropes and stakes, towards Selby – in the opposite direction to that taken by Jem Ward and Young Langan - Bendigo, Caunt and the majority of their followers went with him.

Grear, who was well-known in sporting circles, was keen to bring the fight close to Selby, where he lived. He hoped that the ring might be formed near to the River Ouse, which divided the East and West Ridings, but every time the procession halted for the Commissary to fix the stakes and ropes, the constables appeared and the crowd had to move on. By the time they crossed the Ouse many of the followers, those on horseback as well as on foot, had fallen back through exhaustion. It was now mid-afternoon on Monday and many of the supporters had been on the road and sleeping rough since Saturday.

Monday in Selby was market day. When the procession entered the town the locals stood in amazement. Rumours were rife: one that took hold temporarily was that rebellion had broken out in the West Riding and the crowd was escaping. When the real purpose of the incursion became known, many of the townsfolk forgot their market and tagged along. Thus Grear the sweep had his afternoon of glory, leading Bendigo and Caunt in their separate carriages along the road for another four miles to Skipworth Common.

By the time he turned into a picturesque lane towards a field by the river, most of the several thousand original followers had been left behind. Jem Ward and Young Langan, the latter still holding his old opponent Bendigo's fighting boots, were at the Bell in Hatfield, unable to explain what had gone wrong to the large contingent who had followed them. At the ringside now were a mob of Lambs who had stuck with their hero, some of Caunt's hardiest supporters, those of the original crowd who were possessed of the stamina or the transport to cover the ground and a few hundred Selby folk, among them the captain of the local Badsdale Hunt. He lost no time in backing Bendigo at odds of six to four.

At half past four the men entered the ring, Bendigo first, joking as always. He was attended by Peter Taylor and Nick Ward, brother of the absent Jem. On calling for his spiked boots, Bendigo's high spirits were temporarily dampened when it was realised they had been left with Young Langan, whose whereabouts were at that time unknown. Cursing among the Lambs suggested that Langan had gone absent deliberately, to hinder Bendigo's chances and gain revenge for the fight he had lost to him the previous year. The real explanation was, of course, much simpler. But Bendigo, not to be put off by such a minor matter as essential footwear, soon regained his cheeriness when his seconds procured him a pair of "crab-shells"[32] and the fight commenced.

Many of the local spectators who had not seen Bendigo or Caunt before were astounded by the disparity in height and weight between them. Consequently, Bendigo, despite being favourite with the bookmakers, was considered the underdog. But as always he came out brimming with confidence, dodging back and forth several times to try and draw Caunt forward onto his right hand. Caunt was wary, but when Bendigo feinted with the right and let go his left he caught the big man on the left eye. Caunt instantly closed and grabbed him at which Bendigo went down to the safety of the turf.

In the second round Bendigo was hit with several blows but caught Caunt with a sharp one on the side of the head. In the next he drew first blood, from Caunt's mouth, and Caunt, indignant at the liberty taken, rushed in, lifted him off the ground and tried to crush him against one of the corner stakes. Bendigo only got away by wriggling down to the ground, his huge assailant weighing down upon him. By the fourth, Caunt was bleeding badly from his nose and a cut under one eye, while Bendigo had but a mark on his nose.

---

[32] Slang term for shoes, also known as 'trotter boxes'.

The fight was still in its early stages but Big Ben's temper, always his weakness, was sore tested. He could do little against the Bold `Un's quick, slashing blows and instant back-pedalling. Caunt's lack of defence and slower movement left him wide open to punishment. All he had was his size and strength, which he used to the full in the fifth round by seizing Bendigo in a vice-like grip and trying to strangle him against the ropes. As Bendigo's face began to turn purple there were cries of "Shame" from his Nottingham supporters and the Selby folk, who had no notion of the brutality in store when they followed the trail from their market place.

Bendigo managed to get away after a violent struggle and was thrown to the turf, to be hauled back to the corner by his seconds. Over the next half dozen or so rounds he kept at a distance, jabbing successfully at Caunt's head and going down at every opportunity. This was not generally approved by the Fancy but he had little choice against such a huge opponent. By the twelfth he had changed tactics, targetting the body instead of the head and peppering Caunt's ribs with lefts and rights that could be clearly heard beyond the ropes as they bounced off his ribs.

The thirteenth round brought scenes of unusual chaos, even for a Bendigo fight. Once more Caunt seized him, held him against the ropes and tried to squeeze the life from him. The crowd voiced their disgust, with more shouts of "Shame" and "Thou big, ugly toad, dost thou call that foighting? Whoy, the little `un would lick thee and two or three more such if thee'd foight!" Caunt, however, was not disposed to listen to such opinion and made no effort to let up on his bid to strangle Bendigo, whose eyes were popping almost out of their sockets with the pressure from Caunt's huge hands on his windpipe.

"Cut the ropes" came the cry from the crowd and the Nottingham Lambs, never without a sharp dagger or bayonet to hand, did just that. The ropes were cut in two places and both fighters fell to the ground, Caunt on top. In the ensuing melee, as the mob rushed to rescue Bendigo from under him, Caunt was struck and kicked, while the referee and umpires were jostled and threatened by the remonstrating spectators.

The unscheduled interval while the ropes were repaired gave Bendigo time to regain his composure as well as his breath. The fight resumed and from the fourteenth round to the thirty-eighth the action followed a pattern: Caunt rushed in, Bendigo hit him and immediately went down to escape being choked or thrown or worse. While all this was happening a lone magistrate appeared, wishing to put an end to hostilities, but he soon sensed from the mood of the crowd that his task was hopeless and he retired gracefully rather than risk his own safety.

Round fifty brought a dispute between the respective seconds, the umpires and referee. It was alleged that Bendigo has kicked Caunt as he lay on the ground. Bendigo professed total innocence, claiming he had tripped over him and the referee, aware of the increasingly threatening attitude of the Lambs, said he had seen nothing untoward. Spectators were now pressing forward into the inner ring, where the commissary's men were trying to force them back with cudgels and bull-whips. The out-of-ring fighting and the crush among spectators continued for the next twenty-five rounds as, in the ring, Bendigo hit the lumbering Caunt at will to the head and ribs, darting round him to throw punches from all angles. Caunt responded with some powerful body shots and occasionally managed to get him in a deadly Cornish hug but Bendigo was still moving quickly and the odds remained in his favour.

By the start of the seventy-fifth round, the men had fought for an hour and twenty minutes. Caunt, heaved off his stool by his second, Young Molyneux, was shoved forward with some force. Seeing him coming, Bendigo, who had just reached the scratch in the centre of the ring, fell back and sat on the ground. Molyneux, in the opposite corner, immediately threw his hat in the air and yelled "Foul", appealing to the referee that Bendigo had gone down without a blow. Nick Ward and Peter Taylor protested that their man had slipped, that it was an accident. As he had done earlier, the referee, William Lockwood, who in normal life was a publican on the outskirts of Sheffield, claimed he had not seen what happened but it now became clear, especially to Caunt's corner, that he did not understand the rules of the Ring. Eventually, when the significance of Bendigo's fall was explained to him, he agreed that a foul had been committed and that Ben Caunt was the winner. Before the referee could change his mind, Young Molyneux took Caunt out of the ring.

The row became more heated, Bendigo's corner saying he had slipped only because his substitute shoes, the "crab shells", were without spikes. Bendigo was outraged at the decision and wanted to resume the fight without any further delay. Seeing that Caunt had left the ring, he took the big man's colours, still tied to the post, and claimed that he, not Caunt, was the winner.

Caunt had almost reached his carriage, when a large band of Lambs caught up with him and demanded he return to the ring. He rebuffed them angrily and, with Molyneux, tried to make his way forward. His face was battered and bleeding, his ribs were bruised and broken and his temper had been tested to the limit, not only by Bendigo's superior skill and hit and run tactics, but by the chaos when the Lambs got in the ring. He told those who obstructed him that he had won the fight, he was the champion and to get out of his way. They ignored him and when he tried to climb onto a horse, the Lambs pulled him off. There were more scuffles as a group of Caunt's followers dashed up and, after more struggles, they managed to get him away from the field before he was further knocked about.

Even then, the Big `Un's troubles were not over. After fighting with Bendigo for an hour and twenty minutes, he had to walk the four miles back to Selby. From there he managed to get transport back to his base at the Hawke Arms, where his wounds were attended.

While Caunt's departure was being impeded by the Lambs, Bendigo was still in the ring, appealing to the referee to overturn his verdict. It transpired that Lockwood had not consulted the fighter's respective umpires, and Bendigo's umpire, who had been forced out of the ring before the fall, could thus not say one way or the other. The referee's inexperience was believed to have caused the unruly scenes, but in all fairness such outrages were commonplace whenever fights were resolved by a disqualification. Bendigo's backers gave notice that a lawyer's letter would go to the stakeholder, a man named Hutchinson who kept an inn at Dronfield near Sheffield, warning him not to part with the money until the rival claims had been thoroughly investigated.

When he realised that Caunt had no intention of returning to the ring, Bendigo and his party made their way to Selby, where they stayed the night. Unlike Caunt, he appeared little the worse for the encounter, the only marks on him being a bruise under his right eye, a swelling under the left ear, a few marks on his shoulders and welts and abrasions where Caunt had squeezed him and scraped him along the ropes. A few nights later he enjoyed a benefit at the Theatre Royal, Sheffield, sparring with Nick Ward and Young Langan. Those who packed the theatre to capacity were unlikely to have been readers of the *Sheffield Mercury*, whose brief report that the fight had occurred between Bendigo and Caunt stated:

> "It is a matter of serious enquiry how long the respectable and well-disposed portion of the community are to be sickened and disgusted beyond measure by such exhibitions, got up only for the gratification and entertainment of some of the most depraved and vicious of our species."

Bendigo still seethed at having lost his 100% record, albeit from a disqualification. To anyone who cared to listen he expressed his desire for a return fight "anywhere, anyhow on any terms – tomorrow, next week or next month, I'll do anything to accommodate the big chucklehead."

In the aftermath, there was a great deal of argument in the pages of *Bell's Life*. Vincent Dowling acknowledged that Bendigo "exhibited extraordinary powers of punishment; his hits were terrific, as Caunt's condition after the battle testified, his head and body being dreadfully shattered." But in an indication of the way the newspaper would criticise him in the future, the editor tempered what for his paper was prosaic praise by stating that Bendigo should not be regarded as a fair stand-up fighter: "He was shifty, and too much on the get-away-and-get-down system." As to how he should have fought a man over two stones heavier and five inches taller, the editor did not offer suggestion. Caunt was not a skilled pugilist; he had the physical advantages but he did not have the technique or timing to land a real meaningful punch during the whole fight. Bendigo might have been shifty but he was fast and his punches deadly accurate – as the damage to Caunt's head and body proved. The big man's style of grabbing, tugging, hugging and squeezing were more the mark of a backyard rough-and-tumbler than a man who claimed to be champion of the English prize ring.

While Caunt had won a victory by default, Bendigo did not consider himself to have lost. After all the arguments that ensued he was denied the stakes – the first time his backers had suffered such a setback in seventeen contests, but it was plain to everyone, except Caunt's staunchest friends, who was the best man in the ring. A few days after the fight Caunt offered to fight again for £500, but he obviously had not consulted his backers because the next week he stated that he was ready to make a fresh match "for £100 or as much as he can raise."

Ben Caunt now considered himself the champion. He possessed that attribute much respected by the Fancy - he was "game". So much so that, after two gruelling fights with Bendigo and a decision that owed little to his fighting skills, he could not resist Bendigo's challenge to fight again. Within days, deposits were laid and agreements made for the third contest between Bendigo and Caunt to take place in a thirty foot ring[33] within

[33] Bendigo's backers would probably have stipulated a 30 ft. ring, rather than the usual 24 ft. As a more mobile fighter than Caunt it would give him an advantage.

thirty miles of Nottingham and thirty miles of Sheffield on Monday 30th July.

But the fight did not come off on that date and would not do so for another six years. In May, Bendigo discovered he had bigger fish to fry – Deaf Burke, the official champion, as appointed by the London Fancy, who had been in America for more than two years, returned to England.

6] The Deaf `Un

James 'Deaf' Burke was the clown prince of the prize ring. Just like Bendigo he brought a sense of fun to a tough, brutal sport. Born in the slums of St Giles in 1809, he was two years older than Bendigo. He came from a poor background and lost his father, a waterman who plied his trade from the Strand Steps, at an early age. Burke was illiterate and had a weakness for drink, but was a genial and honest man. His deafness caused him to speak in an odd manner, shortening his words and often adding an "s' on the end, or using a "w" instead of a "v" – e.g. "Gemmen, I's is werry glads to sees you." He gave the impression of being a simpleton, an image he exploited to attract attention to his fighting career, often arriving at fights dressed as a circus clown. On one occasion he caused apoplexy among his backers by climbing into the ring wielding what appeared to be a huge cigar, but in fact proved to be a false one.

There was nothing false or funny about Deaf Burke's ability in the ring. Just like Bendigo, the Deaf `Un, as he was fondly known, rose through the ranks, learning his craft the hard way. He was nineteen and, like his father before him, earning a living rowing people across the Thames, when he won £14 in his first contest. Burke had never seen so much money in his life. Before he was twenty-one he fought eight times, including a near-three hour war against the much more experienced Bill Fitzmaurice. Two months later he fought a man named Bill Couzens on Whetstone Common, but fell exhausted after over two hours and 111 rounds.

It was his only loss before gaining the championship. He met and beat the best men around in the early 1830s, always laughing and playing the fool – until the moment came to start fighting. Facing arrest on a warrant shortly before he fought Andrew Gow at Woolwich, he gave his big hat, cloak and kerchief to an ex-fighter, Jack Carter, who put them on and drove off in a carriage, pursued by two constables. By the time the carriage was stopped and Carter arrested in mistake for Burke, the Deaf `Un had gone in the opposite direction, where he fought Gow without interruption.

In a bout at Shepperton, against an opponent who was known only as 'Birmingham' Davis, Burke was so much the better man that in the twelfth round Davis's seconds shouted "Don't hit him". He listened to their request, walked across the ring and shook hands with his outclassed opponent. The referee awarded him the fight.

Deaf Burke was at the peak of his career in May 1833, when he was matched with Simon Byrne, the Irish champion. Byrne had given Jem Ward a terrific fight for the championship in 1832, Ward's last outing before retirement. Two years earlier, in a decider for the right to meet Ward, Byrne had emerged the winner while his opponent Sandy McKay died a few hours after being carried from the ring following a blow to the throat. The Deaf `Un fought Simon Byrne when an inn-keeper put up £25 to take the fight to No Man's Land, near St Albans. After three hours and six minutes both men were utterly exhausted but only Deaf Burke was still standing. In a grim twist of fate, Simon Byrne died from the injuries he had sustained at Burke's hands - exactly three years to the day since his own blows had brought about the death of Sandy McKay.

Burke was charged with the manslaughter of Simon Byrne. Although he was acquitted and exonerated from blame, he found that his career was about to take a sudden downturn. For five years he had fought regularly – sixteen contests in all – without ever avoiding a challenge. He had beaten the best men in the land. Now, no one wanted to meet him. The Byrne fight, following on from other recent ring fatalities, turned many of the wealthier and respectable Corinthian backers away from the ring. They disliked the attention that court cases brought - and they were irritated by the efforts of the newly-formed Metropolitan Police, who were active in trying to suppress prize fights. Any fight in the London area involving Burke, who now had a high profile, was almost guaranteed to draw the beaks and bluecoats.

The Deaf `Un's lack of opponents did not arise because other pugilists, troubled by Simon Byrne's death, were reluctant to fight him. Neither fear nor superstition played much of a part in the psyche of the bareknuckle prize-fighter. The fact was that Deaf Burke was a top class man and anyone willing to fight him could not raise a side stake. Betting men preferred to have their money on Burke, not against him. Ironically, the one man who could raise the money, Jem Ward - the man Burke was keen to fight - was not interested.

Deaf Burke announced his intention to sail to America at Tom Spring's annual dinner of the Fair Play Club in January 1835, held at the Castle Inn, Holborn. This was the night when the London Fancy declared that

James Burke – the Deaf `Un

Jem Ward must fight Burke or give up his claim to the championship. The Deaf `Un knew that Ward would not oblige him, but he had received a challenge from Sam O'Rourke, an Irishman now resident in America. For two years O'Rourke had taunted and insulted Burke, claiming that he wished to avenge the death of his countryman, Simon Byrne. At Spring's dinner, the Deaf `Un announced that he would fight O'Rourke "or any man in the United States" and prior to setting off he would hold a benefit at the Coach and Horses in St Martin's Lane.

The benefit, described as "a regular bumper" was so successful that Burke realised he was onto a good thing and held back his departure to build up his funds. Not for another fourteen months would he finally board the ship to take him across the Atlantic. Before then he made a tour of the North, doing sparring exhibitions with Young Molyneux and revelling in the welcome he received wherever he went.

"Starring it in the North" was how Burke described his and Molyneux's trip. In Leeds they were made members of the local Buffaloes and a grand supper given in their honour. Forty-nine brother Buffaloes ate and drank until they were unable to stand. On the Deaf `Un's health being drunk with three cheers, he expressed his gratitude in his own eloquent manner, saying that he hoped his brothers would "live to die a natural death". He finished by singing a song of his own composition that went along the lines of "post your pony and make a match, and bring your man unto the scratch." He said he was still hoping to raise the money to fight Jem Ward and was "looking for golden options".

On 18 March 1836 Burke set sail. It was almost three years since he had fought in the prize ring and he was optimistic that in America he could resurrect his career. An Irish immigrant to the States, Sam O'Rourke, was issuing challenges in the press, saying he was "willing to meet any man in the world for 1000 dollars a side, preferably Jem Burke, who murdered my countryman, Simon Byrne." But if the prospect of America cheered Burke, it proved fatal to his old mother, whom he left behind in London. Only a week after he set off, *Bell's Life* reported her death, "in great mental agony at the absence of her son who was dutiful and affectionate." Little in the Deaf `Un's life happened straightforwardly.

When Burke arrived in New York his first move was to inquire after Sam O'Rourke. He was disappointed – the Irishman had gone silent after all the bluster and bombast that he had carried on since Simon Byrne's death. Nor could Burke find anyone else willing to meet him for money in a prize ring. The queue of contenders that he thought would be waiting did not exist. He travelled to Philadelphia, but met with no more success. He earned a few dollars sparring but it was apparent to everyone that he was far too good for the betting men who backed the local fighters to consider putting their money against him.

Yet all was not lost. The Deaf 'Un soon found another means of expressing his curious talents. He became an actor – of sorts. One night in New York he attended a performance by Mr Forrest, the celebrated American tragedian. Deeply moved by the event, he saw a golden opportunity. "Mind ye, this 'ere Forrest is a rum 'un," he said. "Fine actor mind ye. These Kembles and Keens used to pay a tanner to get in the gallery. I shall come out and play the Romans. Why shouldn't I be an actor?"

Why should he not, indeed? Soon a flaming placard outside Conklin's Hall, New York announced James 'Deaf' Burke as an actor "in classic sphere". He was appearing nightly and, so it was reported back in London, "astonishing the weak nerves of the Yankees, appearing on a pedestal as The Venetian Statue, with appropriate change of figure, attitude and expression". This was but one of a series of poses, billed as "beautiful compositions of ancient sculpture."

The Burke repertoire also included Hercules struggling with the Nemean Lion in five attitudes; Achilles throwing the discus or quoit in two attitudes; the slave Eme Leur, the grinder, sharpening his knife while overhearing the conspirators; two positions of a fighting gladiator; Samson slaying the philistines with the jawbone; the African alarmed at the thunder; Ajax defying the lightning; Romulus from David's picture of the Sabines; his brother Remus's defence from the same; Cain slaying his brother Abel and finally Samson lifting the gates of Gaza. He completed this esoteric performance with five celebrated positions of a dying gladiator.

Delighted as he was to be paid for shrugging off imaginary lightning, sharpening his non-existent knife and dying five times a night, Burke's real desire was to fight Sam O'Rourke. Hearing that the braggart was in New Orleans he travelled south and met up with him in a waterside bar. O'Rourke had not bargained for this. He was brave when issuing threats across the Atlantic, but reticent at the realistic prospect of them being taken up. He fell back on his original demand for £1000, which Burke could not match, but such was the excitement at the Deaf 'Un's arrival in town that two local gamblers obliged. They offered to put up $250 each, one on O'Rourke and the other on Burke. Now O'Rourke could not lose face and at last the match was fixed with the man whose challenge in the wake of the fatal Simon Byrne fight had enticed Burke to America the previous year.

Sam O'Rourke was not a classy pugilist, although he had been well-backed in his native Ireland, where his last fight, in December 1833 was for £50 a side. At the side of a top man like Burke he was a rough brawler, a hard case of the bar-room school, with a local reputation among the immigrant Irish community on the Mississippi docks. Nonetheless, as the representative of the New World against the Old World he was well-supported by the local gangsters and gamblers. These were the early days of prize-fighting in the USA and the presence of the English champion had put the whole of New Orleans in a state of hot anticipation.

On 5 May 1837 they met outside the city limits, at the fork of the Bayou roads. Burke, who was used to seeing footpads and thieves at his fights in England, found their American counterparts even more colourful. The crowd, made up of "Creoles, half-breeds, French gamblers, Yankee sharps, Irish roughs" according to one local reporter, openly displayed a variety of lethal weapons, including bowie knives and pistols. The Irish contingent, whether he liked it or not, expected O'Rourke to avenge the death of Simon Byrne. Hostility towards the Deaf `Un had reached an uncomfortable level before he even arrived in the ring.

Perhaps it was inevitable that the actual fight was an anti-climax, especially for those who had backed O'Rourke. His boasts and threats about what he would do to Deaf Burke evaporated in the humid afternoon air as he found the Englishman extremely difficult to hit, while he was himself on the wrong end of the sort of punches that only a trained fighter can deliver.

But if O'Rourke was not too dangerous within the ropes, outside them his second, Micky Carson, certainly was. Besides a towel and sponge, Carson carried a pistol and knife and did not restrict his involvement to merely attending to his man between rounds. In the second, he pushed Deaf Burke from behind, directly into the arms of O'Rourke, who threw him and dropped on top of him. When he rose to his feet, Burke told Carson that if he did it again he would knock him out, at which Carson produced his knife and threatened to slit the Deaf `Un's gizzard. The contest ended in mayhem and Burke, realising his safety was in jeopardy, made his escape by running away from the ring, punching and butting anyone who stood in his way.

The ensuing scenes were reported by the *Charleston Courier*:

> "Matters were coming to a fine pass. Burke was followed by a crowd of Irishmen with shillelaghs, dray-

> pins, whips and other weapons. A well-wisher, seeing him pass, handed him a bowie knife, and another gave him a horse, on which he escaped to New Orleans. The man who handed Burke the knife was cruelly beaten by friends of O'Rourke and we fear killed."

Throughout the afternoon and evening rioting swept the centre of New Orleans, until the National Guard were called out to restore order. Burke, sensibly, was lying low, hiding in a theatre owned by one of his backers. After some days he was smuggled aboard a steamship heading north up the Mississippi and he eventually returned to New York. He went back to doing sparring exhibitions for the next few months, until another fight could be arranged.

After the New Orleans debacle, this bout, against Tom O'Connell, another expatriate Irishman, was an almost genteel affair. Three hundred spectators took a chartered steamer to Hart Island and such was the decorum and good manners of the day that at the first outburst of cheering the umpires halted the fight and asked that "no ebullition of the feelings of either party should be suffered to take place." From then on, between the rounds there was a well-observed silence. Within the ropes O'Connell was no match for the Deaf `Un, who showed his gentlemanly side by suggesting that his opponent's seconds retire him after ten rounds, rather than let him be punished further. The contest was, said one observer, "a doubloon to a shin-plaster and no takers." Still, orderly as it was, the event reached the pages of the *New York Herald, who,* in a tone reminiscent of most of the English newspapers, stated:

> "Although we detest such exhibitions, our duty as chroniclers compels us to make public what we should otherwise bury in oblivion."

In May 1838, two years and two months after he had departed England, Deaf Burke sailed back into Liverpool, his pockets, he said, "lined with dollars". When he left, he was the top dog in the prize ring, the man who no one wanted to fight. Bendigo, at that time, was merely up-and-coming. He had beaten Ben Caunt and Brassey, but he was not considered at that time to be a contender for the championship. Sound defeats of Young Langan and Bill Looney had changed all that, while his disqualification in the Caunt re-match had not harmed him, since it was Caunt, not he, who came out of the encounter battered and bleeding. Now, as Burke returned, Bendigo and Caunt were signed up to fight for a third time.

The Deaf `Un was welcomed back to native soil with a benefit at the Mosley's Arms in Manchester, on his way from Liverpool to London. Just to let him know that little had changed during his absence, Jem Ward, whose refusal to fight had brought about Burke's American adventure, turned out to spar during the evening, wearing his championship belt. Burke moved on to Birmingham where he was booked in a theatre, appearing for several nights as Orson the Wild Man in a dramatic interlude, *Valentine and Orson*. Back in London, his Cockney friends held a benefit at the Grand Shooting and Archery Gallery in Leicester Square. The Fancy turned out in force and Burke obliged them with a performance of his New York statue act.

Bendigo was in a predicament. Deaf Burke was back in England and - so it was claimed - seeking a fight. But the Bold `Un was committed to meet Caunt on 30th July and he was anxious to settle matters once and for all as to who was the better man. Not that he had any doubt himself, of course, but the unsatisfactory ending of the second fight still rankled. Burke, though, was a bigger proposition. He had been declared champion by the London Fancy and was a fighter with an undisputed reputation, unlike the lumbering, hugging Caunt, whose ring record was unremarkable. If Bendigo could beat the Deaf `Un, his claim to the championship would be obvious. While his backers weighed up the situation, he busied himself training another fighter, Joe Lowe, who was known as his pupil. Lowe kept a beerhouse on Trippet Lane, the Sheffield street that lay parallel with West Street, where Bendigo was still resident at the Manchester Arms.

On Tuesday 3rd June 1838, he was in Lowe's corner when he met Dick Cain, a promising Leicester lightweight, at Dore Moor, five miles from Sheffield. It was not a big fight for the Fancy, although plenty of Sheffield men turned out, but the attention of the beaks meant that two earlier locations had been abandoned and it was half past five before the men went to the scratch. Lowe had nearly a stone advantage over eighteen year old Cain, who entered the ring wearing a sailor suit. But Cain, who was trained by Bendigo's old Nottingham mentor, Sam Turner, and had Bill Atkinson seconding, was in excellent condition. Joe Lowe, on the other hand, was, according to a ringsider, "puffy and sleek as a mole as if he'd trained on eggs, sago and calves feet jelly." He was no match for Cain and after half an hour Bendigo threw the towel in.

For a top fighter – a "professor" in the Fancy's terminology, and one so skilled and scientific - Bendigo had little success when training or seconding others. Throughout his own ring career and long after he retired he was to be found up and down the country assisting other pugilists, but it was a rare occasion for him to be in the winning corner.

After the setback suffered by his pupil, Lowe, Bendigo got down to his own business. The Deaf `Un was uppermost in his plans, but Ben Caunt had the most pressing claim for his attentions, since initial deposits of £20 a side had been made and Bendigo's backers had already laid down a second instalment. It was looking as though Burke would have to wait – until, to some surprise, *Bell's Life* announced that the match between Bendigo and Caunt was off, "by mutual consent".

What did this mean? The Fancy wanted to know. A week later Caunt stated he was open to fight "any man in the world barring neither country nor colour" for from £50 to £500 a side. It sounded good, particularly when Caunt's backer claimed that he had pulled out because "it is a pity to see so little a man as Bendigo fight a giant like Caunt, who is anxious to enter the ring with Deaf Burke." In the language of the prize ring, this was mere "chaff", for Burke was no taller than Bendigo. The real reason that the fight was off was because neither Caunt nor his backer could come up with the next deposit, to match that which Bendigo's side had made.

So Caunt forfeited the money already paid on his behalf, whereupon Bendigo hopped on the Sheffield to London mail coach and put up at Tom Spring's hotel in Holborn. Deaf Burke was now within his sights and he needed to be in London, close to the action, rather than out of the way in Sheffield.

For his part, the Deaf `Un made his intentions clear in a letter to *Bell's Life* of 29th July 1838.

> "Sir,
>
> When I was in Yankeeshire, I heard a great deal about 'would-be champions' challenging any man in England. 'While the cat's away the mice will play', and thus the little fry took advantage of my absence to bounce and crow like cocks in a gutter. I hastened back to take the shine out of these braggadocios, and to put their pretensions to the test. I beg to state that I am now ready to fight any man in England for from One Hundred to Five Hundred pounds and as my old friend Jem Ward has retired from the ring, if he will add his champions belt to

> the prize, and let the best man wear it, he will give new energies to the ring, and, I trust, afford an opportunity for deciding the long contested question, ' who is the Champion of England?'
>
> I bar neither country nor colour – age nor dimensions; and whether it be the Goliath Caunt or his hardy antagonist Bendigo, or any other man who ever wore a head, I am his customer and 'no mistake'. My money is ready at Jem Burns, Queens Head etc. Haymarket at a moment's notice; but I will not comment to a less deposit than £25 at starting. If I find the race of old English boxers of the right kidney is extinct, I shall go back to America where an honest man need never want 'a friend or a bottle'.

Burke's letter caused a stir within the Fancy, and not because of its mixture of his own odd language and that of whoever composed it – probably one of his Corinthian backers. If readers were amused by his reference to America as "Yankeeshire", or curious as to why a letter from an uneducated illiterate included the word "braggadocio", no one let on. Instead, the following week came a response from Bendigo, himself not known for his literary talents. His letter, headed "Burke's Challenge Accepted", read:

> "Sir,
>
> Having seen Burke's challenge in your paper of 29th inst., I feel great pleasure in embracing the earliest opportunity of accepting his challenge upon his own terms; which are, to fight me for any sum from a hundred to five hundred sovereigns, and for the Champion's belt of England. I assure you, sir, I shall feel extremely happy to fight the great Venetian – *and I mean nothing but fighting*; and if my friend Ward has retired from the ring and will allow the winning man to have the belt, I am satisfied it's mine. This, I hope, will convince the Deaf `Un, that the mouse is open to be caught equally as when the cat was in America. Further, to convince the 'vaunting Venetian,' my friends have placed £100 in the hands of Peter Crawley, who, according to the invitation in your last, will stake £25 a side as a first deposit and enter into articles on Monday (tomorrow) evening between 8 and 10, and it will then be seen who cries 'Hold, enough!' "

Signing the latter "30th July, Sheffield", Bendigo ended by saying that if Burke didn't come up with the money he would be guilty of boasting as he had complained of others doing.

Such talk of the championship was of great interest to the man who still considered himself to be the champion – Jem Ward. He was not impressed by the suggestion that he should hand over his championship belt to the winner between Burke and Bendigo and he pointed out that there were in fact two belts, both in his possession and both of which he intended to keep. The first had been presented to him in 1825 when he became champion for the first time and the second was buckled on him by Tom Spring and Peter Crawley in 1831 after he defended the regained title against Simon Byrne and then announced his retirement.

Ward reminded Burke and Bendigo that there was no belt which was transferable from one champion to another; those he had been given were with the compliments of his supporters. In a tone befitting his self-perceived role as a patriarchal champion, he said: "Should a battle take place for the Championship, I will feel proud to present to and buckle a belt on the winning man, resigning at the same time all claim to that enviable title, 'Champion of England' which I hope long to find struggled for by brave men, who do not wish to see the fine old English sport of self-defence die and pass away."

Bendigo lost no time in showing the colour of his money to Deaf Burke. Without delay, just as he had said, Peter Crawley, the ex-champion, was despatched hotfoot to Jem Burn's pub to pay over the £25 deposit. But when Crawley arrived, the Deaf `Un was nowhere to be seen. Instead, Jem Burn said he had received a letter from Burke, who was in France, saying that he could not fight for less than £200 and nothing was to be arranged until he returned. Bendigo was annoyed; after waiting for the so-called official champion to return from America, he now had to wait again for him to come back from France.

A week later *Bell's Life's* own laureate penned seventeen verses of doggerel, under the title "HEROIC STANZAS FROM BENDIGO TO DEAF BURKE." Purporting to come from Bendigo himself, the poem poked fun at the Deaf `Un's odd manner of pronunciation and accused him of running off to France to avoid fighting. It began:

"Why truly my nabs of the torpic auricular,
Your conduct of late ha'nt been werry particular,
And I tell you in werse, which I'm no hand at tagging,
That I shrewdly suspect you of bouncing and bragging.

When a challenge you gave and defiance was hurl'd,
To any professor of fives in the world,
Of course I consider that nothing was wrong,
Tho' I fancy you com'd it a trifle too strong.

I knew you were brace and as strong as a horse,
And remembered your sending poor Simon to dorse;
And you told us how Yankees all quak'd at your name,
And 'guessed' they'd ne'er witness'd such bottom and game.

You swore, as Jem Ward had retir'd on the shelf
Your mind was made up to be Champion yourself;
And you dar'd all the world to contend for the prize,
While you barred neither country, nor colour, nor size.

This was all wastly well, but how came you to trot
Ere you knew if your challenge was answer'd or not,
And to cut from your quarters in London adrift
On the cunning consarn between Adams and Swift?

I tell you, my Deaf `un, without any flourish,
Your conduct appears most confoundedly currish;
And as straightforward dealing was always my plan,
If you wish for a customer, I am your man. . . ."

And so it went on, referring to Peter Taylor's attempts to "post the pony" – make the first deposit of £25, to the fights with Ben Caunt, to Burke exhibiting "as statues of worthies wot figur'd of old, Apollor and Wenus" and to the "French polish" his current trip to Paris had given him. According to Henry Downes Miles, who later described the literary effort as "a contemporaneous squib" in his *Pugilistica*, "The public feeling in this matter was not badly expressed."

The "cunning consarn between Adams and Swift" was Burke's reason for travelling to Paris. He was there in the company of the lightweight, Owen Swift, who had fled England a month earlier to avoid prosecution following the death of an opponent, Brighton Bill Phelps. Swift's seconds in the fight were prosecuted and only a week or so before Burke and Swift decamped, Bendigo had sparred in a grand benefit in London to help pay for the seconds' defence. Deaf Burke, who knew what it felt like to have killed a man in the ring, had some affinity with Swift, although this was the second time Swift had been involved in a fatality.

It was a measure of the ruthless dedication to prize fighting of men like Owen Swift that no sooner had he unpacked in Paris than another English pugilist, Jack Adams, arrived and a contest was fixed for £50 a side. There was no shortage of betting men and Corinthians willing to make the journey from the homeland and Deaf Burke, far from being in attendance to offer sympathy and understanding at any trauma Swift might have felt at taking a second life, was there to tend his corner in the fight.

The Swift/Adams fight ended with the French authorities seeking to prosecute the combatants, who, along with Burke, were obliged to leave France in a hurry. But encouraged by his Corinthian admirers to "study Paris graces and parlez-vous", as his carousing was described, the Deaf `Un made the most of his Continental sojourn, although not in a manner appropriate to the life of a professional pugilist.

He was a simple man and easy to lead astray. In Paris he kept late hours, feasted on lobsters, devilled biscuits, cream and devilled kidneys and drank to excess. Burke played up to his fans among the London swell crowd and had neither the sense nor the discipline to maintain the diet and regime necessary to his calling.

After a month away, he returned, saying he would fight Bendigo for £100 a side. The dollars that lined his pocket on his return from America were gone and now he was so keen to make match with Bendigo that he halved the side stake he had originally demanded. "Needs must and better to have half a loaf than no bread," he said. But if his money had gone, his sense of humour was intact. Arriving back from France swathed in a bearskin, which he had acquired on his earlier trip to "Yankeeshire", he was promptly seized by customs officers who thought he was a zoological curiosity. They soon let him go. Said the Deaf `Un: "I gives dem a hugs and dey drops me like a hots potatoes."

At last the match was made for the 15th January 1839, although later postponed to 12th February, Shrove Tuesday. Bendigo v. Deaf Burke would be the first championship contest to be held under the New Rules of Prize Fighting, brought in the previous year following a public outcry at the fatal fight between Owen Swift and Brighton Bill Phelps. There were now twenty-three rules to replace Jack Broughton's seven, which had been in service since 1743. The new rules decreed that men must walk unaided to the scratch before each round and that they had eight seconds, from the call of "time" to do so. The duties of the referee, two umpires, seconds and bottle-holders were stipulated, as were the measurements and fixtures of the ring. Head-butting, kicking, hitting below the belt and falling without a blow were deemed to be fouls, although a man could slip to the turf in a close with his opponent to escape further punishment. Rules governed the holding and payment of stakes and bets and the duty of umpires and referees "in the event of magisterial interference".

Bendigo was not impressed by "the great hero and Yankee celebrity" as he called Burke but he agreed sidestakes of "a cool hundred". Knowing the Deaf 'Un was desperate to fight because he needed the money, he stipulated that the first deposit must be made at his pub in Sheffield, the Manchester Arms. "I see no reason why the Lunneners should have it all their own way," he said. When Burke turned up in Sheffield, he found Bendigo in truculent mood, as the Deaf 'Un complained later to *Bell's Life*. Accusing his forthcoming opponent of "showing the white feather", Burke made his journey worthwhile by sparring with local fighters at a benefit at the local Theatre Royal.

Bendigo was intent on getting his own back for the frustrations of being kept waiting during Burke's foreign travels and did not bother to turn up for the next deposit. Burke had once again been obliged to travel from London to Sheffield, a distance of over 150 miles by mail coach, and this time he performed his Venetian Statues act at the town's Circus Royal, in the Cattle Market. Poking fun at Bendigo, he suggested he try his hand in the character of Guy Fawkes – presumably an allusion to the latter being hung, drawn and quartered. Bendigo declined, but Ben Caunt, who was doing his best to upset the arrangements by offering to fight Burke himself, sparred, as did Dick Cain and some of the local men, including Izzy Lazarus.

Such events were organised to create publicity and interest in the upcoming bout, in much the same way as modern fighters make public appearances and give press conferences. However, Bendigo, had more urgent work to attend to, for while Burke was parading the boards, the Bold One was at Woore in Staffordshire, the scene of his victory over Young Langan. Here, he acted as second to his trainer, Peter Taylor, who fought Joe Birchall. Just as Bendigo was a better fighter than trainer, Taylor was in reverse. And as so often happened to the men Bendigo seconded, Taylor lost - after fifteen rounds he was blind in both eyes and Jem Ward gave in for him.

The Deaf 'Un continued with his theatrical pursuits on his way back to London, stopping off in Nottingham to perform his statues act and his impersonation of the Wild Man in Valentine and Orson. The character, which involved unearthly noises and bellowing and satyr-like antics was said to suit him extremely well, while the inhabitants of Bendigo's hometown were so inspired that for a long time to come they chastised children by threatening them that if they misbehaved they would be taken to the Wild Man Burke.

Both Bendigo and Burke attended the payment of the third deposit, at Jem Burn's pub, the Queen's Head, Great Windmill Street. They were in exuberant mood, Bendigo being described as "full of quaint fun" while Burke tried to claim he was doing his opponent a favour. He had, he said, "lowered me price by £50 to 'commodate Mishter Bendys as he sez his frinds is backards in comin forards."

Shortly before Christmas 1838, Bendigo went into training at Crosby, on the mouth of the Mersey near Liverpool. It was his favourite location for getting away from the distractions of inn-keeping in Sheffield - although that hardly seemed to tie him down - or engaging in rough pursuits with the Lambs in Nottingham. He liked the open air, being able to run along the sand hills and having the variety of sparring partners that his trainer Peter Taylor could provide from Liverpool. Among those who helped out was Matt Robinson, who kept the Molly Maloney beer house in Upper Dawson Street, and was notorious for always being short of money. His favoured mode of dress was a black suit, in which, posing as a bereaved widower, he tried to scrounge money off unsuspecting sympathisers for his late spouse's non-existent funeral.

Deaf Burke, meanwhile, was taking the air at Brighton. As the official champion, he lived up the part fully. Thus, as well as his trainer Tommy Roundhead, he was accompanied by a secretary to read and write for him. "The Deaf `Un thinks no small beer of himself," commented *Bell's Life*. But Burke had hardly begun. The week before Christmas the recently crowned Queen Victoria arrived at Brighton Pavilion, and for the Deaf `Un that was too much for a fellow to bear. His nerves, he said, were far too sensitive for him to be in such close proximity to Her Royal Highness and his devotions to her were interfering with his training. His trainer, Tommy Roundhead, moved him back to London.

Roundhead was not much less eccentric in his ways. On Christmas morning he accepted a wager that he could eat a whole calf's head. When it arrived he was startled by the size of the beast's head. This was not a calf, he claimed, it was "an Essex lion". He lost the bet, when he was unable to chew through its horns, which he declared were too large to swallow.[34] He and Burke settled into new training quarters at Finchley, where the Deaf `Un was said to have "imbibed strange aristocratic notions". While Bendigo ran along the sandhills in Lancashire, Burke sat daily as an artist painted his portrait. He took the attitude of a Grecian philosopher, scratching his head and cogitating on things to come.

By the end of January, Bendigo's backers were happy in the knowledge that their man was "in prime twig". He had trained hard, sparred well and was not distracted even when the house where he was staying, fell down around him.

On a Sunday night Bendigo went to bed at his normal time of 9 o' clock. He soon fell asleep but was woken at eleven by a storm raging around the house, his bed rocking under him and bricks tumbling down the chimney. He huddled under the blankets for several hours, as masonry and glass fell around him, expecting the house to collapse at any moment. At 3 am, he got up, put on his clothes and climbed out of the window. Ten minutes later, the roof fell in and the hurricane all but demolished the house.

The next morning, when he failed to meet up with Peter Taylor for training, Taylor went to the house. He got a great shock to find it in ruins, and Bendigo nowhere to be seen. Fearing the worst, he was relieved to discover the Bold `Un alive and well and sleeping soundly in a nearby cottage, where he had been taken in by a friendly cobbler. He told Taylor "I'd sooner meet three Burkes than spend another night like that."

In the Deaf `Un's camp, concerns were mounting. Their man was not keeping to a strict diet and believed himself to be too great a person to be dictated to by a mere trainer. He had now forsaken serious exercise and taken up boating on the Thames at Putney - an activity which professors of pugilism did not believe was especially helpful in developing speed, stamina or the delivery of punches. He took no notice when told that Bendigo was a fast, tough fighter whose southpaw style made him difficult to both hit and avoid. He did not attend the final deposit at Jem

---

[34] Odd wagers such as this were quite common. In April 1835, at the Jolly Miller, Millbank Street, Westminster, a man named Townsend who was a celebrated pedestrian, was matched to stand on one foot for three hours and during that time to shave himself, eat his supper and to pull off both his shoes and stockings six times and put them on again, without any other support other than the foot on which he stood. He completed the task with ease, at which the landlord offered to back him to stand another hour.

Burn's but told anyone who asked that he was confident that in two weeks' time he would be wearing Jem Ward's championship belt.

Burke seemed to have forgotten that Ward, who was applying the finishing touches to Bendigo's preparations, had no intention of handing over the belt, which he considered his own personal property. Burke's faithful trainer, Tommy Roundhead, declared his man to be "as strong as a rhinoceros and as bold as a lion" but the Corinthians and Cockneys who had observed his half-hearted training schedule were not convinced.

Shrove Tuesday, 1839 was the appointed date for combat. The day before, Monday 11th February, Bendigo, Burke and their close associates met at the Red Lion in Appleby, Warwickshire, to agree where the fight should take place. From there Burke and his party, which included Jem Burn, Tommy Roundhead and Dick Curtis, better known as King Dick, took up quarters at nearby Atherstone, where Burke's presence was seen as a good omen for the annual sports day, held every Shrove Tuesday. Bendigo, watched over by Peter Taylor, Jem and Nick Ward, had a quiet night at an inn closer to the proposed ring.

The fight was planned to begin at ten o'clock on the Tuesday but, as always, spectators began to arrive in hordes the day before. Once they located the Deaf `Un's base they congregated outside, waiting throughout the freezing winter's night. All manner of vehicles had been pressed into service, to get them there, including mourning coaches and even a hearse. Worn-out old nags were taken out of retirement to draw post-chaises and anything else with wheels on and capable of carrying people.

At nine o'clock in the morning the assembly outside Burke's lodgings was vast and increasing. The arrival of a cavalcade of swell drags from Leicester, carrying some of Burke's patrons, was the signal to move off and Burke's party departed for the ring. Those without transport were dismayed to find that it was situated seven miles away, on top of a hill near to the village of Heather. By the time Burke reached there at eleven thirty, thousands of people were waiting, although many more were still treading the frosty roads.

Burke was first in the ring at quarter to one. Accepting the applause of the London Fancy, he posed in a comical attitude and said "Ajax defyings the lightnings. So does I chucks my castors into the rings gentlemens." As everyone waited for Bendigo's arrival, a good-looking, well-dressed woman forced her way through the throng, went up to the ring and seized the Deaf `Un by the head. Prevented from embracing him by the ropes, she seated herself at the ring side and both she and Burke refused to say who she was. He was in very good humour, laughing and joking in a confident manner and clearly believing he was destined to win the day.

Outside the ropes, the Nottingham Lambs were active, as ever. Tom Oliver, the commissary, had hired a large band of 'orderlies' – ex-fighters armed with bull-whips to keep order, but the Lambs still managed to swing their 'twigs' and to sell tickets to a second outer ring they had formed. Here, hucksters wandered through the crowd, selling apples, oranges, nuts, gingerbread and herb beer. Further back, a local publican sold ale from two casks on either side of a cart.

A few minutes before one o'clock, Bendigo made his grand entrance into the ring, amidst deafening shouts of encouragement. Besides the Nottingham Lambs and several thousand more of his hometown followers, large numbers had come from Sheffield, Coventry, Birmingham, Leicester and all the surrounding towns. The newly-built railway meant trains had been laid on from London and Liverpool. By now the crowd was estimated at fifteen thousand, with the largest turn-out of aristocracy that had been seen at a prize fight for many a year.

Bendigo immediately went over to Deaf Burke's corner and shook him heartily by the hand. Burke was seconded by King Dick and Gentleman Jackson, the latter sixty years old and making what would be his last appearance in a ring. The Deaf `Un received Bendigo's greeting warmly, winking at him and stating that he was about to thrash him. When the men then removed their greatcoats and stripped to their fighting breeches, it was seen that Burke's were trimmed with green ribbon and that Bendigo was giving them a great deal of attention. However, it was not the trimming that interested Bendigo, but a belt that the Deaf `Un wore around his waist. Calling over the referee, he demanded that it be removed. Burke explained that it held up a truss which he had to wear since suffering a rupture ten years earlier, but Bendigo was having none of it.

Although the referee declared the belt to be fair, since it was below the waist, Bendigo and his seconds – Peter Taylor and Nick Ward – were adamant that it must be removed. No amount of protesting by the Deaf `Un would change their minds and eventually the belt came off. The referee held it up for inspection, to prove his point that it was harmless and would not have given Burke an unfair advantage.

Stripped and ready, Burke's muscular figure, for which he was distinguished, was not as conditioned as it should have been. He weighed 12st. 6lb to Bendigo's 12st. 1lb, but he looked pale, the missed training sessions and the soft living showing their effects. Unusually, Bendigo had an inch height advantage and as always he looked in fine fettle. His face bore a confident smile as he advanced to the scratch, the underdog with the bookmakers who made Burke favourite at six to four on and found plenty of takers among the London-based Corinthians.

Round 1:Burke came out standing square, his hands high and waiting for Bendigo to make a move. Resolutely on his guard, he could do nothing to stop a right-handed body blow from Bendigo, whose knuckles left a visible impression on the Deaf `Un's ribs. Bendigo brought cheers from the crowd when he scored with a left under the eye but then got involved in trading blows. Some heavy exchanges followed before both men fell together in a corner. Seeing a redness about Bendigo's left ear, Burke's seconds loudly cried "First blood" but the referee, examining the ear, announced "No claret".

As the second round began, Bendigo feinted with his left, hoping to lead off with his right, but Burke was wise to the move. The speed and accuracy of the Bold `Un's right hand soon became apparent as he struck home again under the eye of Burke, who responded with heavy punches to Bendigo's body. Once more they rallied with rights and lefts until both fell. As Burke was carried to his corner, the young lady who had approached him earlier cheered him on, but he was breathing too heavily to notice. Bendigo, who had taken some punishment in the round, appeared untroubled.

Already the Deaf `Un's face was flushed and his body bore the marks of Bendigo's punches. He had a serious expression on his face and "coughed as if the contents of his pudding bag were not altogether satisfied with the disturbance to which they had been exposed." Ringsiders commented that his "cat's meat was out of trim". But when he managed to stop a couple of right hand shots from Bendigo he became more confident and even playful. He went into a fancy dance – which Bendigo stopped abruptly with a left and right to the head. At the ropes, bookmakers were now giving even money on Bendigo.

In a long third round Bendigo jabbed repeatedly at Burke's eye and induced a large swelling on his cheek bone. Burke seemed not to know what to do, as his friends urged him to go in and fight. Even when he did, Bendigo continued to hit on the retreat and the blows he took in return did not tell on him. First blood came from Burke's nose as his left eye closed. Burke looked round almost stupefied as Bendigo jabbed away, taking little in return and finally throwing his man to the ground and falling on him.

When the round ended, Burke desperately tried to make himself vomit by pushing a finger down his throat, but he was unsuccessful. His supporters were astounded at his sluggishness, a London publican shouting "Vake up Deaf `Un! Vats the matters vid you?"

Bendigo came forward for the fourth almost unmarked, while Burke looked much the worse for the previous round. His seconds urged him "Go in and fight" but when he tried Bendigo jabbed at his damaged eye, all the while stepping back as he threw punches. His style was all his own and Burke could not work out how to deal with him. While he thought about it, Bendigo hit him on the nose so hard that it sent him reeling backwards. He recovered and rushed in but Bendigo was so quick on the retreat that he fell over the ropes and out of the ring.

By now the two men had been fighting for sixteen minutes and Bendigo was getting the better of it. Two rounds later both Burke's eyes were closed and the odds were three to one on Bendigo with no takers. In the seventh, Burke was thrown and, on being lifted up by his seconds, claimed in desperation that Bendigo had committed a foul by head-butting him. The referee and both umpires knew otherwise and so the punishment continued. The Deaf `Un was nothing if not brave and continued to rush in, swinging punches, only to be picked off on the face and head.

In the tenth round Burke, agitated and distressed, came in and forced Bendigo back against the ropes. Holding him in that position, he head-butted him twice, at which they both fell to the ground. Jem Ward, at the ropes, yelled "Foul" and, with less uproar and controversy than usual, because it was clear that Burke had butted him intentionally to save himself from further punishment, Bendigo was declared the winner.

The fight had lasted only twenty-four minutes and Deaf Burke had been punished more severely than in any of his previous fights. He had come into the ring as favourite, the officially appointed champion. He was the man who no one, not even Jem Ward, would fight before he left for America, the man whose fists had killed Simon Byrne. He had returned from "Yankeeshire" brimming with vanity, believing that he was unbeatable and he had taken the challenge of Bendigo too lightly. By bitter experience and his own blood he had been reminded that prize fights were not won by rowing on the Thames, less so by posing as a statue or by sitting for portraits. As Vincent Dowling wrote in *Fistiana*, "You might as well try and dam the gut of Gibraltar with a sluice made of wafers as go into the ring without training." After his defeat by Bendigo, Deaf Burke, one of the great fighters of his day, would never be the same man again.

Jem Ward, Bendigo's mentor and trainer, was triumphant. He had sung his man's praises for more than two years and few outside the Midlands had listened, believing that the Bold `Un was a mere flash in the pan who would be found out by a class fighter. His speed and agility were underestimated and his unique hit-and-run tactics – more than a century before their time – were decried by those who regarded 'gameness' as a greater virtue than skill and preferred to see men stand toe to toe, pulverising each other. Jem Ward now reminded them of what he had been saying and *Bell's Life* endorsed his words, declaring Bendigo to be "a better man than has for some years appeared in the ring".

After the fight, Bendigo returned to Nottingham. In the taverns and inns on Long Row and around the Market Place, and in the villages and hamlets for many miles around, toasts were drunk to his success. His friends and supporters were cock-a-hoop at the killing they had made with the bookmakers who had him down as the underdog and there was much merriment for days. The Lambs, whose twig-wielding activities at the ringside were, as usual and with some justification, heavily criticised in London circles, said the ends had justified the means. Two nights later at a dinner held by the Duke of Limbs and other backers at the Star Inn, a subscription was commenced to present him with a silver cup, to mark his victory over Deaf Burke. Bold Bendigo, the pride of Nottingham, was the toast of the town.

7] *Bounce and Claptraps*

Bendigo now declared himself the champion of England. He had beaten Deaf Burke, whose title had been bestowed on him rather than won in the ring, and, as far as he was concerned, the matter was beyond dispute. That *Bell's Life* sneakily suggested he should beat Ben Caunt before claiming the championship was of no consequence. He would meet Caunt anywhere, any time, if the money was right. The "big chucklehead" held no fear for him.

Six nights after the Burke fight, the Queen's Theatre in Liverpool was full to the rafters when he took a benefit, assisted by Jem Ward and all the local fighters. This was to have been the occasion of Ward presenting him with a championship belt, but that part of the celebrations had to be postponed because the belt was not ready. The great moment came a week later at the Royal Circus in Sheffield, when, prior to sparring, his mentor buckled the belt around Bendigo's waist.

The house erupted with cheering as, admiring the belt around him, he moved to the front of the stage and began to address the audience. He said he had arrived at the top of the tree where his ambition had led him for some time. Now he had got the belt he meant to stick to it. He would not accept challenges from all-comers because it wouldn't pay him to leave his business at the Manchester Arms to fight for small sums as he had done before, but he would fight anyone for a good stake. To a man the Sheffielders cheered. The champion was one of their own – for the time being anyway. The night was a resounding success.

Down in London, Deaf Burke was playing the bad loser. He blamed his defeat not on Bendigo being the better fighter, nor on his own foolish lack of preparation, but on having to remove the belt that held up his truss. The loss of this item, to which the truss was attached by a loop, had been a devastating blow to his chances and had affected his ability to fight, so he claimed. Other fighters – he named Jack Langan and Peter Crawley – wore belts to hold up trusses and no one complained. Bendigo had been given a great advantage.

Many of Burke's Corinthian followers were bitter and angry at the way he had succumbed in the fight. They had expected the old Deaf `Un, the one who beat Simon Byrne, but they got a man who had fought only twice in six years and then in America against men who were no match for him. Worse, he had taken his responsibilities lightly, preening and posing when he should have sparred and sweated, taking the easy way out to avoid punishment. They forgot their own part in his dissipation, not least introducing him to the flesh pots of Paris.

Fortunately for Burke, not all his supporters turned against him. Those who stayed loyal attended a benefit at the Bloomsbury Theatre, where he addressed them: "Gemmen, I mean to say as I do not think as I was fairly beat by Bendigo, and I am prouds to say as I am not widout friends what tink de same and as are ready to back me for a cool hundreds against him... Bendigo is werry bounceable now as he says he has licked me but I says he took an unfair advantage in regard of my belt, but dat's neither one ting or toder and if he has friends – and from what I hears, he has not many, at least what respects him – if he's a man he'll give me anoder chance."

As Bendigo moved between Nottingham, Sheffield and Liverpool, taking the compliments of his friends and basking in his success, and as Deaf Burke noisily demanded a re-match, Ben Caunt felt left out. He offered to fight the ubiquitous "any man in England" but did not draw the new champion's attention. Bendigo had a higher sum in mind for his return to the ring. He announced that he would fight anyone except his friend Jem Ward for the sum of £300 to £500 and it was no use "chaffing" him with a paltry sum like £100. His money was ready at the Manchester Arms. *Bell's Life* commented "This is most bounceable but we hope the great man will be accommodated."

From Bristol, where he had taken up temporary residence, Ben Caunt suggested he would certainly accommodate the new champion, saying he would be returning home to arrange the stakes. When he did return home, he was gravely disappointed to find his backers refusing to put up any money. This was a curious state of affairs – *Bell's Life* said Bendigo could only consider himself champion when he had beaten Caunt, but the Hucknall giant's backers did not consider their man's chances good enough to risk the side stake. There was no response even when Bendigo, in nearby Newark for a benefit, said he would do Caunt a favour and fight him for £200. It looked like the big man's opportunity had passed.

If Caunt could not raise a stake, Deaf Burke thought he could. The vice dens of London's Haymarket, where he spent much of his time, drinking, carousing and acting as bouncer for his innkeeper friends, still held plenty of swell coves keen to steal an hour of reflected glory by backing the Deaf `Un in the prize ring. London's night life flourished in such low dives as Goodred's Saloon, The Finish in St James's Street, The Elysium, Mother Emerson's Waterford Arms and a hundred other places where a man could drink, gamble and debauch away his life.

Burke had another attempt to lure his conqueror into a return. On 28th April 1839, he responded to Bendigo's statement that he would fight for £300 to £500 in one of his inimitable letters to *Bell's Life*:

> " Sir,
>
> I seed mister Bendy's challenge in your paper last week and I think as he's coming it too strongs. When I was as great a mans as he now thinks he is I fought him £120 to £100 and would have fought him for £50 or even for love, rather nor he should say as I didn't give him a chance. But now, when I downs in the worlds, he wants to come the grands – and when he knows a man's what's licked can't get as many friends then he's a winner. He crows over him. But what I says is this – if Bendy has so much of that courage for what he has credits, he will give me another shy, and fight me a return match for £100 halfway between Sheffield and Londons. If he picks me again then he may continue to crow, and I'll give him all he can get, but as he knows I was out of condition and I suppose is afraid to meet me as I ought to be and not as I was when he gained so easy a victory. My money is ready if he has the spunk or that manliness to show that it is honour and not 'filthy lucres' he looking after.
>
> Deaf Burke "

As Burke appealed for another chance, Bendigo had other problems. He was embroiled in a row over money he claimed he was owed from the last fight, claiming that he had received only a small portion of the battle money. His backers disputed this, saying that he had been paid the £100 he was due and that another £20 had been deducted for training expenses. And as so often happened, the argument was conducted via the pages of *Bell's Life*, with the editor not slow to hint that Bendigo was showing ingratitude – "the worst of sins and where it exists it severs all friendship."

According to Bendigo, he had been promised the full £120 by his backers, but they had withheld £20 for training expenses, although the expenses only came to £15. Confusingly, he said "Nine shillings and five pence in the pound was deducted from the money which some of my friends stood with me, making the expenses amount to sixteen pounds eight shillings." If anyone grasped what he meant they did not come forward. The editor commented "We do not exactly understand his arithmetic and are prepared to receive a very different version from his Nottingham friends."

It came in a letter on behalf of Bendigo's backers published on 19th May.

> "It is not true that the backers of Bendigo promised him if he won the fight with Burke £120. It is equally untrue that his training expenses amounted to only £15 and that nine shillings and five pence in the pound was deducted to swell the expenses. Bendigo knows as well as any man breathing that in sending such statements to the world he is publishing falsehoods. His expenses came to £67. And he also knows how those expenses were incurred, having been furnished with a copy of the items."

The expenses, as then listed, give an insight into the costs of preparing a pugilist for a major fight in the prize ring at that time:

Ward's bill for training - £15 and he had a present made him of £18 as a testimonial on the feelings of Bendigo's backers for the care, skill and attention he had paid.

£10 was sent to Bendigo to bring him from Liverpool for the fight,
£5 to Nick Ward for seconding him,
£5 to Peter Taylor as bottle holder,
£3 in going to and from Liverpool for the battle money,
£5 to Tom Oliver for the ropes and stakes,
4 guineas for going to London to make the last deposit,
£3.10s for training and fighting boots, and
£6.14s - other wearing apparatus.

The author of the letter, who, like most backers of illegal prize fighting, wished to remain anonymous, continued:

> "I do not wish to appear invidious, nor have I any ill feelings towards Bendigo, but as he has provoked the

> discussion he must take the consequence. It is well known that he behaved anything but properly towards some of his backers here, whom he not only abused but traduced and that he afterwards more than once made a public apology for his conduct and expressed the deep regret he felt, even went upon his knees to beg pardon. He said he had been misled and imposed upon."

The letter was published as "Not signed", with a postscript –

> "I trust I have now completely exonerated the backers of Bendigo from the foul and ungrateful aspersions in which he thought proper to indulge."

Bendigo's triumph in the ring had been tarnished by his attitude out of it. Whether or not the claim that he had gone on his knees to beg pardon was true – unlikely for a proud man such as he was - his backers were annoyed with him. In a fit of pique he had refused to take the prize money, which led to them placing a cheque in a bank, whereupon he asked for it to be given to him in cash. They were so angry they closed the subscription for a silver cup which had been opened at the Star Inn dinner two nights after the Burke fight and returned all the money to those who had subscribed. But such matters did not bother Bendigo too much. His sometimes cheerful, other times truculent attitude meant that he soon forgot the disagreement, even if his backers did not. He knew that, as champion and with his deserved reputation, he would find new backers if necessary. In the meantime he could earn a very good living taking benefits in the Northern towns.

By mid-summer Deaf Burke was still loudly complaining that he had been wrongly done by and deserved another match. Ben Caunt announced his money to fight Bendigo was ready at any sporting house in Sheffield. The new champion, however, was busy dodging beaks and bluecoats elsewhere. In mid June he ventured into new territory with a trip to Westmoreland to face an old rival and would-be opponent, James Wharton, alias Young Molyneux.

Disappointing as it might have been for Molyneux, a good fighter who for several years made noises that he wished to meet him, Bendigo was there only as a second to his opponent, Will Renwick. Ben Caunt, who was not involved with either combatant, was so determined to let his face be seen and to try to goad Bendigo into another match, that he travelled all the way from Nottinghamshire just to watch. Will Renwick was a cobbler, renowned for his sledge-hammer punches, but as so often happened when Bendigo was seconding, Renwick lost, knocked unconscious by a blow between the eyes after one and a half hours. It was beginning to look as if having Bendigo in the corner was a bad omen.

His backers had fallen out with him, but he found someone willing to pen a letter on his behalf to *Bell's Life*. On returning from Westmoreland he lost no time in responding to Caunt and Deaf Burke's recent taunts and half-hearted challenges:

> "Letter from Bendigo
>
> Re Caunt saying his money is ready at any sporting house in Sheffield
>
> Now sir, I have been to many houses that he frequents and cannot find anyone to put any money down on his behalf. As he was in Sheffield for a fortnight previous to my going away to second Renwick I think if he meant fighting he would have made the match when we were both in Sheffield. I will fight Caunt or any other man in England for from £200 to £500 a side . . .. to convince the patrons of the Prize Ring that there is no empty chaff about me as I am going to leave Sheffield this week, my money will be ready any day or any hour at Mr Edward Daniels, the Three Crowns, Parliament St, Nottingham . . . .if Burke wants another shy I will fight him for £150 a side
>
> Signed: William Thompson, alias Bendigo"

As he announced, his sojourn in Sheffield at the Manchester Arms, West Street had come to an end. No reason for Bendigo's departure or his return to his home town was made public. Maybe he thought that as champion he should not be behind the bar of a tap; perhaps he simply wished to be back among old friends and family. Whatever, the Three Crowns in Parliament Street, one of his mother's favourite hostelries and only yards away from his birthplace, was now his base.

Neither Caunt nor Burke rose to his offers to fight them. He made public his opinion of Caunt – "this great Goliath has the courage of a Newfoundland pup, more barking than biting." He offered to give "this bounceable gentleman" a sovereign to travel to Nottingham. Deaf Burke, he said, was of no importance to him. He would fight him for the "cool hundred" Burke had proposed, but only if he put £50 down as a deposit.

Caunt agreed to meet at the Three Crowns in August to make the match. On the night Bendigo was dismayed to find the "great Goliath's" backers had deserted him and the big man could find no more than two sovereigns to put down as a deposit. Caunt was humiliated but he got no sympathy from Bendigo, who declared his "bounce and claptraps" were a disgrace. The big chucklehead, he declared, was nothing but a humbug!

Back in Nottingham, Bendigo kicked his heels waiting for either Ben Caunt to come up with a meaningful deposit or another opponent to emerge with one. The latter did not seem promising. Caunt was the only man around who would attract the Fancy's attention, and then only because of the unsatisfactory ending to their last contest. In both their fights Bendigo had showed himself to be superior, but the Big `Un's size and power always suggested that he might manage to gain a result by sheer physical advantage.

As for the other heavyweights around – taking the word at its contemporary, rather than modern, meaning – Bendigo had beaten all those worth the trouble and none could raise the sort of money he was now seeking. In October, two of his earlier foes, Brassey of Bradford and Young Langan, fought each other at Woodhead, between Manchester and Sheffield, in front of a large crowd. Brassey won after two and half hours.

Bendigo did not attend, preferring to remain in Nottingham, where he was spending an increasing amount of time drinking and upsetting former friends and supporters who did not like to see him lounging about the town with the Lambs. His deteriorating reputation was not confined to his home town; *Bell's Life* made several references to him having offended people and lost friends and even Deaf Burke, who was hardly in a position to criticise, had passed comment. Bendigo took no heed; he said those who recognised him as a brave and honest pugilist would still stand by him "at a pinch".

He showed no interest at old opponents fighting each other, but he could usually be guaranteed to turn up for a contest involving Nottingham men. When Sam Merryman met a Birmingham prospect named Cross at Appleby, Bendigo was one of a large turn-out of fighters at the ropes. Cross was handled by Johnny Broome, a leading light in the Midlands Fancy. Seeing his man losing, he tried to drag him from the ring to deliver him into the arms of a constable, whom he had arranged to be close by in the event of such an outcome. Broome's intention was to avoid paying the side stake but Bendigo, who was present only as a spectator, disapproved of such unsporting conduct. He intervened, dragging Cross back into the ring, where Merryman was declared the winner and all bets had to be paid.

The New Year of 1840 saw him present and active when his old mentor Sam Turner, now thirty-eight years old, came out of an eleven year retirement to fight for the last time. Turner had trained and seconded Bendigo in his earliest fights and set him on the road to the championship. The last time the veteran had been in a prize ring, in September 1828, he knocked out Bill Moulds, known as Winterflood, in the first round. The young William Thompson, aged seventeen and yet to become known in ring circles as Bendigo, watched eagerly at the ropes. He learned a great deal, because five years later when he met the same Winterflood, he too knocked him out in one round.

Now Sam Turner was making a comeback – as a result of a row which arose on a Saturday night in a Nottingham tap, the Filho de Puta, named after the winner of the 1815 St. Leger. Turner was minding his business over a quiet drink when half a dozen rowdies came in, insulting all around them. The biggest and loudest threatened the old pugilist but before he had finished speaking Turner knocked him to the floor with a right hander. Taking him by the collar, he dragged him across the floor and threw him out of the door and down the steps. The man's friends left without further disturbance.

Joe Green, the man on the wrong end of Turner's swift action, felt humiliated. He had fought a few times in small contests, the sort of bye and set-to in which many professionals had begun their ring careers. He challenged Sam Turner to meet him in a ring for a £20 side stake. Although prevailed upon by his wife and friends, the old warrior could not resist the challenge, not even against a man twelve years his junior and two stones heavier. The match was made for 7th January 1840.

The fight attracted all the Nottingham boxing fraternity. Bendigo stood with a group of the Nottingham Lambs, ridiculing Ben Caunt who loudly claimed he could beat any man in the world. "Your backers don't think so," Bendigo scoffed, "or they'd be able to find more than a couple o' sovereigns." Caunt was there to support Green while Bill Broadhead, a great influence on the Bold `Un's early years and still landlord of the Butchers Arms, was in Sam Turner's corner. But the younger, stronger Joe Green was favourite with the bookmakers at four to one on.

After thirty-nine rounds Green had taken the worst of the punishment and was in a hopeless position. He fouled Turner and was himself then struck a mighty blow by Bill Broadhead, who jumped into the ring at the foul. The referee, a local landlord named Jephson, declared Sam to be the winner, but Green's friends cut the ropes and grabbed the ring stakes with which they tried to set about the unfortunate Jephson. Only the intervention of Bendigo and the Lambs saved him from serious harm. When they sprang into action Green's followers soon faded away and the referee was escorted safely home.

A couple of weeks after Sam Turner's fight Bendigo arrived in London and took up quarters at Jem Burn's. Just in case anyone had not heard, he informed the London Fancy that he was willing to fight Caunt or anyone else for £200 a side. A benefit was arranged at Burn's and a large crowd came to see the new champion, including Deaf Burke. The Deaf `Un made a speech saying he refused to be on friendly terms with Mishter Bendy but he would do him a favour and fight him for £100. The two of them excited the crowd in a bout of sparring and Bendigo later sparred a few rounds with Jem Ward's brother, Nick, who many present thought got the better of him. This was not too significant, for Bendigo often looked ordinary when sparring. He was much better at the real, bareknuckle business than he was with the muffs on.

He returned to Nottingham, disappointed that he was no nearer to making a match. It was not unusual for men, having won the championship, to wait several years before defending it, but he was eager to get back in action. He was particularly keen to get Ben Caunt between the ropes again and leave no one in any doubt that Caunt was not in his class.

Becoming bored and frustrated, his life was beginning to drift. A devout trainer when a fight was in the offing, he had always played as hard as he worked. Without a wife or family to occupy him – he was never known to have a relationship with a woman – and with a lifestyle defined by his profession as utterly male orientated, he found it difficult to avoid the daily temptations of the taverns and taps of Nottingham Market Place and Long Row.

The only anchor point in his life was his elderly mother, Mary Thompson. Although his career meant him being away from Nottingham for long spells, and he had lived in Sheffield for two years, he always made sure his mother was supplied every week with her two ounces of Navy Plug, a noxious-smelling tobacco. She smoked it in a broken-stemmed clay pipe, which Bendigo called her "nose warmer".

But his mother, like his late father who had died in a public house, was a drinker. Formidable even in old age, she was notorious for stamping into the Three Crowns on Parliament Street, banging her fist on the bar top and demanding "Half of tuppeny and no slops, mind". Her party piece was taking a taste, spitting it out and telling the barman, "I don't drink slops. Now change this beer, or I'll wash your face with it!"

No wonder then that when he found himself at a loose end and without much reason or motivation to keep in training, Bendigo resorted to that haven of the industrial working classes, the public house. No wonder either, given his energy and exuberance, that when he did indulge excessively in alcohol, trouble was rarely far away.

In mid February he was at Lamley, a hamlet six miles from Nottingham, to watch a fight between a local man, Jack Glann, and William Johnson, commonly known as Leicester Bill. Bendigo arrived drunk and proceeded to offer advice to Glann, in between hurling insults at the referee, umpires and various spectators, and being generally offensive. Some good came out it - Glann took heed of the champion's advice and won on a disqualification, but many of those present were displeased by how he conducted himself. *Bell's Life*, who would have been unlikely to cover the fight had it not been for Bendigo's unseemly presence, said "Men who aspire to the Championship should never forget that deportment which is calculated to gain respect."

Such incidents were only a warning of what was to come. A month later, disaster struck. On 23rd March 1840 it looked like the prize ring career of William Thompson, known to all as Bendigo, Pride of Nottingham and Champion of England was over. Fooling about and showing off to his friends, he suffered an accident that looked like crippling him for life. The accident was widely reported in the local and sporting press:

> "William Thompson, better known by his cognomen of Bendigo has met with an accident which is likely to cripple him for life. On Monday he had been to see the Military Officers' Steeplechase near Nottingham and on his return home he and his companions were cracking their jokes about having a steeplechase among themselves. Having arrived nearly opposite to the Pinder's house on the London Road about a mile from Nottingham, Bendigo exclaimed 'Now, my boys, I'll show you how to run a steeplechase in a new style, without falling' and immediately threw a somersault. He felt whilst throwing it that he had hurt his knee and on alighting he attempted in vain three times to rise from the ground. His companions, thinking for the moment he was joking, laughed heartily, but discovered that it was no

> joke. They went to his assistance and raised him up but the poor fellow had no use of his left leg. A gig was sent for immediately in which he was conveyed to the house of his brother and Messrs. Wright and Thompson, surgeons, were immediately called in. On examination of the knee we understand they pronounced the injury to the cap to be of so serious a nature that he is likely to be lame for life."

He had never suffered any real injury in the ring, even though many of his fights were against men bigger, heavier and stronger than himself, ruthless men who would have thought little of leaving him maimed or even dead. Through his own folly he had done to himself what no opponent could, he had put himself out of action. Now, those who considered themselves his rivals for the title of champion emerged from the shadows where they had been lurking. The backers of men like Ben Caunt, Nick Ward, John Brassey, Deaf Burke and Tass Parker suddenly became more inclined to show their money in making matches. Bendigo, who had beaten them all with the exception of Nick Ward and Parker, neither of whom had shown any willingness to meet him in the ring, was sidelined, perhaps permanently. Over the next couple of years the other fighters would make matches among themselves in a series of uninspiring contests. Meanwhile, Bendigo's future was in the hands of the Nottingham surgeons and the initial diagnosis gave little cause for optimism.

8] Down but not Out

Ben Caunt was not sorry to hear of Bendigo's accident. For him, the champion's injury was good news. Quite apart from the mutual animosity between the two of them, Bendigo's disablement left the path clearer for Caunt to fight again for the title. Whoever the opponent might be, and there were less than a handful of likely men, he could not be as problematic as Bendigo. Caunt's backers, previously reluctant to even make a deposit for a fight against the Bold `Un, now became enthusiastic and articles were agreed for him to meet John Leechman, better known as Brassey of Bradford.

In the build-up to the contest it became apparent that Caunt's capacity for acrimony and bad feeling was not unique to his dealings with Bendigo. He objected to almost every aspect of the arrangements and the few details he did let pass met with objection from Brassey. By the time they met, at Six Mile Bottom near Newmarket in October 1840, the Fancy was weary of hearing their complaints and eager for them to settle matters in the ring. "Verily, this splitting of hairs is anything but rational and looks very like trifling," said *Bell's Life*. The newspaper sought the opinion of Bendigo, who had beaten both Caunt and Brassey, as to the merits of the two men. He said he would "give the palm" to Brassey whom he pronounced as the better tactician, if not the gamer man. Betting men, always keen to hear the words of a "professor", wondered if he might be influenced by his dislike of Caunt.

While expressing Bendigo's expert opinion, the oracle of the ring was able to inform its readers that the injury which had put Bendigo out of action did not now look to be as serious as first feared. In the immediate aftermath of his accident the surgeon's opinion was that he would be crippled for life, but he had not bargained for Bendigo's strength and willpower which was already suggesting a more positive outcome. Over the year he made a remarkable recovery and declared that, given time, he hoped to be back in the ring.

News of Bendigo's progress was of no interest to Caunt, who received severe punishment in labouring to beat Brassey over a hundred dreary rounds. The sporting men of Newmarket were not impressed, but Caunt lost no time in announcing himself once again Champion of England and said he would meet any man for £100 a side within fifty miles of London. He was king of the ring, but not for long - five months later he met Nick Ward, younger brother of Bendigo's trainer Jem, and after only twelve minutes he was disqualified for a foul. Loud and long Caunt had crowed that he was the top man, now he had lost his title. To make matters worse, he was bitterly annoyed by rumours, no doubt circulated by the crafty Ward brothers, that he had struck Nick Ward a foul blow deliberately to save himself a beating.

Such tales were unfair because, for all his shortcomings, Ben Caunt's bravery or, as the Fancy called it, gameness or "bottom", was never in doubt. He quickly signed up for a return and in May 1841 made no mistake in soundly beating Nick Ward. This time it was Ward who was criticised for giving in too easily, earning harsh words even from his own brother. Caunt was so pleased with himself that he left the ring by leaping clear of the top rope, a height of four feet six inches, and on the way home ran a race against a Corinthian across a ploughed field for a bottle of wine, which he won.

Once more, Caunt was proclaimed champion. Prior to jumping over the ropes he was presented with a belt which had been funded by a subscription started at Jem Burn's pub, the Queen's Head in Haymarket. The presentation of championship belts by backers was not new, but this belt was different in that it was transferable if a holder was beaten or retired from the ring.

The new belt was seen for the first time when it was held up to the crowd's attention moments before Caunt and Nick Ward had come to the scratch. The official orator of the prize ring, Cicero Holt, announced that it had been "prepared by a number of liberal gentlemen as a spur to the honest and manly feeling which it was desirable should ever pervade the minds of men who seek distinction in the prize ring." After the fight, the belt was buckled around Caunt and an official presentation was later made at a dinner at the Queen's Head.

The belt was made of leather and purple velvet, in the centre a pair of clasped hands surrounded by a wreath of the rose, the thistle and the shamrock, entwined in embossed silver. On each side were three shields of bright silver on which the names of all the champions of England were to be engraved, Caunt's being the first. It was the first official championship belt in boxing.

Little was heard of Bendigo during these months, although he was now getting about with the help of a stick. His association with Jem and Nick Ward ensured his presence at Long Marsden, near Stratford-on-Avon, when Caunt regained the championship he himself had been forced to give up, although he took no part in the proceedings. His interest lay in the supporting bout, between his old pal from the boxing booth days, Levi Eckersley, who at the age of thirty seven faced Peter Taylor, more usually seen in Bendigo's corner.

Taylor was the reverse side of the coin from Bendigo – a successful trainer who was not much of a fighter. Neither he nor his opponent had any place in a prize ring and both were gasping for breath after only three rounds, whereupon Eckersley fell without a blow and would not rise. Johnny Broome, the Birmingham fighter and publican, who had bet on him, was so disgusted he jumped into the ring and delivered a mighty kick to the unfortunate Levi's backside.

Ben Caunt was now enjoying his most successful period. One of his first public appearances as the new, undisputed champion was to return to his home village, Hucknall Torkard, in Nottinghamshire. Many of his old friends and neighbours had been present to see him regain the title against Nick Ward. Now, a month later on a hot June evening, he came back home.

Excitement did not come often to Hucknall Torkard. Thus, the village was buzzing with anticipation for hours before the great man arrived. His reception was planned in detail. A large door was laid across a cart drawn by a number of young men, in the centre of which was fixed an armchair and a beanrod graced with a large handkerchief as a substitute for a flag. As Caunt arrived, clad in a plum coloured waistcoat with a big yellow handkerchief round his neck and the champion's belt at his waist, he was met by a brass band and drummer and encouraged to mount the armchair.

A procession set off through the village, led by the band and local boys carrying green oak boughs, while men and youths hauled the cart on which the hero was enthroned. Unfortunately the chair broke and the Champion of England fell off the cart onto the road. He was unhurt but his dignity was offended and he refused to climb back into the chair. Amidst toe-curling embarrassment and general shock that such misfortune could occur on this day of days, Caunt's annoyance was eventually appeased by profuse apologies. Still he refused to climb back on the cart and insisted on walking to his quarters at the Coach and Six Inn, where a party went on until the early hours of the morning.

Ben Caunt was an exceptionally fine specimen of a man, with an ego proportionate to his size. Now he was the champion of all England, the domestic ring seemed small and limited. He had fought and beaten all the best men and the only thorn in his side, Bendigo, was no longer in the reckoning. He decided he needed a new challenge and only one place came to mind: America.

In this plan he was retracing the steps of Deaf Burke who had returned from a year across the Atlantic with glorious tales of his own great success. Caunt was no admirer of the Deaf 'Un, and needed no convincing that whatever Burke had done, he could do better. And like Burke, he was certain that the New World would welcome him, the Champion of England, that American pugilists would line up to be thrashed by him and that he would make his fortune.

Bendigo, recuperating in Nottingham, recalled wryly that less than a couple of years earlier Caunt had been unable to show more than a meagre two sovereigns towards a deposit for what would have been the deciding fight with him.

Ben Caunt

On 10th September 1841 Caunt sailed from Liverpool. He said he was going "to show the New World an Old World Champion" and boasted he would be "a big thing in a country of big things". The voyage took nearly two months and Caunt's optimism received a further boost when his arrival merited a notice in the *New York Spirit of the Times* of 13th November:

> "Caunt, the Champion of England arrived on Monday week last in the packet ship Europe, bringing with him the Champion's belt. He has appeared several times at the Bowery Theatre in *Life in London,*[35] being introduced in the scene opening with Tom Cribb's sparring room. He is an immensely powerful man, two or three inches above six feet in height and well proportioned. Caunt's reputation at home is that of a liberal, clever, manly fellow; prodigious strength and thorough game have won him more battles than his science, though he is no chicken. The following challenge has appeared in some of the daily papers: 'Challenge to Caunt, the Champion of England – Sir, I will fight you for five hundred dollars, three months from this date, the forfeit money to be put up at any time and place you may name. You can find me at 546 Grand Street. Yours, James Jerolomon.' "

Whoever James Jerolomon was, if he even existed, he was never heard of again. It was perhaps for the best, because Caunt was doing so well exhibiting his somewhat limited skills in sparring - when he was not donning greasepaint on Broadway - that he admitted he had no wish to enter a ring in meaningful combat. Nonetheless, he was keen that the folks back home knew how well he was doing and in January 1842 a letter from him arrived on the desk of the editor of *Bell's Life*.

An uneducated man, Caunt, like Bendigo, was illiterate and his letter, as the editor suggested was more likely "the hand of some Yankee Barnum, rather than the fist of burly Ben." It read:

---

[35] *Life in London* originated as a cartoon by the satirists Robert and George Cruikshank. The words were written by Pierce Egan, an Irish sporting journalist who also wrote the first chronicle of the prize ring, *Boxiana* (1812). The cartoon featured Corinthian Tom and his country cousin Jerry Hawthorne. Turned into a play, it became a huge hit in London, the provinces and, later, America and was adapted to suit different audiences. The inclusion of a scene in Tom Cribb's sparring room indicates the social importance of the prize ring in London life. Americans were impressed by the ring's connections with royalty and the aristocracy, although by the time of Caunt's visit, those heady days had mostly passed. Cribb's name was known in New York for his two defeats of Tom Molyneux, the black American fighter.

> "Sir, upwards of three months have elapsed since I left England, and, holding the championship, I think it necessary to let you know where I am. Since I arrived in this country, I have only been at New York and Philadelphia, which latter place I came from on Thursday last. With respect to this place and its people, I am proud to say that no man ever could be better received in any place. I believe the Americans to be the best-hearted and kindest people in the world; the only danger I have to counter is their killing me with kindness. When I came here first I published my intentions, that I really came to see the country and exhibit sparring, and I think I have given the public satisfaction as to my knowledge of the art. I have set-to with several professors."

The "professors" were in fact amateurs who frequented Hudson's Sparring Rooms and Pistol Gallery on the corner of Broadway and Chambers Street in New York. At Hudson's, Caunt gave exhibitions with the gloves on and made an impression on the locals who were keen to learn to box in the English manner. Prize fighting in the United States had not moved on since Deaf Burke's earlier visit and there were no trained pugilists who betting men thought worth backing against the English champion.

None that was until a challenge came forth from a man who would make Big Ben look diminutive. Word of Caunt's fistic skills had travelled and a challenge was made by a man who was referred to as the Michigan Giant. Back home Caunt was known as a giant, but the American version was truly gigantic. Charles Freeman was his name, he was twenty two years old, stood 7ft. 3inches tall and weighed 23 stones of hard muscle. He could hold a large man off the ground at arm's length and, rather than being cumbersome or awkward in his movements, he was double-jointed in his limbs, jumped eleven feet from a standing start and could turn twenty-five somersaults in succession. In Halifax, Nova Scotia, he had been matched with a worthy opponent who, on seeing him, decided against the plan, agreeing instead to spar with gloves on the stage of the local theatre. With his first punch, Freeman knocked the unfortunate fellow head over heels into the orchestra stalls, where he caused considerable damage to kettle-drums and big fiddles.

Caunt was dismissive of such tales and made all the right noises about meeting Freeman in the ring. He went so far as to claim in his letter to *Bell's Life* that his New York "friends" had offered to back him for

$10,000 a side. "I have all the reasons to believe a match will be made," he wrote but clearly did not believe any such thing, as in the next sentence he continued: "I expect to be in England in a short time if the above match is not made, when I shall be ready to accommodate Bendigo."

So, in one breath he was talking about fighting a 7 ft 3 inch, 23 stone man-mountain, in the next, Bendigo, a man half the weight and more than a foot smaller, whose fists had already twice made a mess of him. Caunt had mastered hyperbole but did not recognise the onset of absurdity.

He never fought Charles Freeman, although the Michigan Giant was willing. They sparred in New York, at Washington Hall on Broadway, an experience Caunt survived without getting knocked off the stage, unlike the man in Nova Scotia. Instead of meeting as foes in earnest, the big man and the bigger man became firm friends and when Caunt arrived back on a packet ship in England in March 1842, he was accompanied by Charles Freeman.

First stop was Nottingham and a meeting with Bendigo, whose fractured knee was now well on its way to recovery. Six months earlier he had quashed rumours that he was about to go to the scratch with Brassey of Bradford for £100, saying that he would not fight anyone until the outstanding matter of who was the better man between himself and Caunt was resolved, and he would be ready in the coming Spring.

That time had almost arrived and Caunt had returned from America with this massive fellow who could lift 1,532 lbs. above his head and could ride two horses at once, while carrying Big Ben on his shoulders. At less than five feet eleven inches to Freeman's seven feet three, Bendigo had to stand on tiptoes and look up, just to meet his gaze.

Nevertheless, when he met Caunt and his huge friend in Nottingham, all went well. Both the Bold `Un and the man who had taken his championship were on their best behaviour and it was agreed that the following Tuesday they would all appear at the Nottingham Theatre – "to show what warriors can accomplish".

The day before the planned exhibition, the town was covered with placards and bills, announcing the coming event. On the night, hundreds of people gathered outside the theatre. Pugilists and Corinthians arrived from all over the Midlands, eager to see for themselves just what the American giant was like with the gloves on. Many of them were equally keen to check out the extent of Bendigo's recovery, for he was billed to spar with Freeman – a curious prospect, given the disparity in height and Bendigo's frustratingly unorthodox style.

But it was not to be. A local clergyman, concerned that such an unholy event was about to take place in Passion Week, objected and the show never went ahead. Greatly disappointed, the crowd were left to speculate on what the outcome would have been if Bendigo had met the giant.

They never had another opportunity. Outside of Nottingham, Bendigo did not figure in Caunt and Freeman's plans. The pair moved on to Manchester where a well-known comedian and impresario, Mr Sloan, hearing of the Nottingham mishap, booked them at the Queen's Theatre. Here, in what was known as "the city of soot", there were no zealous vicars to object and the two pugilists appeared for a week, sparring and doing their best to imitate the thespian art in 'Tom Cribb's Chaffing Parlour', a scene from *Tom and Jerry*, the mini-drama adapted from *Life in London* which Caunt had featured in on Broadway.

Although Bendigo was now fit to fight again, Ben Caunt had more grandiose plans. He could see the opportunity to make a great deal of money by appearing in theatres with Charles Freeman, at no risk to his person or reputation. For all his boasts, his bombast and bluster, Caunt knew that if and when he fought Bendigo again, it would be a painful experience. The previous matches had been so, regardless of the manner in which he had gained the verdict last time out. Right now he was keen to tour the country with his freakish friend, not minding even that while he was billed in some places as the Champion of England, Freeman was styled Champion of the World.

From Manchester they moved to Huddersfield, then to Caunt's home village, Hucknall Torkard. There he married his childhood sweetheart, Miss Martha Bond, said to be a distant relative. Back on the road, Caunt and Freeman filled halls in Bolton and Salford and at the Queen's Theatre in Liverpool, where Bendigo had made his first appearance as champion after beating Deaf Burke. Here, there was so much interest in the giant that an extra show had to be put on.

The London Fancy got their chance to size up the big man at Tom Spring's Castle Tavern. While in London, the American decided to drop in at Buckingham Palace for a chat with the Queen. Being American and of unsophisticated disposition, he did not realise that a certain etiquette, not to say invitation, was necessary in visiting royalty. He was disappointed when he turned up at the Palace but left his card, which a Palace flunkey assured him would be passed on to Queen Victoria's husband, Prince Albert.

The climax of Caunt and Freeman's stage success came in May in the unlikely setting of the English Opera House. Large as it was, the theatre was crowded to excess, the balcony, boxes, pit and gallery thronged, even the sides of the stage. The crowd, not the usual opera audience, became impatient at having to sit through two farces featuring the Irish comedian, Mr Sloan, the man who had booked Caunt and Freeman in Manchester. They had not paid to see farces, they wanted to see the champion shape up to the Giant. According to the reporter from *Bell's Life,* when Caunt did so, wearing his belt, he stood "particularly high in his own estimation".

Seven months later, after starring at York and Doncaster races, Charles Freeman was matched for his first appearance in the English prize ring. His opponent was William Perry, a Birmingham man widely known as the Tipton Slasher. They met twice within a fortnight, both fights dreary affairs. The first meeting brought little action before bad light caused an early finish and the second was given to Freeman on a foul, when the Slasher went down without a blow. The Slasher was outraged and, forgetting Freeman for a moment, offered to fight Caunt there and then for the championship. Caunt replied: "Fight me? You can't even beat my novice!" It was a telling remark: Caunt had been happy for Freeman to be called "Champion of the World" to attract crowds in the theatres, now, after a mediocre debut in the prize ring, he referred to him as "his" novice.

Charles Freeman never fought again and, after the dull show against the Tipton Slasher, Caunt distanced himself from his protégé. The giant remained in London, where he died of tuberculosis in October 1845.

While Ben Caunt had been parading himself and his large friend around the theatres and halls, making more money than either of them had ever seen, Bendigo was feeling left out. The championship had been taken from him by cruel fate – or by his own foolish behaviour. Caunt would not have been able to strut the country with Freeman, making money everywhere they went, could not even have gone to America proclaiming himself champion, had he not injured his knee. He would walk with a limp for the rest of his life, and his knee would occasionally give way, causing him to fall, but it was much improved and he could now spar and do exhibitions. In May 1842 he and his old friend Bill Atkinson, the Nottingham Pet, appeared at the Circus in Huddersfield, before a good crowd. And just in case anyone had forgotten who was the real champion, Bendigo wore the belt presented to him following his triumph over Deaf Burke three years earlier.

Two weeks later, *Bell's Life* announced his imminent return to the prize ring. A group of his old Nottingham backers, returning from The Derby at Epsom, had stopped off at the Rising Sun in Air Street, Piccadilly, a hostelry kept by the renowned fighter, Johnny Broome. Originally from Birmingham, Broome was still influential in Midlands ring matters. One of the fighters he looked after was Tass Parker from West Bromwich, who had beaten Brassey of Bradford and made other good men look awkward. Bendigo's Nottingham friends were in ebullient mood, having cleaned up at the Derby on the winner, Attila.[36]

Flush with their winnings, they announced they were keen to "post the coal" for Bendigo to meet Tass Parker and an agreement was made for £100 a side, to fight in a 24 foot roped ring on Wednesday 24th August, within twenty miles of Wolverton in the direction of Nottingham.

The match was on. Bendigo went to London for a benefit at Jem Burn's, where he drew a full house, with some would-be spectators left outside in the street. The night ended with him sparring with the Australian champion John Gorrick, known in the ring as Bungaree, who had recently lost to Johnny Broome. He then went into training and the second and third deposits were made.

By mid-June, when the fourth deposit was due to be made at the Three Crowns in Nottingham, rumours were circulating that all was not well in Bendigo's camp. His fitness was the obvious question, but those in the know said this was not in doubt. What could be amiss? The deposit was made but he did not appear in person and for a few days it seemed as if the rumours had no substance.

The next week it became clear that they did. On the 22nd June Tass Parker's fifth deposit was forwarded to the White Swan, Salford, as agreed, but there was no sign of Bendigo's friends or their money. Then, to the consternation of his backers and to the amazement of the Fancy, national as well as local, the reason was revealed. Bendigo's brother, John Thompson, had successfully applied for a summons for him to be bound over to keep the peace, to prevent him fighting Tass Parker.

Bendigo was deeply embarrassed. He was thirty-one years old, a pugilist by profession, a proud man, a man who could look after himself in any situation. If he wanted to fight in a prize ring, no one should be able to stop him. That the blues and beaks tried and occasionally succeeded was all part of the game – but to be prevented by his own brother was beyond his comprehension.

Nevertheless, that was the situation. Brother John maintained a lifestyle almost as far removed as it was possible to be from that of Bendigo, or Bill as he knew him. Wiser and without the stigmatising experience of the workhouse in his youth, John had taken opportunities

---

[36] Attila, owned by Colonel Anson and ridden by W. Scott, won the 1842 Derby by two lengths at 5-1. Colonel Anson, who had served at Waterloo, is credited with his skilful handling of a duel between Lord George Bentinck and Squire George Osbaldeston, which saved Bentinck's life. Osbaldeston would later referee the third fight between Bendigo and Ben Caunt.

that were denied to his brother, who followed his natural athleticism and aggression from an early age. As Bendigo climbed from childhood poverty to become a successful prize fighter, John Thompson, although also illiterate, took a more conventional route and built up a business as an optician in Nottingham with a shop and small factory in Carlton Street. He described himself in advertisements as "surgical instrument maker, anatomical machinist &c. to the General Hospital and Dispensary, Leicester Infirmary, Loughborough and Newark Dispensaries, and all the principal Unions in the district." He was also a sports outfitter, selling "Archery goods, consisting of bows, arrows, targets &c.; also cricket bats, balls, stumps, leg guards, and every article connected with the above fashionable games."[37]

John Thompson is the only one of Bendigo's brothers or sisters who was ever referred to in newspapers of the time, or mentioned by the fighter himself. His opposition to prize fighting was given as the reason behind his action, but why he did so on this occasion and not others is unclear. Maybe he believed that Bendigo was not capable of holding his own, for his lameness was plain to see and it was this that had encouraged Tass Parker's backers to put their money down.

It emerged that after the third deposit had been made, John, who was aware of the date of the impending bout, informed the police. Bendigo was summoned before the Nottingham magistrates where he admitted that he was planning to fight Tass Parker on the 24th August and that this would amount to a breach of the peace. The court bound him over to be of good behaviour for twelve months in his own surety of £100 and he had to find two more of the same amount before he could be released. Such sums were extremely high in the circumstances but Bendigo had no trouble finding either his own £100 or two from his backers, the landlord of the Three Crowns and another town publican.

Seventy pounds in all had been paid down by each side in the first four deposits. Bendigo's backers argued loud and long that they should not forfeit, claiming magisterial interference, but on Parker's side Johnny Broome was having none of that. The arrival of the police or magistrates at a fight could not be avoided, but a pugilist's own brother taking out a summons to prevent him fighting was unacceptable. To Bendigo's further embarrassment, his backers lost their deposits.

---

[37] *Nottingham Daily Guardian*, 13 June, 1925, reminiscences by a correspondent, 'EB'.

Inconvenient and problematic as it was, the summons probably came as a blessing, for he was still a long way from the level of fitness required for what would have been a gruelling encounter with Tass Parker. But now he was back in the doldrums, his fighting restricted to town centre brawls while under the influence of alcohol, skirmishes with his Lamb friends and the rest of his time taken up with fishing in the River Trent, cock-fighting and ratting evenings.

Whatever his fitness, or lack of it, his backers remained loyal. For over a year there was not a word of a challenge and during this time Ben Caunt was content to rest on his laurels as champion and plan how to invest the money he had earned touring with Charles Freeman. His size and reputation made him a natural innkeeper and he moved to London to become landlord of a well-known haunt of the Fancy, the Coach and Horses in St Martin's Lane. Here, he held exhibitions of the pugilistic art and amused himself at musical evenings, where the clientele sang heartily and Big Ben took the chair. For eighteen months he and Bendigo exchanged barbs in the sporting press, but whenever a match looked likely, Caunt retracted on side stakes he had previously agreed.

In December 1843 a letter from Bendigo appeared in *Bell's Life*, denouncing Caunt's claim to the championship. It was said the big man preferred "bounce and benefits" to fighting and Bendigo called upon him to accept a £200 challenge. Caunt's response was positive and characteristically brash. He said that he would be happy to accept the challenge, adding that he would fight Bendigo, Tass Parker and the Tipton Slasher within six months, and would immediately lay down £20 deposit for each match. He said "Should this not be a 'go' within four months, I shall beg most respectfully to decline the ring altogether."

As Bendigo expected, Caunt's money failed to appear to back up his boasts. He had no more wish to fight the clever Parker or William Perry, the up-and-coming Slasher, than his old Nottingham foe, even though he knew that Bendigo's fitness and agility had been affected by his knee injury. Caunt could not be persuaded, cajoled, insulted or in any other way lured into a match with the Bold `Un. He was enjoying the title of Champion of England, why risk everything by getting in with the notoriously tricky Bendigo?

Then, in October 1844, Caunt had an unexpected setback, one beyond his control. With much vaunting and swagger from the champion, his younger brother made his debut in the prize ring, at a location on the Kent coast. Twenty years old and trained by Ben, Bob Caunt was not as imposing a figure, but he still had the advantage of height, weight and reach over his opponent, Nobby Clarke. What he did not have was

Clarke's ring experience and from the outset this told. After only fifteen minutes, Bob Caunt, taking a severe beating, failed to come to the scratch. He was still on his feet, but he gave in.

Ben was devastated. His brother had been soundly beaten by a better man, but, while no one could doubt the result, there were many questions asked at the ropes about the way he had given in so quickly. Spectators and backers had anticipated young Bob would be made of similar stuff to the champion and they were not happy. Caunt junior had failed a bigger test than the mere fight – he had showed himself to be lacking in gameness. Big Ben was renowned for his courage, his capacity to take punishment without ever backing off. His pride was sorely bruised, he felt his family name had been shamed. He suffered more pain from the accusations against his brother than he ever had in the ring.

With Bendigo a greater thorn in his side than ever, bantering and insulting him and his brother at every opportunity, Caunt tried to arrange another fight for Bob, but there was no interest. Bob Caunt's career was over before it began,[38] but Ben now had to decide what to do about his own title. He had rested on his reputation for four years without defending it and the London Fancy, of whom he was now a leading member as landlord of the Coach and Horses, were impatient. There were mutterings about the old days of Jem Ward and no one wanted to go back to that situation. Tom Spring, Jem Burn and their Corinthian friends thought it was about time Caunt either put his money on the table or surrendered the title.

Bendigo made several forays from Nottingham to try to stir up proceedings, but Caunt did his best to avoid him. Bendigo always stayed at Jem Burn's pub, the Queen's Head and whatever the company, he was always welcome to join in. On one occasion he was entertaining Lord Longford and Lord Caledon and half a dozen officers of the Household Cavalry with his tales when in walked Caunt. The landlord, Burn, a man noted for being courteous to all his customers, greeted him with "Here is the champion, gentlemen." Bendigo, the worse for drink, jumped to his feet and shouted "Him, champion? I'll let him see who's champion. I'll fight him now, and anybody else!" Matching his words with action, he

---

[38] Bob Caunt later redeemed himself in the eyes of the Fancy. He took a similar route to that taken by Ben a few years earlier and sailed to America, earning a living doing exhibitions in small halls. He fought an ex-convict saloon-keeper, Yankee Sullivan (real name, Frank Ambrose) at Harper's Ferry in 1847 for $1000 a side but although he was considered to be the victor, he did not get his winnings. He had a second fight in the English ring in 1849 at Six Mile Bottom, Newmarket, losing a bloody battle with Bill Burton. On this occasion Bob Caunt was severely beaten but would not give in and it was Ben who prevented him from going out for the 24th round.

leaped at Caunt, who swung a vicious blow with his left hand. But speed was never his strong point and Bendigo ducked. Caunt's huge fist smashed into the wooden panelling as Bendigo hit him with a sharp punch under the ear, which sent him staggering into the wall.

It looked like the much-discussed third fight between the two of them had at last begun – without a purse and with few spectators. But with aristocratic authority Lord Longford stepped in and commanded both men to drop their hands. They obliged – Caunt sulkily rubbing his jawbone and Bendigo jibing that "the big navvy dun't look like a champion to me." The pressure was now on Big Ben. For more than four years he had basked in the title of Champion of England. The time had come to prove it was his by right.

9] Riots at Ringside

The punch that Bendigo delivered to Ben Caunt's jaw in their unscheduled encounter at Jem Burn's pub in Windmill Street had a decisive effect on the champion. Comfortable as he was as landlord of the Coach and Horses, and determined to hang on to the title as long as possible, he could not go on suffering Bendigo's insults. His pride had taken two knocks – once by his brother Bob's failure in the ring and now by coming off worst in the skirmish at Burn's. He now had no choice but to prove himself. So, on 17th April 1845, he entered into an agreement to fight either Bendigo or William Perry, the Tipton Slasher. At that point only Johnny Broome knew which one of them would be the actual opponent` and he was keeping his secret in a green bag that held all his ring documents and personal papers. Broome's green bag was well known within the Fancy.

Ten days after Caunt signed to fight, Bendigo arrived in London. He was accompanied by the Duke of Limbs, his publican backers from Nottingham and a Lamb or two, on hand to hurl a few insults at Caunt. Bendigo, of course, needed little assistance in that department. Tom Spring's Castle Tavern was crowded almost to suffocation when Johnny Broome opened his green bag and revealed that it would be Bendigo who would fight Caunt for the championship. The two fighters shook hands with a good humour that surprised many present. Bendigo was sober but nonetheless in buoyant mood, stipulating that on the day the championship belt should be displayed in the ring, as he intended to wear it as soon as he had beaten the Big `Un. Caunt laughed and made a rare joke about Bendigo being a patient fisherman who should wait until he had caught his fish.

The fight was now arranged, to take place on 9th September for £200 a side. But before the ink on the agreement had time to dry, an early dispute arose when Johnny Broome, acting on behalf of Bendigo, proposed a location half way between Liverpool, where Bendigo trained, and London. Caunt might not have been educated but he was knowledgeable enough about the geography of England to realise that the Nottingham area was being suggested. He objected strongly, saying he didn't agree to any locality where instead of having to fight one man, he should be likely to have to fight a dozen. He said that from earlier experience with Bendigo he knew that if he, Caunt, looked like winning the fight he would be subjected to every type of outrage. He said he might as well be called upon to fight in Nottingham Market Place as he knew what chance he would have of winning if he was in reach of Bendigo's friends.

Bendigo laughed off Caunt's words, but did not contradict him. The location was agreed as half way between Nottingham, where for most of the time Bendigo lodged in various houses, and Caunt's base in St Martin's Lane, London. At the final deposit, the location was changed to "at a safe locality" in the Newport Pagnell area. Bendigo was not too bothered where it would take place, but he was pleased that Caunt showed concern about the Lambs and what they might get up to. In the build-up, as well as on the day, psychology would be important. He could also see that in spite of his own damaged knee he had a fitness advantage, for Caunt had blown up to seventeen stones and would need to work extremely hard to get down to a fighting weight.

Both men engaged in a series of benefits to stir up interest. In mid-May, Bendigo drew a packed house at the Wheatsheaf in Nottingham, putting the gloves on with his old mentor Sam Turner, while one of his earlier opponents, Bill Moulds, alias Winterflood, sparred with Sam Merryman. The following week he was back in London at Jem Burn's, going out to Fulham Fields to run and doing an exhibition at the Tennis Court in the Haymarket. All the elite of the Fancy were in attendance and he requested the presence of Caunt on the stage, saying he wished "to squeeze the hand of good fellowship". He said that he wanted "nothing more than a fair, manly fight in the good old English style and may the best man win." The next night, when both men attended at Johnny Broome's for the fourth deposit, Bendigo was in a loud, exuberant mood, so much so that *Bell's Life* commented sniffily "were he more quiet it would show better taste."

As he had done before, Bendigo went to Crosby, near Liverpool, to train under the watchful eye of Jem Ward, the old Black Diamond. In the past, Peter Taylor had done the day-to-day work, getting him up in the morning, joining him in runs along the sand dunes, sparring with him, mixing the potions for pickling the skin on his hands and face and checking his diet and overall preparation. But Taylor's reputation had suffered from his poor fight with Levi Eckersley four years earlier. Shortly after that dismal contest he broke his arm, then he lost his sparring rooms in Liverpool, since when he had faded away from the prize ring scene. His role was now filled by Jem Ward's brother, Nick, the man from whom Caunt had regained the championship in 1841.

The last two deposits were made at Tom Spring's Castle Tavern in Holborn, without appearances from the fighters. At the final meeting, a ticket-only dinner at the high price of fourteen shillings, attended by backers and Corinthians, it was announced that both men were in splendid condition, Bendigo being certain of success, while Caunt, who was reported to have lost a great deal of weight, considered defeat impossible. Big Ben was in training at Hatfield in Hertfordshire, under the supervision of his uncle, Ben Butler, with Tom Spring making regular visits to offer advice.

Extraordinary interest in the fight was gathering all over the country. *The Sportsman's Magazine* of August 16th featured caricatures of both fighters on its front page. Caunt was depicted wearing a tailed coat, holding a top hat in one hand and supporting himself with a knobbly stick. Bendigo, also top-hatted and in gentleman's finery, was smoking a cigar. For weeks *Bell's Life* printed poems and ballads in praise of Bendigo, while wagers on the outcome were made by people who had no possibility of being there as spectators. Not for decades had a prize fight attracted such anticipation, especially among the general public, whose interest was generated in the main by word of mouth.

There were many aspects of the coming contest that attracted public attention: - both Bendigo and Caunt were genuine and worthy contenders for the title of champion; this would be the deciding contest between them; the decisions in the two earlier fights were unsatisfactory as they each resulted from fouls; the differences between them – Caunt's size and Bendigo's skill – made the outcome harder to predict; there was uncertainty about Bendigo's damaged knee and he was now thirty-three years old, while the ill-feeling between the two men meant that neither would give an inch.

On Sunday 7th September, two days before the event, *Bell's Life* announced:

> "The great tilting match between Ben Caunt (the present champion of England) and the renowned Bendigo who seeks to deprive him of the distinction which he has so hardily won and so honourably maintained, is to come off on Tuesday next within 70 miles of London. The

> precise ground on which 'the lists' are to be formed has not yet been selected."

The paper went on to express concern that "every possible pain" be taken to preserve order on the day. As usual, an inner ring for the accommodation of the wealthy swells and Corinthians was to be formed twelve yards from the ropes. For weeks, rumours had been circulating that the Nottingham Lambs were planning to cut the ropes and break into the ring, if Bendigo appeared to be losing. In view of the Lambs' customary conduct, this was a distinct possibility, yet *Bell's Life* dismissed the rumours as "foolish threats", believing a large contingent of ring stewards armed with whips would be able to repel all trouble-makers.

The same evening, amidst a great fuss and furore, Bendigo, arrived in Newport Pagnell, accompanied by Jem Ward and Sam Merryman. All day the constabularies of Buckinghamshire and surrounding counties had been on full alert, watching with ever-increasing anxiety as hordes of hopeful spectators headed into the area. Bendigo's boisterous arrival, loudly hailed by a large band of his supporters who had preceded him, was the last straw. In quick time a constable of the hundred arrived and announced that he had a warrant and orders to arrest anyone attempting a breach of the peace. Jem Ward immediately took Bendigo out of the village and installed him at a nearby farmhouse until Tuesday morning, the day of the fight. The Lambs and other followers remained in Newport Pagnell, to the displeasure of most locals, but the constable seemed interested in arresting only the principals, should occasion demand. He perhaps wisely concluded that an ever-expanding horde that would move on in the morning was best left alone.

On the Monday evening, Ben Caunt arrived at Wolverton railway station, two miles west of Newport Pagnell, on the four o'clock train from Euston. He had gone down to London from his training base at Hatfield on the Sunday and made an appearance at Tom Spring's, where he gave out two hundred handkerchiefs in his colours of orange with a blue border. The recipients of these were to pay him a guinea each if he won, nothing if he lost. Caunt, Spring and the rest of his party took lodgings at the Cock, an inn in the neighbouring parish of Stony Stratford, while Bendigo's supporters continued to pour into Wolverton by the trainload. These were the early days of rail travel and never again would the small station see as many travellers pass through as it did on those two days in September, 1845.

The Nottingham Lambs and other hard-line followers of Bendigo from the Midlands towns, from Sheffield and Liverpool – "some of a most questionable aspect" as one report described them – set up base in Newport Pagnell. A few who arrived early enough put up at the Swan but it was not long before every available room, barn and outhouse for miles around was taken and it was a lucky man who could find even a chair to spend the night in. Taken by surprise the Buckinghamshire folk might have been, but they quickly realised that some of the ruffians had money to spend. Food and drink were provided at exorbitant prices; carts and gigs in all sorts of disrepair were hitched up to carry folk to the ring on the morrow at a sovereign a head. Some of the more enterprising locals did six months' business in a few hours.

For the time being the Lambs had things their own way, terrifying the locals with their leering swagger and their heavy twigs. Caunt still had followers from Nottinghamshire, the miners and farm hands who had supported him all his career, but as landlord of the Coach and Horses in St Martin's Lane, he was now very much the London man-about-town and most of his supporters from the capital travelled up on the Tuesday, the morning of the fight.

On Monday evening a meeting took place at the Swan Inn between Jem Ward - on behalf of Bendigo, the commissary Tom Oliver, and Tom Spring, acting for Caunt. Spring was not happy at the disorder in and around Newport Pagnell and was worried that the constabulary would find it too easy to interfere in Buckinghamshire, where Bendigo wanted to fight. Spring proposed Lillingstone Level,[39] ten miles to the west, where Nick Ward and Deaf Burke had met in 1840, but Bendigo refused on the grounds that Caunt and his party were staying close by and it would be unfair for him to have to make a longer journey. After heated argument, a site further south, at Whaddon, which they believed to be in Oxfordshire, was agreed upon and at first light the Commissary, Tom Oliver, headed off to set up a ring.

Tom Oliver had fought in his younger days as The Battersea Gardener and took over as official keeper of the ropes and stakes on the death of the previous incumbent, Bill Gibbons. His eye for a site was legendary throughout the Fancy and many were the days he had travelled England by gig, and later by rail, armed only with his sooty pipe and an Ordnance Survey map, scouring the landscape for a patch of turf suitable for the prize ring's finest to do battle. He knew the fields, inns and hamlets of

[39] Now shown on maps as Lillingstone Lovell, to the east of the A413 Buckingham - Towcester road

every county boundary from Yorkshire down to Sussex and even in old age it was said he could leap a ditch or hedge and clamber through a gorse bush better than young swells a third his age.

On fight days Oliver travelled by horse and cart, taking with him his equipment and an assistant. His movements were always watched closely by those who liked to keep close to the action and this time, as always, when he set off for Whaddon a procession of people "on the prad and toddle", as horse and pedestrian were known, followed on behind him. He was the man who would lead them to the fight. Oliver, who did not court attention – to do so would only attract the blues and beaks – tried hard to escape from the head of what was fast becoming a travelling carnival, by taking short cuts down narrow lanes and over fields, to no avail.

By the time Oliver had covered the ten miles to Whaddon and put up the ring, a crowd estimated at five thousand strong had gathered, and the Nottingham Lambs were breaking heads to force out those who could not or would not buy tickets at between one and five shillings for the enclosure they had formed around the ropes. Bendigo was by now at the ringside. He was later criticised for failing to prevent the excesses of his Lamb friends, but in the circumstances it would have taken a lot of energy to try, energy that he no doubt felt better saved for fighting Ben Caunt.

The arrival of Caunt was now eagerly anticipated, but the champion was nowhere to be seen. Unbeknown to Tom Oliver and to Bendigo, as well as to the huge crowd who waited in the hot afternoon, a constable had visited Tom Spring at the Cock in Stony Stratford and informed him that the village of Whaddon was in Bucks., not Oxfordshire as Spring and Oliver believed, and that if Caunt or Bendigo tried to fight in his county he would arrest them. The Buckinghamshire magistrates were determined to prevent the fight at all costs.

Spring immediately sent a messenger to Whaddon, but when he arrived his news was greeted with scorn by the Nottingham men who refused to allow him near Oliver and ripped up the letter he had brought from Spring. They wanted to remain where they were and were not about to give up their profitable enclosure and set off another trail round the countryside on the word of one man on a horse.

The situation was now becoming ludicrous. Five thousand people waited in a field, Bendigo was in attendance, but Caunt was miles away and no matter how much the Lambs disliked the idea of moving, there could be no fight without the Big `Un. Eventually, men were despatched to accompany the messenger back to Spring, who confirmed the situation and a new site was agreed at Sutfield Green, near Lillingstone Level, the place Caunt had first proposed. Tom Oliver now led a second procession another eight miles.

Bendigo was annoyed by the inconvenience and he blamed Caunt. Along the road, when his pony and trap passed the Big `Un's party he shook his fist at the champion and swore to punish him. It was irritation Caunt did not need, rolling along a dusty road on such a hot afternoon. The followers, too, were weary – and there were many of them. At half past two, as Oliver began to erect a second ring with an outer and inner enclosure, the crowd, which now numbered ten thousand or more, was becoming dangerously impatient.

When Caunt and Bendigo arrived at the new site, unruliness broke out all around. Spectators struggled to find positions where they could see the men and climbed on the carriages of swells and on each other, pushing, shoving and punching, their tempers worsened by the heat and frustrations they had endured to be there. Suddenly, at the ropes, a large contingent of Nottingham Lambs dashed into inner ring, swinging cudgels and forcing back all those not in possession of tickets purchased at either Whaddon or the present ring. The stewards, men from the London Fancy and most of them ex-fighters, although armed with sticks and bull-whips, were left powerless. The highly-organised incursion took full advantage of surprise, while interest was diverted by the combatants' arrival.

No one was spared. A party of Corinthians, stalwarts of the London Fancy, had been promised tickets by Tom Spring, but he had not yet arrived. They tried to assert their upper class authority only to be jostled and beaten without fear or favour. The Nottingham Lambs did not hold with airs, graces or social contacts; at times like this a cudgel was more useful than a public school accent. Bendigo, standing close by, lapped up the cries and good wishes of his supporters, without attempting to interfere.

At twenty past three the fighters finally entered the ring. Caunt came first, with Young Molyneux and Jem Turner as his seconds and his uncle Ben Butler taking charge of the water and brandy bottles. Bendigo brought a full complement of assistants – his trainers Jem and Nick Ward; the London publican, Jem Burn, and a well-known lightweight, Jack Hannan, known as the Holy Land Pink. Tom Spring had now arrived with tickets for his London friends, but the few who were still around had been forced to cough up five shillings each to the Lambs. Spring brought the championship belt into the ring, and, in accordance with the articles of agreement for the fight, he showed it to Bendigo to prove it was the genuine article.

Bendigo immediately took the belt and buckled it on, shouting to Caunt in the opposite corner that he would bet him £50 that he would win the fight. Caunt shook his head; he found Bendigo's sense of humour trying at the best of times and at that moment he wanted to fight, not place bets.

What neither of the combatants knew was that a referee had not yet been appointed. Two umpires were at the ropes, one from each camp, but in all the mayhem at, first Whaddon and now Lillingstone Level, the commissary had been unable to recruit a suitable person to act as final arbiter. Various names were put forward by each side, only to be ruled out by the other, until one was proposed that was mutually acceptable. Squire George Osbaldeston was a renowned sportsman of the country school. In his younger days an athlete and cricketer, a duellist, oarsman, pigeon shooter, racehorse owner and a Master of the Quorn Hunt, he once rode two hundred miles on horseback in ten hours.[40] The Squire, now in his late fifties, was a popular choice, but he was nowhere near the ring, having retired to his carriage to avoid the crush and unruliness.

A deputation approached him and appealed to his sporting instincts to act as referee. He had seen enough trouble that afternoon to want nothing at all to do with the proposal, but he succumbed to moral blackmail when it was pointed out that if he would not be referee then the fight could not take place. The Squire did not need to think too hard about the consequences if that happened. He agreed to the request – a decision that very soon he would bitterly regret.

All was ready for Caunt the champion and Bendigo the challenger to begin. With ten thousand voices urging them on and the championship belt secured to the ropes, they looked hard at each other across the ring. Caunt had won the toss for choice of corners and stood with his back to the sun that still burned hot in the late afternoon. At a pound under fourteen stones he had shed three stones in training and was the lightest he had ever been in the ring. His ribcage was prominent and the muscles on his chest and arms gleamed. But the finely honed body could not hide the ugly scars of earlier battles, so apparent on his almost gaunt features, in contrast to Bendigo, who at 12st.1lb. brimmed with vitality and was unmarked. Both men's faces were stained with 'pickle' to toughen the skin and as a prevention to cuts. They stripped off their coats and approached the scratch mark in the centre of the ring.

---

[40] See earlier footnote re Osbaldeston's duel with Lord George Bentinck.

The first round began. Caunt stood erect and ready, his hands up, as Bendigo dodged and weaved about him in his crafty style. Any concerns about his knee limiting his mobility seemed unfounded as he feinted and swayed, tempting Caunt to drop his defence. Caunt swung a blow which missed and Bendigo responded with a resounding smack in the right eye. A few more shuffles and the Lambs were excited to see an old cut opening up on Caunt's cheek. "First blood to Bendigo," was the cry as the bookies were called upon to pay up. The round ended when Caunt used his strength and weight to force Bendigo down in a corner.

For the next two hours they would do battle, although as Caunt came out for the second round his cheek and eye were already showing damage to an extent that would cause a referee in modern day boxing to immediately stop the fight. A pattern was set in the early stages – Caunt throwing hard, vicious but often wildly inaccurate punches, Bendigo dancing round him, picking him off and making fun of him, before dropping to one knee at any slight blow, to end the round. Alternatively, Caunt rushed in and grabbed him, and then either pressed him against the ropes or fell on him with all his weight.

By the sixth round, Caunt's breathing was showing signs of distress and to close observers it seemed that he had over-trained. He had certainly punished his body to lose three stones. Two rounds later Bendigo got within his guard and delivered yet another slashing left hand to Caunt's cheek bone. Caunt missed with his return but he managed to grab his man and flung him against the ropes. His manoeuvre was misjudged for, in leaning over to force his weight down, he fell out of the ring and landed on his head, at the feet of Tom Spring and Vincent Dowling, the editor of *Bell's Life*. Bendigo, who tumbled with him, was unharmed.

Thirty seconds after being carried back to his second's knee, Caunt was on his feet and the routine of Bendigo dancing and popping in blows, Caunt hugging and throwing and spilling more blood from his injured face, continued. Caunt's followers frequently shouted "Foul!" and "Unmanly! as Bendigo slipped down to gain time, but the referee did not agree. Bendigo was doing all the boxing and in the thirteenth the Nottingham Lambs erupted with shouts of "Knock down!" when, despite giving away such weight and height, their man showed the power in his left hand by hitting Caunt on the old spot on his left cheek, knocking him clean off his feet. The blow was so hard that, as it connected with Caunt, Bendigo rebounded onto a ring-stake. Now he had won first blood and first knock-down.

The mood of his supporters turned very quickly in the next round as Bendigo rushed in confidently but was grabbed by Caunt, who tried to strangle him by pressing his neck against the ropes. The Lambs' presence at the ropes was becoming ever more menacing to good order – but encouraging to Bendigo who came up for the fifteenth, in the words of *Bell's Life*, "as lively as a kitten". Another two rounds and a blow to the Big `Un's mouth left his upper lip completely split, blood flowing from it in torrents.

Whenever Caunt managed to grab their hero and press him to the ropes, the Lambs howled with anger and abuse and waved their twigs at him. His own followers, mostly London men and in particular Tom Spring, protested vehemently to the referee at Bendigo's tendency to slip, trip and tumble to the ground, often when he had not been struck a blow at all. In the twenty-fourth round a tumultuous roar of "Foul! Foul!" went up as Bendigo cracked Caunt's ribs with his left and immediately hit the ground himself. The Lambs swarmed through the inner ring to ensure "fair play" and their protests were sufficient for Squire Osbaldeston to decide after some argument that there had been no breach of the rules. In the course of the row, Nick Ward, Bendigo's second, somehow became incapacitated and had to leave the ring, his place taken by Nobby Clarke, the man who had so soundly thrashed Bob Caunt in his first prize fight.

Bendigo continued with his hitting and getting down to avoid the return, as Caunt became more and more frustrated. On several occasions Bendigo went down as he rushed in, causing the Big `Un to fall over him, not on him, and in the twenty-sixth Caunt swung a wild blow which missed and he hit the corner stake, injuring his right hand. Four rounds later, in a rally, Caunt's left cracked Bendigo's right brow and blood flowed, a rare experience for the Bold `Un. In return Caunt received a hard smack on the nose.

The thirty-second round became eventful after Tom Spring and Young Molyneux protested to the referee and umpires that Bendigo was going down without blows being struck. They demanded that he be disqualified. The Lambs did not approve of such unsporting appeals and one of them tried to punish Spring with a cudgel to the head. The blow missed its target, hitting him on the shoulder and causing him pain for several days. This assault was a signal for more Lambs to climb through the ropes, twigs swinging and heads cracking all over the ring. Squire Osbaldeston turned down the protests made on Caunt's behalf and, after some delay as the ring was cleared of brawling rival supporters, the two fighters came to the scratch.

Insults and complaints were being hurled at Osbaldeston now from all those whose money was on Caunt, but the Squire refused to declare against Bendigo. Vincent Dowling, the editor of *Bell's Life*, who was no supporter of the Bold `Un at the best of times, reported that the referee's position was far from enviable:

> "He must have been possessed of no small nerve to have presumed to decide against the arguments that were so significantly shaken in the vicinity of his knowledge box and to this must be must be attributed his reluctance to give a candid opinion."[41]

If the referee was disinclined towards a candid opinion, the Nottingham Lambs had no such reluctance. Just as Caunt's followers complained about Bendigo hitting and going down, his followers were incensed at the way Caunt kept falling against him over the ropes and trying to suffocate him. When it happened yet again in the forty-first, one of the Lambs swung his twig at Caunt's head – but counter-productively, for the blow landed on Bendigo's shoulder.

This marked a long spell of chaos around the ring, with sections of the crowd pushing forward and others, close to the ropes trying to get away. At one point the *Bell's Life* editor had six or seven bodies pressed against him from behind, and Caunt and Bendigo, who had both fallen out of the ring, thrashing about at his feet. The London Fancy, responsible for preserving order, hit out with their bull-whips and sticks but were no match for the Lambs, who approached mayhem in a notoriously organised manner. Of the many stewards there on behalf of the organisers, only Johnny Broome and another pugilist,Jack McDonald, tried to help the spectators at the ring-side who were in distress. The rest, wrote Vincent Dowling, "looked on with modest timidity, evidently afraid to interfere with the 'club law' of the Nottingham bands, who obeyed the signals of their leaders with a discipline worthy of a better cause."

Meanwhile, inside the ring, Caunt seized Bendigo by the neck and twice swung him round like a cat. Although Bendigo continued to cause more damage to the bigger man's seriously distorted face, he was showing signs of fatigue when several more rounds ended with Caunt throwing him and falling with all his weight upon him.

On and on it went, the familiar pattern of Caunt's punches missing their target, Bendigo's connecting, Caunt hugging and throwing, falling on his smaller and lighter opponent, Bendigo going down to end the

---

[41] Henry Downes Miles, who was also present at the ring-side, included Vincent Dowling's report of the fight for *Bell's Life* in his later book *Pugilistica.* Miles, who favoured Bendigo, described Dowling's opinion of the referee as "partisan writing" and *Bell's Life's* criticism of Squire Osbaldeston as "a gratuitous and unjust imputation on a most honourable sportsman". According to Miles, Caunt was a beaten man by the 32nd round.

round. Not that the crowd's cries of "Claret" were all good news for him; he had already sustained a cut to the brow, now, in the sixty-sixth he caught a blow in the mouth from Caunt and more blood flowed. But when he was hit he leaped back in to the fray and punished Caunt again and again, causing him to wince with pain as he pounded his body and face.

Outside the ropes, even more pain was being dispensed. Nowhere close to the ring was it possible to watch the fight in safety, as whips and staves flashed through the air and rival supporters fell with gaping wounds and broken bones. Time between rounds was being very erratically kept, with a minute and sometimes longer elapsing before the fighters were called to the scratch to resume.

A strange episode occurred in the eighty-second when Bendigo retreated to the ropes and fell backwards, but then jumped up and threw punches. Caunt immediately turned and ran across the ring to his corner with his head down and Bendigo, chasing after him, hit him on the back of the neck and jumped on him in a rough scramble. Shouts of "Coward" were aimed at the champion, but when he came out for the next he hit Bendigo straight in the mouth, once again drawing blood.

The Nottingham Lambs were by now at boiling point. The hot sun and long day had affected them almost as much as their man, whose fatigue was obvious. Time and again their hatred for Ben Caunt caused them to rush the ring to try to get at him. The inner enclosure, where the umpires and referee were supposedly protected by the stewards, became a battleground, and in the eighty-fifth round Squire Osbaldeston was forced to abandon his seat and join Bendigo and Caunt in the ring. The editor of *Bell's Life*, Vincent Dowling, was pulled from under a pile of spectators, his clothes ripped and torn. Jem Ward managed to restore the referee to his position but even the hearty Osbaldeston was in a dither now, as sticks flashed by within an inch of his hat. It was two hours since the fight had commenced and it was clear to the few with time and space to consider such matters that it could not go on much longer.

Despite the punishment he had suffered, Caunt was still able to throw punches of murderous intent with both hands. Bendigo at this stage was dancing away, though managing to get back inside sufficiently to cause more damage to his man's eye and cheek. In the eighty-seventh he connected with a sharp rap to the face and then fell down as Caunt's friends again appealed to the referee. Two more rounds and Bendigo's right struck Caunt's ribs with such force that the blow was heard around the ring, over the ongoing racket. For two more rounds it went on, the seconds - Molyneux on Caunt's side and Hannan for Bendigo - claiming fouls to no avail.

Finally, in the ninety-second, after a fierce exchange of blows, Bendigo stooped down to avoid Caunt's left. As he did so, he hit Caunt in the groin and fell backwards himself. Caunt dropped to the floor, writhing in pain, as, in the words of *Bell's Life*:

> "An indescribable scene of turmoil ensued; shouts of 'Foul' and 'Fair' escaped from a thousand tongues – a thousand pairs of iron lungs, many evidently influenced by their desires and not by their convictions."

Under the rules, the blow was clearly a foul – if struck intentionally. The umpires could not agree whether Bendigo had meant to do it and deferred to the referee, who, due to the roaring of the crowd, could not be heard. When Osbaldeston did manage to get his words across, he said he had not seen the blow, and Molyneux and Hannan had no alternative but to return to their men and send them out one more time.

The ninety-third round was to be the last. Incredibly, given the punishment that had been endured over more than two hours hard fighting, both men came quickly to the scratch. Caunt threw lefts and rights, catching Bendigo on the forehead. He was forced back on the ropes but got up, only for the Big 'Un to knock him down. What happened next would become a matter of great controversy. For years after, whenever old supporters of Bendigo or Caunt got to arguing the merits of their men, the events of the next few seconds – and the minutes that followed as the referee was pressed for a decision - would be raked over and over again.

Caunt, thinking – and not without good reason – that the round was over as his opponent was on the ground, half turned from him to return to his corner. But Bendigo was up in a flash and, just as he had done before, he chased across the ring to continue the battle. Caunt saw him coming and seemed about to deliver a mighty punch, but instead changed his mind and sat down on the turf. In Bendigo's corner, Jem Ward, Hannan the Holy Land Pink and Nobby Clarke leaped forward yelling "Foul!", based on Caunt going down without a blow. Their claim was a bit rich since their man had been doing it all through the fight, but it was loudly taken up by the Lambs who, without waiting for confirmation from umpires or referee, lifted Bendigo into the air and bore him off in triumph to his carriage.

The end came so suddenly that many of the thousands present did not know what had happened or who had won. Word buzzed round the field that Bendigo had been disqualified following the low blow in the previous round and only those very close to the ring knew what had actually occurred. In his corner, surrounded by an angry Tom Spring and Young Molyneux, Caunt was dumbstruck by the turn of events. He and his party rushed after the referee, who had made his escape from the ring, but, when confronted, Osbaldeston said he had seen Caunt go down without a blow and that as such conduct was unfair he had pronounced against him. He had judged what he saw from the overwhelmingly difficult position in which he had been forced.

Spring argued that the round was in effect over and Caunt had gone down to avoid being drawn in by Bendigo as had happened earlier, but the Squire stood by his decision, telling Spring and anyone else who cared to listen that he had been chosen referee by both parties and he had accepted the office against his own inclination. In discharging his duties he had done so impartially to the best of his abilities and had no bias in favour of one man or the other. The matter was now at an end, he added. In that, he was very wrong.

The result and the manner in which it arose were in keeping with Osbaldeston's erratic decisions throughout the fight. It was pointed out by impartial observers, as well as Caunt's followers, that the umpires had not been consulted for their opinion and that according to the rules this should have been done before the referee gave his decision. But the rules were not created in an atmosphere of intimidation, violence and sheer mayhem. In the heat of the moment, although many criticised Osbaldeston at the time and later, it was no surprise that when Caunt sat down in the ring, the referee saw his chance to get out without being murdered by the Nottingham Lambs.

The fight had lasted two hours and ten minutes. Many bets had been laid that Caunt would win within half an hour and many more that Bendigo would not be beaten within an hour. These bets were easily settled, as were those on first blood and first knock-down, both going Bendigo's way. Although he was not too badly marked – he had a cut over his right eye, a swollen ear and contusions on his cheek, mouth and forehead - by the time he reached his carriage he was in a state of exhaustion. The repeated heavy falls and the hot sun left him barely able to stand, but he soon recovered and was taken to his quarters to celebrate, along with Jem Ward, his seconds and backers.

The evidence of Bendigo's superior skill could be seen in Ben Caunt's battered face. But the physical pain he felt was as little compared to his mortification at having lost the championship. Tom Spring declared himself "dead beat" from his efforts to see fair play and the assaults that had been made upon him by the rampant Lambs. Dejected and feeling robbed, the losing party returned to the Cock at Stony Stratford, intending to return to London the same night on the first available train from Wolverton.

Unfortunately for Caunt, many more people had the same idea. Hordes of Londoners descended on the small town and a terrible crush developed as the station was closed with more than two thousand fight followers trying to force their way in. There were delays well into the night as the railway company did its utmost to shift the crowds heading south. Meanwhile, in London, the sporting houses were besieged with anxious enquirers as to the result. St Martin's Lane and New Street, opposite Caunt's Coach and Horses, were blocked and nobody could get in or out of the Castle Inn, Tom Spring's pub in Holborn. Rumours abounded that first Caunt and then Bendigo had won and it was not until the ten-thirty train arrived at Euston that the correct information was discovered.

Bendigo stayed overnight at the farmhouse where he had lodged before the fight. He travelled up to Nottingham on the Wednesday. Word of his victory had reached there the night before and he was met at the station by thousands of well-wishers. He seemed little the worse for the fight, despite the blows he had taken, the falls he had suffered and the times Caunt had his neck pressed against the ropes. The working people of the town were in a high pitch of excitement, but the delight at Bendigo's success was not shared by the *The Nottingham Review*.

Reporting the fight at some length, in a style considerably more flowery and elaborate than even the sporting press, the paper offered no praise to the local hero, but instead castigated everyone involved:

> "It would be well that everyone who attends a prize fight felt, along with the pugilists, each blow given. Those who abet and countenance a prize fight are worse than the fighters. Talk of "national courage" may be the practice of such brutal demoralising scenes in the nineteenth century! 'Tis a national disgrace. How is it that magistrates who license publicans (many of them pugilists and ex-pugilists) who have given their houses for matching prize fights, and boxing glove exhibitions? If they were to refuse licences to those who keep such houses, prize fighting would soon shut down. By their not doing so, they openly give encouragement to the brutal exhibitions that take place. And, query; do not magistrates violate their oath of office in not suppressing

> the houses named? At the brutal exhibition last Tuesday there were present many of the nobility as well as mobility."[42]

The editor of *Bell's Life*, Vincent Dowling, had plenty to say on the subject, albeit from a rather different perspective. His paper gave the fight a great deal of coverage and throughout Dowling was scathing in his contempt for the whole proceedings. He wrote:

> "During the last thirty years it has been our fate to witness almost every important battle in the Prize Ring, but we confess, although we have occasionally had to record transactions of the most discreditable description, and to administer castigation to wrong-doers in no measured terms, the proceedings on Tuesday far exceed in enormity anything we had before witnessed. . .
>
> We were prepared to expect that at such a season we should have to encounter much disorder and confusion, especially as the members of the ring have of late ceased to use any exertion to maintain the decency of their order. But on an occasion when the very existence of British boxing was at stake . . . we did expect that we should have at least the semblance of good order and fair play.
>
> We have already alluded to the Nottingham roughs, men of the most reckless character who came prepared with bludgeons to force their opinions and who from first to last struck terror into all who dared to dissent for their dictation. These men were congregated at Newport Pagnell on Monday night and by way of keeping their hands in cracked a few heads, one poor fellow flying for refuge into the Swan Inn. The next morning they were regularly called over one by one by their leaders and answered to their names like so many policemen going on duty. . .
>
> We heard their war whoops and watched their signals – the slightest appeal against the conduct of Bendigo was drowned or opposed by their cries and exclamations, rendered more terrific by the flourish of their bludgeons which were shook with significant meaning over the heads of the referee and which in one instance ended nearly in the prostration of Spring and in another in the death of Caunt at whose head a deadly blow was aimed –

[42] *Nottingham Review*, 12th September, 1845

> although it unluckily fell on Bendigo's shoulder as he lay across the ropes with Caunt upon him. The last of appeals to the referee were accompanied by similar indications of personal violence, the effect of which could be sufficiently understood by a declaration of the Squire at Wolverton that had those who censured him been in his situation they would have acted precisely in a similar manner. He did not think his life safe and self-preservation left him no option.
>
> Now we will ask, by whom were these persons paid and organised and for what purpose?
>
> Was it for the purpose of securing for both men a clear stage and no favour? Or was it to render the success of one – we incline to the latter opinion. If we are informed correctly there was a pre-determination that Caunt should not win under any circumstances and those roughs were the chosen instruments to carry this plan into effect, hence the avidity with which certain parties were ready to take all the odds that were offered on Caunt. Jem Burn, who acted as Bendigo's mentor, repeatedly declared that if Caunt hung himself upon his man on the ropes, he would cut them. We pointed out to him the folly of such threats and they were happily not carried into execution but if men of his stamp and influence will hold out such threats and afterwards associate with those who do worse, what chance is there of sustaining the character of fair boxing matches?"

Elsewhere in the paper, Dowling declared: "A more disgraceful and disgusting exhibition never stained the annals of British boxing." He justified the amount of space he gave to the events at Lillingstone Level on the grounds that "The great interest attached to this fight in all parts of the kingdom has induced us to be thus prolix". Not everyone agreed with him: his great rival in the sporting press, Henry Downes Miles, was critical of many of Dowling's comments and assertions, claiming that from the position the *Bell's Life* editor had taken, by one of the centre-stakes, he had not been able to see much of the action and had relied on Spring and other pro-Caunt sources in his report. He considered that Caunt's followers were equally ruffianly in their behaviour and that Dowling was partisan towards the big man.

Besides his journalistic duties, Vincent Dowling had another great responsibility regarding the fight: he was the stakeholder, the man who held the £400 put down in total by the men's backers. As the rows and recriminations over the result gathered pace, and Caunt's backers served legal notice that the stakes be returned to each set of backers, rather than be awarded to Bendigo, Dowling's position became an increasingly awkward one.

No less discomfited in the aftermath was the referee, Squire Osbaldeston. Rumours were rife that he had admitted being intimidated by the Lambs and had admitted not actually seeing the last round. On 18th September, nine days after the event, he wrote to Dowling, as stakeholder, clarifying his position, asking the editor to pay over the stake money and expressing regret that he had ever agreed to act as referee:

> "SIR, - An appeal having been made to me, as referee, by Mr Spring, to reverse my decision in the late fight between Bendigo and Caunt, on grounds unworthy of my consideration, I request you will confirm that decision by paying over the stakes to Bendigo, who, in my opinion, is justly entitled to them. It was with the greatest reluctance and at the particular request of my friends and the unanimous solicitations of the backers of the men, that I accepted the office; but I shall always consider it one of the greatest acts of folly that I ever was guilty of in my life."

He went on to say that he had endeavoured to do justice to each side to the best of his abilities and judgement and that he was completely convinced of the justness of the decision he gave and not influenced in any way by the behaviour of the "roughs". He wrote:

> "In no one instance, in my judgement, did Bendigo break the law of fair fighting. I must also deny, in the most positive manner, that I ever stated to any person that I did not see the last round. I saw every round distinctly and clearly and when Caunt came up in the last round he had evidently not recovered from the 92nd. After the men were in position, Bendigo very soon commenced operations and Caunt turned round directly and skulked away, with his back to Bendigo, and sat down on his nether end.
>
> He never knocked Bendigo down once in the fight, nor ever got him against the ropes in the last round. In my opinion Caunt got away as soon as he could from

Bendigo, fell without a blow to avoid being hit out of time, and fairly lost the fight.

...I am, your obedient servant, The Old Squire, Doncaster"

His letter was one of many printed in *Bell's Life* the Sunday following the fight. Vincent Dowling, stuck between the two parties – Bendigo asking for his winnings and Tom Spring, on behalf of Caunt, demanding that the result be declared void - had announced he would withhold the money until the referee explained himself. Osbaldeston had now done that, but his comments only whipped up the furore to even greater levels and still Dowling refused to part with the £400.

A great deal of talk was going on about a fresh match between the two fighters at Doncaster, with a purse of thousands of pounds mentioned. Amidst two full broadsheet pages of post-mortem and many letters from supporters of both sides, a surgeon wrote in, telling how he had attended Ben Caunt the day after the fight and "carefully examined every part of his person". His description of the big man's wounds was not at all consistent with the blows he was reported as having sustained from Bendigo's fists, but the point of the letter was his confirmation of a blow sustained to the lower abdomen "just above the pubis, which occasions a good deal of tenderness."

Caunt was, of course, convinced he had been wrongly disqualified. Two nights after the fight he aired his grievances at the Tennis Court, Windmill Street, at a benefit for the Commissary, Tom Oliver. It had been hoped that Bendigo would also attend, but he remained in Nottingham, leaving the Big `Un to complain loudly and bitterly to the capacity audience that he had suffered an injustice at the hands of the Lambs. They had intimidated his friends, he said, while Bendigo had struck him in "the most tender part of my person", causing an agony from which he had not yet recovered. He said "If I had fair play I'd lick three Bendigos in one ring", adding that he would put £300 down with whatever stakes were laid by backers.

Bendigo's Nottingham supporters were not surprised at the attitude of Ben Caunt and Tom Spring, but they were livid at what they read in *Bell's Life*. They were especially angry at all the blame for the trouble at the fight being placed at the Lambs' door, and pointed out that the so-called "roughs" were not just from Nottingham, but also from Leicester, Liverpool, Manchester and Sheffield, while Caunt had his own supporters from the Nottinghamshire villages as well as the swells of London. It was in part true, but the reality was that when it came to havoc and ensuring "fair play" for the Bold `Un, the Lambs led and others followed.

The arguments would rumble on for months. Caunt instructed a solicitor in Gray's Inn Square, who sent a letter to Vincent Dowling at *Bell's Life*, threatening him with legal proceedings if he handed over the stake money to Bendigo. He followed up the letter with a writ from the Court of Exchequer, but Bendigo's backers were not taking the matter lying down. While bets were offered that Caunt would never get a farthing of his money, stalwarts of the Nottingham Fancy met at the Poultry Hotel in the town and opened a public subscription to oppose Caunt's legal action. While they were at it they heartily condemned Tom Spring for not paying up on his bets and banned *Bell's Life* from the public houses of Nottingham

Dowling defended his paper's stance, in robust fashion. On 26th October, six weeks on from the event, he wrote:

> "Abuse has been privately heaped upon us for our strictly impartial account of the fight . . .We have encountered many a breeze but never such a blow as this and as we like a fair stand-up fight we shall give a counter-hit and promise not to fall down to avoid the return."

He was intending a dig at Bendigo's fighting methods, but Caunt, never one to let a slight pass, was unsure whether it was he who should be offended, since it was through him going down without a blow that the fight had ended and the controversy begun.

He had already sought a re-match in a letter to Bendigo, saying he would fight him for £500 on a stage – beyond the reach of the Lambs – anywhere in England, Ireland, France or America "where we can have fair play and no favour". He even offered to pay his travelling expenses, but Bendigo had not replied to the letter, although he did suggest that if Caunt upped the figure to £1,000 he might consider it. In one of many letters printed under Caunt's name in *Bell's Life* at this time, he now said he would accept the challenge of £1,000 - "and if Bendigo or his friends decline the offer I shall continue to sign myself as heretofore, Your humble servant, Benjamin Caunt, Champion of England."

As expected in many quarters, Caunt abandoned his action against Vincent Dowling,[43] who, in the New Year 1846, finally paid Bendigo the £200 that represented Caunt's part of the stake money. The championship belt had been in Bendigo's possession since he took it from the ropes at Lillingstone Level and he had already shown it in benefits before the Nottingham and Liverpool faithful. Once again he was the Champion of England. He had regained his title and proved to all fair-minded folk that when it came to fighting skills he was the best man in the land. His critics, and there were many, accused him of adopting shifty tactics, of being unsporting, of falling to avoid being hit, but his response to such talk was to ask: "What am I supposed to do when they're bigger and heavier than me?"

[43] He was advised that, as prize fighting was outside the law under the 18th clause of the Games and Wagers Act, he had no legal recourse.

10] The Needle Pointer

No betting man in the land would have wagered a guinea on Bendigo and Ben Caunt becoming friends. Their mutual animosity had festered for over ten years. It seemed inconceivable that they could ever settle their differences, grounded as those differences were in jibes and ridicule on one hand, envy and bitter frustration on the other - and sealed in blood spilled over three relentless fights. The hotly disputed outcome of their last encounter was never likely to rest easy on the proud Caunt, while Bendigo might have remained long aggrieved of the way in which the bigger man had tried repeatedly to strangle him against the ropes.

But in early 1850 the unexpected happened. They met in London, dined together at Jem Burn's public house, shook hands and buried their arguments of the past. On Monday 4th February they even took a joint benefit at the National Baths, Westminster Road, where a packed crowd watched eagerly as the two ring heroes sparred together. Afterwards Bendigo attempted to gird the loins of Big Ben with what was described as a "championship belt". It was actually the belt he had himself been presented with eleven years earlier by Jem Ward, after beating Deaf Burke.

This act of goodwill was in keeping with the Bold `Un's new-found friendship towards his old foe, but no consideration had been given to the difference in size between them. As Bendigo placed the belt around Caunt's waist, he tried to draw the ends together on his stomach but discovered they would not meet – there was a gap of ten inches. Amidst ribald comments from some members of the audience, he suggested that Ben might care to submit to a steam press, but Caunt declined the offer and the belt was hastily put back in its box by Bendigo's friends, to be returned to Nottingham. This embarrassing episode could have been a test of their new-found friendship, but bumper takings of £200 for the benefit ensured both men went home happy.

Four years had elapsed since their third and final match. From the day it was announced the fight was always destined to be a classic of the mid-century prize ring and the events within and without the ring lived up to all expectations. National and local newspapers, the sporting press, the chaunters and street singers and hawkers of poems, they all nourished the legend. One broadsheet ballad, sold only days after the event, began:

> "On the ninth day of September
> Eighteen hundred and forty five
> From London down to Nottingham
> The roads were all alive.
> Oh! such a sight was never seen
> Believe me it is so
> Tens of thousands went to see the fight
> With Ben Caunt and Bendigo
>
> And near to Newport Pagnell
> Those men did strip so fine.
> Ben Caunt stood six foot two and a half
> And Bendigo five foot nine
> Ben Caunt a giant did appear
> And made the claret flow
> And he seemed fully determined
> To conquer Bendigo.
>
> *Chorus:*
> With their hit away and slash away
> So manfully you see
> Ben Caunt and Bendigo
> Has gained the victory.[44]

For all its celebration, the fight signalled the beginning of the end of the prize ring. The disruption by law officers, the extortion of swells and Corinthians by the Nottingham Lambs, the intimidation of the referee and the cudgel blows aimed at the combatants - all marked the fight as a spectacle of sporting disorder at its worst. Prize fighting had been in terminal decline for decades and, although it would manage to survive for many more years, never again would crowds gather in such numbers as they did at Lillingstone Level on that hot September Tuesday in 1845.

---

[44] From *The Victorian Underworld*, Kellow Chesney. Temple Smith, 1970. This ballad is one of many such 'accounts', low on accuracy of detail as to the actual events. They were often sold by the foot and written before the event. Another, *Bendigo, Champion of England*, is to be found in *Modern Street Ballads*, John Ashton (Ed.) Chatto & Windus, 1988.

In the immediate aftermath of the fight, Bendigo appeared to have retired from the ring. He did not make a formal announcement, but he had hinted before meeting Caunt that this would be his last contest. He was thirty-three years old and had proved his worth once and for all against the best of his peers. Though not wealthy, he was comfortably off for a man of his class and lifestyle and as he became older the effort required to prepare for fights had become harder to summon. Nor was it made any easier by his drinking habits when not in training. He decided to call it a day, to relax and live off the fame he had achieved in thirteen years as a prize fighter.

And so, for four years after the last meeting with Caunt, Bendigo had been absent from the public gaze. There was little reference to him in the sporting press and, as time went on, few demands for him to defend the championship. He stayed in Nottingham and, when he was not roistering with the Lambs in the town pubs, or winning bets by catching flies in flight between his thumb and first finger – just to show he had lost none of his speed - he was fishing in the River Trent.

Angling had always been a pastime, since he was a small boy in New Yard. With the river barely a mile away, it was easy to walk down, cast a line and while away a peaceful afternoon, far away from the violence of the ring and the hurly-burly of town life. In the years after the third fight with Caunt he became a regular sight, wandering through the town carrying his fishing tackle, clad in a velveteen coat, corduroy knee-breeches, thick worsted stockings and heavy hob-nailed boots.

He was the best-known man in Nottingham, the hero of the common people, a street urchin who had climbed out of the mire of workhouse, mill and factory to be hailed by lord and labourer alike. His status in the town was evident in the wake of the General Election of July 1847. As the new Conservative Member of Parliament, John Walter, grandson of the founder of *The Times*, took a victory parade through the streets, it was Bendigo who was chosen to lead the procession. To give due gravitas to the proceedings he rode a white horse and wore his championship belt.

The *Nottingham Journal* reported:

> "He appeared to exert himself very greatly to preserve order among the rougher portion of the throng, on the shoulders of whom he used his whip with characteristic liberality but no one seemed in the least to resent his energetic proceedings.
>
> On the contrary, to esteem a cut from the best bruiser in England seemed rather an honour than an affront."[45]

The new MP was so pleased with Bendigo's efforts that he gave him a fishing rod in appreciation.

Occasionally he attended fights as a spectator. In May 1846, when Paddy Gill, a Walsall lightweight, fought Young Norley at Whitney before a crowd of three thousand, Bendigo arrived to find Ben Caunt at the ropes. It was only three months since he had finally received Caunt's £200 after a protracted dispute and he soon engaged his old foe in argument. Caunt repeated his offer to meet again in the ring for "anything from £500 to £1,000", telling those standing around him "If I fight him again I'll bring some Derbyshire pickaxe men that'll be more than a match for his Nottingham Lambs."

The following year Bendigo went to Lindrick Common, near Worksop for Paddy Gill's next contest, against a Liverpool carpenter, Tom Davis. The fight ended in scenes most familiar to the champion – when Gill was given the decision, Davis's friends attacked the referee with fists and sticks, smashed a bottle over his head and ripped his clothes to shreds. Only the intervention of Bendigo and the Lambs, who grabbed the referee, escorted him to a chaise and sent him on his way, saved the unfortunate fellow from serious injury and possible death.

But for most of the time he was happy to take life easy in the tap rooms of Nottingham Market Place or on the banks of the Trent. The title that he had regained but not defended fell into abeyance. It was assumed although never confirmed that he had retired, but no one else came along with a pressing claim and so he was still in effect the Champion of England.

Then, in the New Year 1850, rumours began to circulate of a possible challenger to the title. Johnny Broome, who had been involved in the matching of Bendigo and Caunt nearly five years earlier, was said to have an "unknown" who wanted to fight for the championship. For several

[45] *Nottingham Journal* August 1847

weeks this anonymous challenger was discussed within the Fancy, some claiming to know his identity, others sceptical. Such mysteries were a hallmark of Broome's way of doing ring business; on the last occasion he had held out until the last moment as to whether Bendigo's opponent would be Caunt or the Tipton Slasher.

But whoever he was, would Bendigo want to fight him? Would he be interested? He was thirty-eight years old, middle-aged by the standards of the time and he had been in the ring only twice in the past decade. He walked with a noticeable limp from the old knee injury, which had been aggravated still further while playing quoits a couple of years earlier. If this claimant came forward and issued a challenge, the chances were – so the Fancy believed – that the old warrior would dodge it.

They were wrong. All was revealed at the National Baths, on the occasion of his joint benefit with Ben Caunt. Bendigo was delighted by the reception he got from the capacity crowd and, at the conclusion of the evening, after the performance of trying to fit the belt on his new-found friend, he stepped to the front of the stage to give a speech. He said he was willing to meet any man in the world for £200 or upwards and he hoped that this "unknown" of Johnny Broome's, who everybody was talking about, would come forward with his money, to put an end to all the "tall talk".

What happened next was not what he expected. A tall, robust young fellow in a long dark overcoat could be seen pushing his way through the crowd. When the man, who looked like a farmer or a shepherd, jumped onto the platform with his arm outstretched and waved three five pound notes, the Bold `Un, for once in his life, was nonplussed. He stared open-mouthed as the young man shouted, in an excited voice, "I'm Johnny Broome's unknown. I'm Tom Paddock of Redditch and I've come here to take thee on, Master Bendigo. 'Ere's my brass, down with thine and I'll fight thee as soon as thee likes."

As he finished speaking, the National Baths erupted with applause. All eyes were now on Bendigo and he was urged to respond to the challenge. He did not disappoint – recovering from his surprise, he seized Paddock's hand and, leaping and cavorting about the stage, he dragged the bewildered fellow after him. The crowd went wild and, eventually coming to a halt, he waited for the noise to subside before going to the edge of the platform and saying "Gentlemen. This is the happiest moment of my life. This is just what I wanted. You'll have a fight for the belt and you'll see what old Bendy can do when he tries." He then left the stage as the audience began to ask themselves, who was this Tom Paddock and who had he fought?

Paddock was twenty six years old, from Redditch in Worcestershire and known as 'The Needle Pointer', after the local trade of needle-making. He had youth on his side and was a hard puncher, but with only five fights behind him he lacked experience. He had been taught by the best men in the Midlands in Johnny and Harry Broome and had twice beaten Nobby Clarke, conqueror of the unfortunate Bob Caunt. Many among the Fancy thought Bendigo had taken on one opponent too many.

Two nights after their first meeting, he and Paddock came together with their backers at Peter Crawley's pub and arrangements were drawn up for the fight, to take place on Tuesday 4th June 1850[46]. Paddock made much of his lack of fear of his opponent or his unruly friends, saying he would be happy to fight in Nottingham if Bendigo wanted to, but the location was fixed for half way between the Lace City and London. The stakes were fixed at £200 a side, along with the championship belt. Each party left £25 deposit, to be passed to the editor of *Bell's Life* who was appointed stakeholder.

Over the coming weeks, publicity for, and anticipation of, the fight built up. At the second deposit, held at Johnny Broome's pub in Piccadilly, it became clearer as to why Bendigo was making a comeback, and the reason was not the one which the Bold `Un liked to give to journalists later in life.

In that version, he claimed that he had only returned to the ring because of his mother's urging. "She was a wonderful old woman. She was mainly the cause of my last fight – that with Tom Paddock. Well, I went to see her; she was eighty-two years old then, and I found her at her lodgings, smoking her pipe and reading Bell's Life. 'There you are then, mother,' I says. 'Yes,' she says, answering me sharp, 'here I am. Have you seen this?' It was the paper she meant. 'No,' I says, 'I ain't.' She says 'Have you seen this Tom Paddock?' 'No,' I says. 'I have,' says she, 'a needle-pointer at Redditch; a fellow with no more breadth to his shoulders than there is between the eyes of a mouse, and he challenges you to fight. And I'll tell you this, Bendy, if you don't take the challenge you are a coward. And I'll tell you more, if you won't fight him, I'll send and take up the challenge myself.'"

---

[46] Later changed to the next day, Wednesday June 5th

That was the story he told James Greenwood, a correspondent of the *Daily Telegraph* in 1874.[47] But Mary Thompson, like Bendigo, could not read and it is unlikely that she played any part at all in his acceptance of Paddock's challenge, which had anyway taken Bendigo by surprise. The reality of his decision to enter the prize ring again was that he was running short of money, as he hinted in Broome's pub, saying that although he had been fighting since the early age of fifteen, he was no nearer independence now than he had ever been.

Unlike many of his contemporaries, Bendigo had never gone into business. His only excursion into the licensing trade had been years earlier when he kept the 'tap' in Sheffield, the Manchester Arms, but that seems to have been more a convenient arrangement with the proprietor than Bendigo becoming a landlord on his own account. The only way he had traded on his name was in giving exhibitions of his skills, which had been profitable once, but opportunities for these had faded away with his apparent retirement, until the joint event with Caunt at the National Baths.

At Broome's pub, where he appeared full of his usual good spirits and wearing a Quaker's hat, he told Paddock that his experience was a lesson that he hoped the younger man would take advantage of. Paddock, he said, should "make hay while the sun shines", for if he was beaten in the coming struggle the world would not look upon him with favour. The young challenger, who stood taller and heavier than him, just smiled. At the side of Bendigo, who looked his thirty eight years, the Needle Pointer, seemed to brim with health and strength, his ruddy cheeks the colour of a beetroot.

While in London, Bendigo appeared at a benefit at Jem Burn's for the dependants of his old second, Nick Ward, who had died earlier in the week. Many of the London pugilists turned out to spar, including the Bold `Un's former opponents Caunt and Young Langan, and the deceased's brother Jem Ward, the old Black Diamond, now forty nine years old. *Bell's Life* declared Bendigo "The star of the night, as electric in his movements as ever and throughout the evening he showed that his heart was in the right place."

A month later found him in training at Farnsfield, a hamlet thirteen miles from Nottingham. It was a departure from previous habits, when he would always train near Liverpool with Jem Ward. Now, he was back with Sam Turner, his earliest mentor, the man who had guided him

[47] Published in *Low Life Deeps*, Chatto & Windus, 1881

through his first fights in the ring – and rumours were circulating as to what had gone wrong in his relationship with Ward.

Ward was quick to dispel tales that he had forsaken his former protégé in favour of Tom Paddock, who, it was said, he was backing for part of the stake money. He wrote to *Bell's Life*, "I fear I have lived so long from the friends of my early youth, they must have entirely forgotten my general habits." He said he never exchanged "old" faces for new ones and he imagined Bendigo understood that. He said he was too occupied with his own business and could not have undertaken the training had it been proposed to him.

Confusing the matter further, Bendigo wrote the following week:

> "Mr Editor, You sometimes style me 'the bold but eccentric Bendigo' but I beg to assure you sir with all my peculiarities, I am not unmindful of the many obligations I am under."

He had settled back into the old routines, taking long walks and runs and sparring in the paddock behind the White Post pub at Farnsfield with Sam Turner and a local man, Matthew Haze, who stood six feet three inches tall. He knew that to beat Tom Paddock he would have to be fitter and stronger than ever before.

The week before the fight, reports surfaced that both sides had "engaged roughs" to intimidate each other. Such action would have been quite unnecessary on Bendigo's part, as nobody came rougher than the Nottingham Lambs and they did not require any engagement for a Bendigo fight, they were as certain to be there as was the man himself. The allegation came from Johnny Broome, Paddock's chief advisor, but he was then counter-charged with having travelled to Birmingham to line up a force to ensure Paddock's success. Broome claimed that at the time he was said to be there, he was ill in bed.

The final deposit, held at Jem Burn's, was attended by a large contingent of supporters of both men. Articles for the fight stated that the stakeholder, Vincent Dowling of *Bell's Life*, should name the place where it would be held. This he did, by handing to the backers of each man a sealed packet, containing the location, with instructions that it should not be divulged until the morning of the fight, Wednesday 5th June. He spoke long and eloquently on the topic of "the manly sport" and how the confusion which prevailed at the last contest for the championship – when Bendigo met Caunt five years earlier – had created disgust in the minds of all true patrons of the ring. Dowling dismissed the rumours that "roughs" had been hired by each side, saying that he believed it was the wish of both sets of backers that they should see a fair and honourable fight.

Bendigo's training quarters at Farnsfield proved a mixed blessing. He had no difficulty getting down to business with Sam Turner and Matthew Haze, but the proximity to Nottingham brought an endless stream of friends, supporters, well-wishers and the plain curious who thought they would venture into the countryside and exchange pleasantries with their hero. The residents of the small hamlet were not pleased with this insurgence of townies, many of them rowdy and exuberant. When, in the final week, large bands of Lambs turned up in mischievous mood, creating their usual disturbance around the place and terrorising the gentle rustics, a complaint was made to the local magistrate.

Fearing legal interference that would disturb his fight plans, Bendigo departed Farnsfield and moved to the home of a friend near Lowdham, eight miles away from Nottingham. But word of his move travelled and so it was that on the lunchtime of Monday 3rd June, two days before the scheduled fight, as he and a friend were about to step into a railway carriage at nearby Lowdham Station, a constable stood in his path. Brandishing a warrant of arrest, the lawman asked him if his name was Bendigo.

As he did, he grabbed hold of the Bold `Un, never a safe thing to do. Bendigo immediately struck the constable's arm with the flat of his hand, and he fled. Dashing from the platform, he shot straight into a neighbouring house, where he bolted the door behind him and went out of the back, clambering over pigsties and through a garden. The constable summoned assistance on horseback but the fugitive had escaped. Bendigo ran as fast as his damaged leg would allow until he reached the main road. Here, his friend, who had slipped away from the scene unnoticed, picked him up in a horse and fly and they sped off. With a good start on the police they soon reached Newark, catching the next train to Stamford, where they spent the night.

The following day Bendigo caught a train to Mildenhall in Suffolk, the place secretly designated as the actual location of the ring. He put up at the Railway Tavern, slept well and on the Wednesday, the day of the fight, rose at half past six and went for a walk. He was in chirpy mood, greeting his supporters as they arrived in droves by train and all the other means of transport that drew men to prize fights.

Mildenhall, thirteen miles from Newmarket, was a wise choice of location, although it favoured the London Fancy for whom special trains were laid on,[48] whereas the Nottingham men had to change three times. The population was small and scattered and nobody could ever recall seeing a policeman in the vicinity. Johnny Broome, who occupied the same role with Paddock that Jem Ward did previously with Bendigo, had himself fought there against John Bungaree, an Australian, and he knew the lie of the land. By half past twelve the Commissary had formed an inner and outer ring only half a mile from the railway station, on a flat piece of land surrounded by woods, and about two thousand people were congregated.

Back at the Railway Tavern, Bendigo refused to move. He had learned that a train carrying supporters from Nottingham was delayed and he intended waiting for it to arrive before he set off for the ring. Paddock was already there, lying in the shade under a tree. He had less experience of these occasions than Bendigo, and less guile in how to inconvenience an opponent. Growing tired of waiting, Paddock approached the ring with his seconds, Jack McDonald and Solid Coates, and threw in his broad-brimmed billycock hat. There was a round of applause from his followers and some concerned looks from those who had bet against him, for all had to agree that he looked well-prepared, strong and impressive. Still there was no sign of the champion, so, after striding around and testing the turf for springiness, Paddock had no option but to return to the shelter of a large umbrella and continue waiting.

At one o'clock, along came Bendigo in a chaise. He jumped out and was greeted noisily and enthusiastically by the large number of his supporters already present. The day was as hot as for the Caunt fight but he seemed unaffected, although not as exuberant as on that earlier occasion. Tom Paddock did not provoke the same degree of animosity that Ben Caunt once had, and Bendigo knew that the Needle Pointer had youth on his side. Nevertheless, it was he, not the grim-faced Paddock, who seemed more optimistic as they shook hands and, as he had done with Caunt, he casually produced fifty pounds from his pocket and offered it as a side bet. Paddock declined with a shake of his head.

Bendigo's nonchalance remained intact when, after winning the toss for corners, he chose to face the sun. No one could understand what this was about, but most agreed that an old hand like Bendigo must know what he was doing. In the inner ring, a large turn-out of aristocrats and Corinthians sheltered beneath umbrellas. Their equilibrium was soon

[48] Only first and second-class carriages were provided, at £2 and £1 for the return trip from Shoreditch Station. Third-class was rejected on the grounds that such passengers would be disorderly.

upset by an invasion of Nottingham Lambs, but there were none of the wild scenes that marked the prelude to the Caunt fight.

The men stood in their corners, under umbrellas, waiting. The greatcoats they wore to protect them from the sun did nothing to help them stay cool, but they would have to wear them a while longer. Then, as happened so often at this point in prize ring proceedings, a dispute arose over the choice of referee. Johnny Broome and his sidekicks wanted Vincent Dowling, who was already holding the stakes, but Dowling, no doubt recalling the treatment meted out to Squire Osbaldeston in Bendigo's last fight, was not keen to take charge. Nor did Bendigo's people want him to; Dowling had been highly critical of the Bold `Un in the pages *of Bell's Life* over the years and they were concerned that he would be biased against their man. But time was passing and the crowd had become restless, so eventually, at the third time of asking, Dowling accepted the invitation and Bendigo reluctantly agreed.

Stripped to their breeches, the difference in physical appearance between the two men was marked. Paddock stood taller and was four or five pounds heavier, his muscular frame and ruddy-faced youthfulness contrasting sharply with Bendigo, who seemed thinner than usual. Besides his gammy knee, he had been troubled by rheumatism and – although Paddock did not know it – he was suffering from a bruised big toe, which was swollen to the size of a duck egg. The *Nottingham Review* commented that he had "a paternal looking countenance" although appearing ten years younger than on the previous evening.

Older and battered by life he might have been, but he had trained harder than ever and despite his thirty-nine years was favourite with the bookies. His backers had put down large sums on him at 2-1 on and he did not want to let them down. More than that, so he said, his mother had told him before he left Nottingham, "If you don't lick him, I'll slap your chops for you when you get home." He waited, quieter than anyone could recall ever seeing him before a fight, talking to his seconds, Young Molyneux and Jack Hannan. At twenty minutes to two, the two men stepped to the scratch, shook hands once more and the contest began.

There was little to shout about in the early stages. Bendigo employed his usual cagey tactics, dodging out of range and frustrating Paddock so much that after several attempts to land a punch, the bigger man stopped short and folded his arms across his chest with a look of bewilderment and disgust on his face. Bendigo made no move until he resumed a normal stance and the first two rounds passed with hardly a blow being struck.

Come the third and the Bold `Un`s backers began to think his return to the ring might have been a mistake. Having difficulty using his right hand, because Paddock was fighting southpaw too, he looked awkward and the round ended with him taking a heavy blow to the ribs which knocked him on to his back and brought loud cheers from the Needle Pointer's supporters. First knock down to Paddock.

At the ropes, between rounds, Johnny Broome and his brother Harry urged their man to force the fight, to bustle Bendigo about the ring and wear him out with unrelenting attacks. It was sound advice, for to play the waiting game with such a wily campaigner as Bendigo was to invite failure. Paddock, strong and not afraid of being hit, got into his stride, once again delivering a rib-cracker and, as Bendigo fell in the fifth, kicking him in the thigh.

First blood went to Bendigo as he cut Paddock's eye in the sixth, and now the challenger lost his temper, throwing Bendigo on his back and stamping on him. Cries of "Foul" and "Shame" rang around the ring, but referee Dowling saw nothing unfair. The Lambs, who had until now showed remarkable and uncharacteristic restraint, became agitated, more so in the eighth when their hero was thrown over the ropes and the Broomes chorused "Where's your Bendy now?" That question was soon answered when Paddock was floored with a punch to the jaw. The champion was not at his old best, but those who had put money on him breathed a little easier.

Paddock's bad temper was much in evidence from now on, although the Lambs were fretful that Bendigo was taking punishment. He tried a cross buttock, one of the moves he had always executed to perfection, but the pain it caused in his weakened knee caused him to avoid trying another one. His left eye was cut and his back and neck were scraped and bleeding from contact with the ropes. In the sixteenth he came back, knocking Paddock out of the ring, and in the next, three lefts and a quick right brought a flow of blood from the Needle Pointer's left eye.

The Lambs were happier –"Paddock's licked now" was the cry, along with "The old `uns not beaten yet" - but on three separate occasions the challenger hit Bendigo after he had gone down to end rounds. Not once did Dowling, who seems to have been shameless in his prejudice against Bendigo, uphold the calls for a foul. The time had come for the Lambs to make a point. They could not let such injustices pass and at the end of the thirty-sixth round a group of them went up to Dowling, waved their twigs in his face and threatened to kill him.

THE GREAT BATTLE BETWEEN BENDIGO AND TOM PADDOCK.

After such an unambiguous warning, Dowling kept a wary eye on the Lambs. The next round brought an appeal from Young Molyneux in Bendigo's corner that Paddock's hands were smeared with resin and turpentine - intended for Bendigo's eyes to temporarily blind him. The referee declared the allegation to be correct, but to the loud protests of Bendigo's corner he refused to disqualify Paddock, saying it could not be proved that the substances had been put on during, rather than before, the fight. Paddock was allowed to continue, after returning to his corner and washing his hands.

Two or three minutes elapsed before "Time" was called to begin the next round, which enabled Bendigo to gain second wind after all the bustling he had received. Over the next ten rounds he showed his superiority, several times hitting Paddock so hard in the stomach that he vomited. The only reply that caused Bendigo discomfort was a heavy punch to the back of his ear, but by the close of the forty-sixth round, bets of six and seven to four on were offered about Bendigo, with no takers.

Paddock by this stage was slow coming to the scratch. As he sat on his seconds' knees in between rounds he seemed to be losing control of himself, such was his temper and frustration. In the forty-ninth round it all boiled over, as the Bold `Un hit him with a punch so fierce that he himself lost his balance and fell over the ropes. He sat, both arms spread and his legs flat on the ground, whereupon the enraged Paddock stormed in and hit him two heavy blows to the head. Even Vincent Dowling could not claim to have missed this blatant foul. He had warned the Needle Pointer's seconds earlier that a further transgression would bring about disqualification - now Molyneux and Hannan demanded it, on Bendigo's behalf. Dowling had no alternative but to agree; anything less would have brought about a riot. After a battle lasting fifty-nine minutes and at the age of thirty-nine, the Bold Bendigo had proved once again that he was the best man in the land, the undisputed Champion of England.

Chaos followed the referee's decision and the next few minutes surpassed even the uproar of previous Bendigo fights. This time, however, the culprits were not the Nottingham Lambs. Their conduct had been remarkably restrained, especially given the referee's failings regarding Paddock's repeated foul play. They had of course threatened to kill Dowling, but only the once, and they had neither cut the ropes, invaded the ring nor seriously assaulted anyone to such a degree that it was worthy of remark. Both before and during much of the fight, it seemed as though they were depressed by fears that their man had bitten off more than he could chew and they were awaiting the worst. Now they were relieved to be able to celebrate a victory.

The trouble now was instigated by Paddock's supporters. As Bendigo approached the referee for confirmation of the result, the Needle Pointer leaped forward and struck him two hard blows. Bendigo fell at the feet of Dowling while Molyneux and Hannan jumped on Paddock. As a rare old melee gathered force, the referee left the ring, but immediately he was dealt a mighty blow on the back of the head by one of Paddock's friends, wielding a bludgeon. The assailant, a well known Birmingham villain known as Long Charley Smith, was about to repeat the treatment when Tom Spring, now fifty-five years old, delivered an uppercut that sent Long Charley spinning off into his friends. They made to set upon Spring, but quickly backed off as Ben Caunt and Peter Crawley, who had been watching the fight at the ropes, came to Spring's aid.

Bendigo's supporters were overjoyed with the result. His trainer, Sam Turner, announced that the champion would fight any man in the world for £500 at the end of a month. There were no takers. The Bold `Un was carried from the field in triumph, albeit in a worse condition than after any of his previous fights. Both his eyes were cut as well as the back of one ear, but the worst damage was to his left hand, which had been obliged to do most of the work, due to Paddock's unexpected southpaw tactics on the day.

He returned to Nottingham the same night, arriving at nine o'clock by express train. News of his success had been telegraphed soon after the fight ended and he was greeted at the station by a huge crowd and a band playing 'See the Conquering Hero Comes'. He walked across the road to the Railway Hotel where he took a drink, before travelling in a cab to the Flying Horse, where he stayed a short time. Moving on to another establishment in Pelham Street, he took a warm bath before proceeding to his brother's house a few streets away, where he spent the night.

The following day, for the first time ever after a fight, he remained in bed. A doctor was summoned to check out his injuries. One eye was blackened, another cut underneath, while his ribs, which it was now revealed had been broken in the last Caunt fight, would cause him severe pain for weeks. The old warrior knew the time had finally come to retire from the ring.

Vincent Dowling recovered sufficiently from the concussion he received at the hands of Long Charley Smith to report on the championship fight for the following Sunday's *Bell's Life*. Even though Bendigo had showed himself to be the better man overall and Paddock bore far more marks of battle, the editor/referee was less than enthusiastic in writing about Bendigo's victory. The Champion had, he said, been clearly overmatched and "soon discovered that he had caught a tartar and not, as he imagined, a yokel." He wrote "Bendigo has not added to his fame; a man who has won a fight by foul blow receives the profits but he adds nothing to his reputation."

It was a churlish attitude from a man who, having agreed to act as referee, had showed partisanship towards Tom Paddock, only to then be attacked by one of his supporters. Dowling's opinion was not shared by the professionals who had been present. Ben Caunt, Peter Crawley, Jem Ward and Jem Burn all said that Paddock, who eventually left the ring in tears, could not have lasted much longer and Bendigo was undoubtedly the better man. While Paddock had tried to make excuses after the event, his mentor Johnny Broome had voiced no serious complaint about the result.

Bell's Life's report on the fight aroused outrage and indignation in Nottingham. Bendigo's backers wrote to the newspaper, complaining that their man had not been "lauded as a hero of the first water," as he should have been. Vincent Dowling replied the next week: "We have never questioned his courage but we have often said that he is not a fair stand-up fighter, for the man who will strike and then fall to avoid a return does not come within that category. We admit that this is his crafty style of fighting but it is not popular." The Nottingham Lambs disagreed. Although few of them could read, they were sufficiently informed to show what they thought of *Bell's Life* by burning it in the Market Place.

After a fortnight's rest in the Nottinghamshire countryside, Bendigo travelled to London to be presented with the stake money. A large crowd turned out at the Queen's Head, Jem Burn's public house in Windmill Street and the returning champion was in good form, which even *Bell's Life* acknowledged:

> "Bendigo appeared to have lost none of the whimsicality of manner, peculiar patter and odd antics for which he has been so long known. His appearance when standing forward to receive the £400 awarded to him by the referee was the signal for a hearty cheer from his admirers, many of them up from Nottingham. The money, consisting of three crisp Henry Marshalls of £100 each and a brace of fifties, was handed to Bendy with the presenter accompanying it with an address in which he took a rapid survey of the champion's career. From the

> age of fifteen years to nearly forty, the man before them had been known to his fellow townsmen as a skilful, fearless and incorruptibly honest boxer."

Within the space of a fortnight, Vincent Dowling's opinion of Bendigo had taken a remarkable upturn. He now delivered a eulogy, concluding with a toast to his health and his prosperity in retirement. Bendigo responded by thanking those present for the honour done him and observing that he had always studied the "rules of the ring". He said that by those rules he had abided and by them he had won. He thought his duty to himself was always to try to win by methods allowed by the laws of fighting. He also owed it to his friends not to lose their money by rashness. He did not see the judgement of standing up and exchanging with a man much bigger and stronger than himself when real skill might mean saving the battle.

To great cheers he went on to say that he couldn't bear the thoughts of being beaten but he knew he had many friends, poor men in Nottingham, who risked their all on him. He couldn't sell them, even if he might not so much mind the rich losing their money. He said he was retiring from the ring having never shrunk from any challenge on account of size, strength, country or colour and he would leave future honours and money to be struggled for by younger men.

Thus the Bold Bendigo announced his retirement from the prize ring, which he had graced with skill, style, courage and humour for eighteen years. In that time he had won nineteen fights and lost once on a disqualification. He had never been beaten and, unlike almost any other fighter, he had never suffered serious punishment. Now it was all over. He was a man with boundless energy, who thrived on excitement and mischief. Training for fights and the need to keep himself in reasonably good condition during the long lay-offs had been just about enough to occupy him in the past, but his propensity towards alcohol and unruly company did not auger well for a trouble-free life in the future. The next years would not be as rewarding or successful as those that had passed, but they would never be dull.

11] The House of Correction

Retirement was never likely to be easy for Bendigo. His spirit was too strong to settle into quiet domestic life and anyway he had no domestic life. He had never married nor showed any interest whatsoever in women. His life remained focused on the same pubs and sporting activities that it always had. He had rubbed shoulders with the highest in the land but his real friends were low fellows - fighters, publicans, betting men and the rough and rowdy Nottingham Lambs.

Early on, Bendigo found no difficulty coming to terms with his new situation. After fights he had always returned to his regular routine of drinking, helping other fighters and doing a bit of fishing, and so the first months after the Paddock fight brought little change. As the next twenty years rolled by, his life, like those of many pugilists before and after him, would deteriorate into an alcoholic haze and downward spiral. His fame and reputation would turn to ignominy as his conduct caused those who had once admired him to look on in dismay. But the dark days were yet to come; for now he was the Pride of Nottingham, the undefeated Champion of England.

To celebrate his retirement and mark his successful career in the prize ring, his backers commissioned a portrait in oils by Thomas Earl, a noted artist of the mid-century. The painting tells us much more about him than the earlier sporting prints. The eyes are alert and the face bears a knowing expression, only the partly flattened nose suggesting his recent profession. He has long sideburns and the shaven pate of his fighting days has given way to a thatch of dark hair. He is dressed in a black jacket and blue and white spotted cravat. The portrait was presented to him in London by two of his main backers for the Paddock fight, Alfred Edwards and Thomas Dayson.[49]

---

[49] The portrait was acquired by the National Gallery in 1961 from Henry Hall of Ruddington, in whose family it had been for some years.

Bendigo's departure from the ring opened the door for the two men now considered to be the best around - Tom Paddock, his last opponent, and William Perry, better known as the Tipton Slasher. The Slasher was keen to prove himself where Paddock had failed, by getting the great Bendigo in the ring and beating him, but his challenge went unanswered. Instead he had to settle for meeting Paddock on Woking Common on 17th December 1850. Perry won after meting out heavy punishment to the Needle Pointer throughout their forty-two minute contest, which ended in disturbances when Paddock was disqualified for felling him after the close of a round.

As the New Year began it looked as if Bendigo's retirement might be short-lived. Barely six months had passed since he bade his farewell to the ring, but now there were indications that he was showing more than a passing interest in the Tipton Slasher's challenge, which was repeated after he became champion. On 12th January 1851 a letter, apparently from Bendigo, was published in *Bell's Life*. It was preceded by a note of caution - "We give the following as we receive it without pledging ourselves to its authenticity." The letter read:

> "Mr Editor, I beg to inform you that I have this morning received a communication from my Nottingham friends, wishing to know if it were my intention to fight any more. I wish by the medium of your paper to inform my friends and the public in general that I will fight any man in the world for £500, bar neither the Tipton Slasher nor anyone else. I would prefer "the New Rules" by *moonlight*. Any communication can be made to me at Mr John Long's, 2 Vicar's Croft, Leeds. Respecting the belt, it was not paid for: Captain Ongley made me a present of it and I mean to keep it. I shall be at Nottingham in a week with my friends. Respecting the last affair with Paddock and the Tipton, I consider it a mere humbug as also do my backers.
>
> Signed William Thompson, whether by Bendigo or anyone for him we cannot say.
>
> Bendigo's money is always ready at the Dog and Bear, Nottingham."

The letter appears to have been genuine, for no rebuttal or correction was printed in the following weeks. However, the seeking of £500 side stake suggests, in the parlance of the Fancy, that it was merely "bounce", such a sum being beyond the reach of the Tipton Slasher - and probably

Bendigo too. As for what he meant by "the New Rules by moonlight", the editor was probably no wiser than anyone else, hence his use of italics.

Perry the Slasher, was sufficiently encouraged by the letter to place £50 in the hands of Tom Spring, to make a match for £500 a side. He recognised, however, that he might be wasting his time, when he suggested to *Bell's Life* that Bendigo might be "playing the game of brag".

And that was the last time Bendigo's name was mentioned in connection with William Perry, who would lose his title to Harry Broome later in the year. Perhaps the Tipton Slasher became complacent or succumbed to the temptations of the flesh, because the following month he was reported as having "abandoned the arms of Mars for those of Venus and is now in Liverpool, accompanied by a fair fugitive from a certain hostelry in Sheffield."

There would be more rumours and reports of proposed comebacks, but nothing that ever seemed likely to happen. Meanwhile, Bendigo was still involved with ring matters, helping one of his Leicester friends, Bill Burton, prepare for a fight against Tass Parker. This was the opponent he would have met himself in 1842, had the warrant from his brother John not prevented him. Burton and Parker fought in May 1851 at Ashbourne, Derbyshire, a location described by Vincent Dowling as "a wild and retired district".

The fight was refereed by a Sheffield man, Swanky Greaves,[50] who held the position of commissary for the area. It was a bad-tempered affair which ended with Tass Parker falling without a blow and a group of Burton's followers, including some of the Nottingham Lambs, attacking the referee. The unfortunate Swanky was bludgeoned about the face and head, sustaining a gaping wound above one eye. He had been accused of taking two sovereigns from Parker's friends, with the promise of fifty more, to decide in his favour. While this was happening, Bendigo, who had stirred up the trouble by confronting the referee, got Burton out of the ring, leaving the Lambs and company to their mayhem.

In July there was brief speculation that he would make a comeback against Con Parker, an Islington gravedigger, for £100. The same month

---

[50] Edward and James Greaves, known as 'Swanky' and 'Leggy', were active around Northern prize rings. In 1850 they were each imprisoned for two months at Doncaster Quarter Sessions after acting as seconds to Nick Lannigan who fought a Nottingham man, Patsy Clay. Although the Nottingham Lambs were out in force to support Clay, reports do not mention Bendigo being present on that occasion.

he attracted a good crowd for a joint benefit with Bill Burton in the Castle Yard at Nottingham. In August, a ball was held at Saville House in London to raise funds for the erection of a monument to him in Woolwich Churchyard. Many of Bendigo's friends attended, including Ben Caunt, Jem Ward, Jem Burn and the Holy Land Pink, but the Bold `Un – who could not be envisaged at any sort of ball, whether in evening dress or not - was absent. Nor was he among the large contingent of fighters past and present who paid their last respects to Tom Spring at his funeral a couple of weeks later. Spring, landlord of the Castle Tavern for twenty-three years and a stalwart of the London Fancy, had often been critical of Bendigo and the Nottingham Lambs.

Late September saw him at Norman's Heath, near Appleby in Leicestershire, meeting up with his old foe Tom Paddock, who had demanded a return match after losing their fight the year before. But this time the Needle Pointer would have to make do with Bendigo's pal, Harry Paulson, making only his second appearance in the Prize Ring.

Paulson, from Newark, was a ballast-heaver by occupation. He was thirty-two and had a reputation as a hard man among his peers, the Trent bargemen. Bull-necked and barrel-chested, he was similar in height and weight to Bendigo, who trained him for the Paddock fight, and his backers hoped he would take up where the retired champion had left off. But on the day, when they arrived at Norman's Heath, they found the ground occupied by the blues. Fighters and followers hastened to Castle Donington, but no sooner was a ring set up than two coachloads of constabulary arrived.

It was clear that the fight was not about to happen. A meeting was held between the men's patrons and umpires and the match was put off until the following day at a location known as Gonerby Moor. In the early morning a large contingent headed across the Moor on foot, but they had been fed a red herring, intended to fool the police and their informers. Paddock and Paulson along with their backers and those in the know – including a contingent of Lambs - were at the same time travelling by train to Sedgebrook, near Grantham in Lincolnshire.

Here the fight did come off, Paulson getting the better of ninety minutes brutality that was halted when a lone constable appeared and forced his way through the crowd to the ropes. It is a measure of the respect that people of all classes had for those in authority that he was able to get so far, let alone to call upon the fighters to stop and then to read the Riot Act, telling the crowd to disperse.

Where he over-stepped the mark was entering the ring and attempting to grab Paddock, who immediately slipped through the ropes, to the amusement of the Lambs, who shouted "He's off!" Their mirth was short-lived as they realised that Paulson, who was winning, might not now be declared the winner, and so they turned on the constable and chased him away from the ring. In the end their man did get the verdict, Paddock's seconds throwing in the towel to save him from returning for further punishment.

Three months later Harry Paulson and Tom Paddock fought again at Belper in Derbyshire. As was happening all too frequently now, the police and magistrates arrived again to spoil the sport, but this time they were met with violent opposition. On a cold December day the Lambs and Paddock's Birmingham friends joined forces and when the Superintendent of Police climbed into the ring to read the Riot Act he was bludgeoned to the floor, trampled on and kicked insensible. Cudgels and twigs flew and as the battle raged one of the Lambs picked up the apparently lifeless body of the police chief and threw him out of the ring, over the heads of the mob. He was rescued by two of the more responsible bystanders and taken to Belper where surgeons managed to restore him to consciousness. Paddock and Paulson fled to Derby but were arrested and sentenced to ten months hard labour in Derby Gaol for their part in the fight which had brought about the riot. Bendigo was not mentioned in any reports; if he was present, for once he managed to keep out of trouble.

According to legend, it was during this period that Bendigo was offered a position at Oxford University as boxing coach. Such appointments were not uncommon, given the traditional Corinthian interest in the prize ring, but those retired pugilists who were hired tended to be of a type more servile and less prone to eccentricity and excess than the Bold Bendigo. There is no conclusive evidence that he did grace Oxford, although in later years occasional references were made in the Nottingham newspapers by correspondents reminiscing about old times. One such in the *Nottingham Evening News* of 28th September 1905 refers to him spending a "season" at Oxford, "where, in order to get within its more classic precincts, the under-graduates disguised him as a professor of the university." It was also said that he could not settle away from Nottingham and returned because his mother had fallen ill.

Later on, when short of money and there were no fighters to train or second, he was employed at the Trent Bridge Cricket Pavilion as a waiter on match days. He had always been keen on cricket and was no mean player, as well as being able to throw a 5 1/2 oz. cricket ball two hundred yards. For wagers he took part in single wicket matches against some of the best batsmen around. Ishmael Wilson's pamphlet quotes him:

> "I have played and beat at Cricket, Gerland of Leeds, one of the great All England Players at that time; also Thomas Burton, the tutor of Burton Cricket Club; we played at Aldres, near Lichfield."

He was backed against George Parr, the All-England captain and the best batsman of his generation, for £50 in single wicket but turned up on the day suffering from gout and the match fell through. According to Richard Daft, captain of the Nottinghamshire team and one of the top cricketers of the mid-century,[51] Parr's backers had been confident that he would win easily, but the cricketer himself told Daft he did not think he should have done, as the wicket would have been a rough one and "Bendy bowled underhand 'grubs' at a great pace". Daft recalled:

> "Bendy was little above middle height but was very strongly made, specially round the shoulders. He bore little or no traces of his long career as a pugilist. He was always on the move and was continually joking with someone or other. He was hardly ever seen without his fighting colours - blue with white spot round his neck."[52]

On wet days, when there was no cricket, Bendigo would entertain players and gentleman alike in the pavilion with tales of his career in the ring –"Fighting me battles o'er again" as he said. One of his party pieces was to stand in front of someone, holding his hands behind his back and invite the person to try to hit him on the head. His reflexes even in late middle age made the task almost impossible.

At other times he also liked to prove his toughness by taking blows to the head, as Daft, who was a great follower of the prize ring and had been taught to fight by Patsy Clay, recalled in a later book, *A Cricketer's Yarns:*

> "Bendigo possessed a skull of adamantine hardness and would allow any man to give him a hit on the back of

---

[51] Richard Daft was a great rival of the young W.G.Grace. Over a century before batsmen wore helmets for protection, on one occasion he arrived at the crease wearing a towel wrapped round his head.

[52] From *Kings of Cricket*, Richard Daft. Tillotson & Son, 1893

> the head with his fist as hard as he liked. The striker who took him at his word was always a good deal more hurt than the struck. I've seen Tom Butler[53] give Bendy a few smacks in this way but I think he never quite put the full force into the blow as Bendy was known to be a queer tempered fellow who, whenever he got accidentally hurt in a friendly encounter immediately turned it into an unfriendly one which was by no means pleasant for the amateur who was opposed him." [54]

Single wicket cricket was an occasional sport to Bendigo, his participation usually involving a bet on the result.[55] In his younger days he had been backed to take part in handicapped running races and, as the biographical pamphlet by Ishmael Wilson describes, he was noted for cock fighting and badger baiting, both activities which were organised for and by betting men. Away from the hurly-burly, he continued to spend a lot of time on river banks, relaxing with rod and line. Not that his competitive spirit was at rest in this sport, for, as he told Wilson, " I have succeeded in carrying off the 2nd, 3rd, 4th and 5th prizes at York Great All-England Fishing Match."

Bendigo took his fishing seriously. One of his friends in Nottingham was the champion angler William Bailey, who had started his working life as a shoemaker but gave up his awl and stool and took up the rod for a living. He had a fishing tackle business at 170 Annesley Terrace, Kirkwhite Street in Nottingham, making rods and reels, and he instructed gentlemen in the art of angling.

As in almost every working class recreation or sport, betting also figured in angling, with big money to be won at the large fishing matches. On other occasions private wagers were made between individuals as to who would catch the most fish within a set period. In both public and private matches Bailey was successful: one afternoon in 1855 he caught 84lb of bream in 4 hours on the River Lea near London, in a one-to-one against a rival from Sheffield he caught 50lbs more trout than the other man and he once landed twenty-two fish weighing 65lb in two and a half hours.

---

[53] A Notts. player and the brother-in-law of the earlier mentioned George Parr.

[54] Published by Chapman and Hall, 1926

[55] Single wicket involved each player having two innings. Sometimes the bowler had to field for himself, on occasion he was allowed a fielder. Andrew Ward in *Cricket's Strangest Matches* (Robson, 1990), describes a match in 1838 for 100 guineas, which attracted 5,000 spectators. The winner scored 34 and 89, his opponent "0 and very few".

William Bailey spent his life studying the habits of coarse fish and the best ways of luring them onto his hook. He believed he knew everything there was to know about what they got up to underwater and his wisdom brooked no argument from anyone. Even Bendigo, the former bare-knuckle champion of England had to bow to his superior authority, and when he committed the sin of ignoring the master's advice on over-baiting for bream in winter, his misjudgement was published in Bailey's book as a lesson for all anglers to heed:[56]

> "Bendigo of Nottingham and myself had been taking a fair number of good bream out of the Clifton Water in the early part of one February when the weather, although cold, was not too cold for the fish to bite, with careful treatment. As we were retiring one night, my mate said 'I've got here about seven hundred lob worms; I will bait this place for tomorrow.' I replied, 'If you do such an absurd thing as bait a place for bream in winter, you will not have my company in the morning.' However, he threw them into the water. On our way home he said 'I suppose you think I shall not catch any bream tomorrow; but I shall and will bring you a basket full just to show you what baiting for bream in winter will do.' 'No,' I said. 'You won't. I consider you have done a very stupid thing. I will tell the story some time to prevent others from acting as foolishly as you have done; for I feel satisfied if it were possible to see the bottom of the place you have baited tomorrow morning you would see every worm you have thrown in untouched.' 'Oh,' he said. 'That's all nonsense. I don't believe it.' And so we parted.
>
> The next morning Bendigo called on me as usual to accompany him, but I refused to go, saying 'You may have all the sport to yourself today,' at which he growled 'All right.' I believe it is a well-known fact that Bendigo in all his pugilistic career never got a good licking but on this occasion he returned to me at night just like a thoroughly beaten man for he had not caught a single fish of any description.' 'Ah! Bill my lad,' he said. 'You spoke the truth last night for I have not caught a fish. I feel so vexed I have a good mind to hit myself on the top of the head for being so stupid. It will be a lesson to me

[56] *The Angler's Instructor – a Treatise on the Best Modes of Angling in English Rivers, Lakes and Ponds and on the Habits of the Fish.* 3rd Edition 1879, Longmans 1879.

> for the future. I shall never again bait a place for bream in winter.'"

He did not venture far from Nottingham now. So rare were his appearances at prize fights that when he turned up in London in early January 1856 to supervise the training of Harry Paulson for his fight with Tom Sayers, *Bell's Life* welcomed "the eccentric and lively ex-champion," with the comment: "We have been asked twice this week whether he is not dead."

The clientele of the Rising Sun in Piccadilly, now kept by Jem Burn, could confirm that he was very much alive, as he kept the patrons amused with his tales and jokes into the early hours, once he had seen Paulson to bed. He found time to look up his old trainer Jem Ward, the Black Diamond, who had moved from Liverpool to keep the Champion Stores public house at 429 Oxford Street, where every Friday night he held a musical evening.

After a short stay in London, Bendigo and Paulson moved to Bognor Regis on the south coast, to finish off training. They were soon joined by Burn, who travelled down to be treated for an attack of sciatica. When he was not honing his pal Harry's fitness, Bendigo could be seen manipulating the legs and back of the portly publican. Customers at their base, the Beach Inn, were intrigued by this odd trio. Three weeks later when they all returned to London, Burn was walking straight and Harry Paulson was in the best condition of his life.

Tom Sayers, Paulson's opponent, was, like Bendigo, one of the great bareknuckle fighters. His later fight with the American Tom Heenan – styled as the first 'world championship' and for a £5,000 purse - would be the last gasp of a dying prize ring. He was a middleweight who moved up to heavyweight because of a dearth of opponents and he fancied his chances against Harry Paulson. They met at Appledore in Kent on a freezingly cold day at the end of January. Giving away more than a stone and underdog with the bookmakers, Sayers showed his class by knocking out the Newark man after 109 rounds lasting three hours and ten minutes.

As had happened so many times before, Bendigo's presence in the corner brought no luck to his man, but the reception he received in London was extraordinary. *Bell's Life,* for so long critical of him when Vincent Dowling had been editor,[57] now held him up as example to behold:

---

[57] Dowling had died in 1852.

> "We may be pardoned for paying passing tribute to excellent conduct of the Bold Bendigo who, from first to last, comported himself with all the gravity and decorum of the Chief Baron (Nicholson)[58] himself."

Readers were urged to attend a benefit in London at Saville House in Leicester Square, and were reminded how the "Nottingham heroes" had earlier sparred to raise money for the defence of another fighter, Mike Madden, who faced trial for manslaughter. "The gallantry of Harry Paulson can never be too highly appreciated and the eccentricity and kindliness of heart of the Bold Bendigo are themselves attractions which ought to draw a full house." Praise indeed, and the London Fancy responded, turning the night into a great success. The "Nottingham heroes" sparred, Bendigo sang a few ditties and the pair went home with £65 between them.

The warm reception he received in London was the high spot of Bendigo's post-retirement years. Over the next decade and a half he would earn little credit by his behaviour and his reputation in Nottingham, where for so long he had been idolised, plummeted. In the words of Ishmael Wilson – it is doubtful that they were strictly Bendigo's own: "After finishing my career as a prize fighter, I took to drinking heavily until at times I was nearly mad with it. I have suffered nights and days from delirium tremens through the cursed drink."

The extent to which alcohol affected Bendigo's life is no surprise given his family history and chosen occupation. His father's exceptional talents had been dissipated by drink and he died at the bar of a public house, while his mother's affection for beer was well-known. But besides the parental influence, a prize fighter's life was centred on public houses. In every town they were the places where the Fancy gathered, and for years Bendigo had been plied with as much ale as he could drink as soon as he walked through the door of any pub in Nottingham

But there was another reason why he went off the rails. In September 1854 his mother died. Robust, rough and truculent as she was, Mary Thompson had been his guiding light since boyhood. She had been the driving force behind his career as a pugilist from the start. Fighting came

---

[58] There may have been a touch of irony in this comment: The self-styled `Baron` Nicholson held mock trials in Covent Garden - *The Judge and Jury Show*. In the adjoining premises he produced the more risque *Poses Plastique*.

naturally to him, but he said did not fight because he liked it – "I did it to get a living. I could do it better than anything else and I had my mother to keep. She didn't mind me doing it – not she; she encouraged me to it. If anybody came to her in a fright and said, 'Lor Mrs Thompson, your boy's being half killed,' she would say, 'Ah you leave him alone; he'll come off all right.' If ever I came home when I was a youngster and she found out that another boy had licked me, she would say, 'Now just you go back and lick him, or I'll lick you.' She would too."[59] He often said that he become a prize fighter to keep his mother from the workhouse and, from what is known of her lifestyle, without his support she might well have ended up back there.

A great encouragement to him throughout his ring career, she it was who told him, when Ben Caunt was pressing his claim for their first fight, "fight the hulking lout and shut his rat-trap mouth." She was reputed to have urged him to settle matters with Big Ben prior to their third encounter in similarly un-ladylike terms and her threat to Tom Paddock suggests that, for such a rough and ready woman she certainly had a colourful imagination.

During his fight with Deaf Burke, she was said to have known he was winning because the clock on the wall ticked "Ben-dy, Ben-dy." She said "If it had said 'Deaf-`Un, Deaf-`Un,' I'd have smashed that clock's face in." Earlier in his ring career, going along to watch him train, she found him sparring with a man much taller and heavier than her youngest son, Bill. "What's that brute doing to my poor boy?" she demanded. "Leave him alone you big bully, leave him alone." Nor, according to reputation, was she averse in her younger days to joining in when trouble broke out in tap room or dram shop, wielding a twig with the best of them.

Once he was able, Bendigo supported his mother, with help from his brother John, who by then had become successful in business. John might have opposed prize fighting but there seem to have been no hard feelings between the two of them. In an interview much later, Bendigo recalled how they had an uncle, an optician, who left them his stock-in-trade and his tools: "I says to my brother, 'You take the lot and allow mother six shillings a week on my account, like," and so he did. And I used to buy the old lady her winter clothes and he bought her her summer clothes and so she did pretty well until she died at eighty-three."[60] Announcing Mary Thompson's death on 15th September 1854, the *Nottingham Review* did

[59] James Greenwood, *Low Life Deeps*. Chatto&Windus, 1876
[60] ibid.

not mention Bendigo, stating only that she was the "mother of Mr Thompson the optician of Carlton Street" - his brother John.

There was little to divert him from the ale-house. He had no home of his own as such, lodging some of the time with his nephew Ben Thompson, who kept a fishmonger's shop in St Ann Street, at other times with backers or friends. In the pubs there was always companionship to be had and an audience ever eager to hear again tales from his fighting days. And of the company he kept, the audiences he entertained, none were more appreciative than his old friends and supporters, the Nottingham Lambs.

The Lambs now had no sporting hero to follow around the country. Bendigo, Sam Merryman and Sam Turner were all safely - if not soundly - retired. The old days of causing mayhem at the ropes of the prize ring were fading memories, the long trips by horse and carriage or on foot, in latter days by train, terrifying all around them, were no more. Not that they were inclined to lay down their twigs and join their sporting heroes in retirement. They went back to politics, where their brand of dark menace had long had a market. Not for the first time in their history they became political thugs for hire.

Disrupting elections was of course not new to the Nottingham Lambs. Generations of their number had been employed in causing mayhem at the hustings, all the way back to the turbulent years of 1780-1812, when seventeen riots took place in the town.[61] Every election until 1812 had some conflict, quite apart from other disturbances that brought the townspeople onto the streets. The Luddite, Reform Bill and Chartist troubles brought later violence – like the Battle of Mapperley Hill in 1842, when 400 people out of a crowd of 5,000 were arrested by troops and marched four abreast to the House of Correction - but after 1848 the atmosphere in the town became calmer.

The arrival of Sir Robert Clifton to fight the 1861 election soon put paid to that. Clifton, a baronet and old Etonian, was thirty-five and known as a great wit and rumbustious public speaker. He won the seat for the

---

[61] An undated cutting from the *Notts Guardian*, probably ca 1920: "Recollections of the Past by a Nottingham Old Boy – It was at the time of a Parliamentary election that the Nottingham 'lamb' was seen in his greatest glory. It was then that he had more money in his pocket at one time than he had seen for many months . . . His duties were peculiar but very congenial. He had to thrash anybody and everybody if necessary, especially the opposition 'lambs' and constables, to kidnap opposition voters and keep them drunk and hidden till the election was over, to prevent the opposition candidate from being heard if he tried to make a speech, especially on nomination day. In short, he was to do anything that would tend to defeat the opposition party."

Liberals after fighting a campaign against his opponent, the Earl of Lincoln. A contemporary diarist, Samuel Collinson, who regarded Clifton as being "of scampish notoriety", commented:

> "The town seemed to be given up to ruffianism, mobs of people were about every polling place insulting the voters for Lord Lincoln; towards afternoon all the shops in the Market Place, Pelham Street, Clumber Street and Bridlesmith Gate were closed – Ruffians insulted all decent looking people, tearing their hats from their heads &c &c pocket picking was carried on extensively & the whole scene was a disgrace to the town & the times we live in." [62]

Clifton was dropped by the Liberal Party for the next election, in 1865. Instead, an anti-Corn law campaigner and prominent dissenter, Samuel Morley, was chosen to stand with Charles Paget, a local Justice of the Peace. Sir Robert Clifton, however, who considered himself "the people's idol,"[63] was not to be deterred. He stood against them on an extreme Liberal ticket. While Morley, a teetotaller, railed against drunkenness as a nuisance to self, family and society, Clifton attacked all temperance reformers as a minority who were trying to impose their will on the majority. The second official candidate, Charles Paget was no match for the eloquent, slanderous Clifton who commented that he would rather have a gorilla for a colleague in parliament. "Lord Cowjuice should be his name," he said.

Little doubt exists that the Lambs had been active on Clifton's behalf during the disorder of the 1861 election. In Nottingham, political harassment was their work. This time, however, although it was alleged that Lambs were hired by both sides, there was strong evidence that Clifton had close links with them. At the last election he had fought a dirty campaign, but the events of '61 paled against what would happen this time.

Sir Robert Clifton got down to business on 29th May, six weeks before the election, at a meeting in the Market Place, attended by an estimated 15,000 people. He attacked the Government, the temperance reformers and especially his opponents whom, he said, wished to put licensed victuallers – "a fine body of men who give great sums of money to

---

[62] Published in *Transactions of the Thoroton Society of Nottinghamshire Vol XLVII* (1943)
[63] ibid.

charity" - out of business. Of his rival, Morley, he said "If he stands on his head he will never have any sense in it." At a later meeting at the Nottingham Castle Inn, he asked those present to "draw your swords for me in this glorious fight".

His opponents, Paget and Morley planned to address the people at a meeting in the Market Place on 26th June. In the days beforehand Clifton held several meetings where he engaged in rabble-rousing language to denounce his rivals. If anyone dared to speak out in opposition, he invited the crowd to deal with them. Although he had entertained a contingent of Lambs at his committee rooms - later named as Frederick Smith, James Smith, a pugilist called Cope, David Cole, John Davy, Warmer Cummings and Samuel Owen – he claimed that his opponents were hiring ruffians. One of his close associates, a man named Dring, produced what was said to be a list of names of Lambs hired by Paget and Morley at two shillings and sixpence, plus a quart of beer, a man.[64]

Matters reached a head with the 26th June meeting, which had been billed as a grand open-air demonstration. Train-loads of Paget and Morley's supporters, arriving in Nottingham in the late afternoon, were ambushed by a large crowd of Clifton's men who lay in wait outside the station. The visitors, mostly from surrounding villages, were greeted by a hail of stones. Earlier, Clifton had been heard speaking with two prominent Nottingham Lambs, Cabbage Smith and 'Besom' Jack Wigley, whom he asked "Are you going to be driven out of town by a lot of cock-stockingers?" After a running battle, the villagers managed to fight their way to the specially erected platform in the Market Place, where a brass band welcomed them.

Between three and four hundred men – some Lambs, others Clifton's regular supporters – had gathered to disrupt Paget and Morley's meeting, with another five thousand or more also in the square and many others looking on from windows. The rival supporters hurled stones at each other for fifteen minutes and then the Lambs charged the platform, set it on fire and sent the band and their instruments flying. A full scale riot now ensued, as the mob ran up and down surrounding streets, smashing windows and fighting with anyone they could find. Sir Robert Clifton was reported as having been present when the mob wrecked his opponents' committee rooms, and as having shaken hands with the leaders, urging them to "Go to it".

---

[64] A detailed account of these events can be found in an unpublished M.Phil. dissertation (1972) by David Cutting, *The Nottingham Parliamentary Election of 1865.*

Not until the police baton-charged the crowd did the riot come to an end, in the early hours. Arrests were made but several men were rescued on the way to the police station. In all fifty people were injured, mostly suffering scalp and face wounds. A few days later, twenty-one people, described in the local press as "working men", were put before the mayor and magistrates. As a large crowd gathered outside the Town Hall they were all discharged after promising to be of good behaviour in the future.[65]

No documentary evidence has been found to show whether or not Bendigo took part in the riot. He was fifty-three years old at the time but going through a period when he came into conflict with the law on a regular basis and no one had a closer bond with the Lambs. Certainly a man named Thompson was close to the action when Clifton was speaking with rioters outside Paget and Morley's wrecked committee rooms and he told the politician that he was going to vote against him. Resorting to his favourite epithet, Clifton said "Who are you, you bloody cowjuice? I'll knock your head off in a minute?" at which Thompson replied, "You're a finer gentleman than I took you for."[66]

Was this Bendigo? If so, Clifton did not apparently recognise him, but the response to the threat was a not untypical Bendigo remark and while in other circumstances he would respond violently to such words, he might have hesitated to engage in fisticuffs with a land-owning politician, particularly as Clifton was a friend of his brother, John. This came to light at the later Parliamentary Inquiry into the election, when John Thompson gave evidence that on Clifton's behalf he had hired committee rooms in the Market Place.

In any event, he was getting into plenty of trouble on his own account. He would have one more big day out in the prize ring, the following year when an aspiring champion, Andrew Marsden, whom he and his pal Harry Paulson had trained for three years, fought Ned O'Baldwin for the second time. In their first match Marsden had won in three minutes but since then he had become a Nottingham publican and piled on weight. Unfit, he was knocked senseless in eleven rounds. Bendigo, who had bet heavily on Marsden, was disgusted and told him to go back to pulling beer.

He himself went back drinking it, with, on many occasions, unfortunate consequences. His behaviour was becoming marked by

---

[65] The riot is depicted in a painting by John Holland Walker, in the collection of York Municipal Art Gallery

[66] M.Phil dissertation (1972) by David Cutting, *The Nottingham Parliamentary Election of 1865*,

outbursts of bad temper, as described many years later in a nostalgic letter printed in the *Nottinghamshire Guardian*. The correspondent, identified only as "F.R.", told how as a young lad in 1856 he came across the old champion as he sat waiting for a bite on Trent Bridge. Curious, he approached, trying to see if he had caught any fish, but as he did Bendigo turned round sharply and kicked him with his heavy boots. "It was a mercy my leg was not broken," the writer recalled. "As it was, the skin was broken and my leg was sore for days."

Better days saw Bendigo hailed as a hero after saving people who had fallen in the Trent. He claimed that he had saved three lives there – "the last one being a young woman; I was then in my 59th year"[67] – but on this occasion at Trent Bridge, although faced with nothing more irritating than childish curiosity, he quickly resorted to violence. It was a dark side of his character that had surfaced years earlier, according to another correspondent in the same newspaper, whose letter appeared on 16th August 1919. John B. Riley was in his eighties when he wrote the following:

> "In 1843 I went to Mr George Whitehall's school in Newcastle-street, off Parliament-street. Going home one dinner-time I was passing the Old Dog and Bear, Bridlesmith-gate when I saw Bold Bendigo talking to the landlord on the causeway. Lad-like I stopped to listen, and all at once, Bendy left off talking and gave me a sounding smack on the side of my head. The landlord said 'You shouldn't have done that, Bendy. That's John Riley, the slater's lad. You'll hear about it again.' So he did, for my father took me with him and asked him what he meant by it. Bendigo said he was sorry for what had occurred and gave me some money to buy toffee."

This incident occurred long before Bendigo retired, although at the time his future was uncertain following the knee injury sustained while performing somersaults. Even taking into account his own anxieties, and working class society's attitude to children in these times, his behaviour showed a serious lack of self-control.

His conduct in later years was heavily affected by alcohol, but at times it also begged the question, was he to some degree punch drunk? He boasted "I was engaged in 21 matched fights and was never beaten in one and what is more I never in my life had a hit on the nose hard enough to

---

[67] *The Life, Battles, Conversion & Death of Bendigo, Champion of England.* Ishmael Wilson, 1889

make it bleed and in all my battles I never got a black eye."[68] He was ignoring the cumulative and debilitating effects of the many blows to the head he had taken in his eighteen years in the prize ring.

Nostalgia was popular with readers of the *Nottinghamshire Guardian* in the post-First World War years. Anecdotes regarding Bendigo – some good but most bad – were forthcoming from time to time, one sparking off another then the correspondence fading until another event or comment revived the subject. A favourite theme was Bendigo's habit of causing trouble in public houses. In one account, of events in the Horse and Groom Inn in the late 1860s, he took a tankard belonging to a bricklayer named Fife and drank the contents – at which Fife punched him in the chest, knocking him down. Helping himself to other men's beer had become an unpleasant habit – a regression to his childhood when he fought and stole food from other urchins in the streets. Now, in the tap rooms and dram shops, victims would often not protest too loudly, fearful of his reputation as a prize fighter.

He had become little more than an alehouse bully. Not that he always got his own way - arriving drunk at the Pelican Inn one night, he began to knock off customers' hats. The nineteen year old pot boy, Tip Flinders, who had no idea who he was, thought he was just another drunken nuisance, someone to be moved on swiftly. Without any ceremony at all, he knocked the ex-champion out and threw him through the front door.

On another occasion, he bit the hand of Lord Chesterfield's gamekeeper during an altercation in the Ferry Boat Inn, Stoke. A stand-up fight developed in which Bendigo, now sixty years old, was knocked into the fireplace by a heavy blow to the face. He looked around for the poker, an implement that had saved him in similar situations before, but the landlord, anticipating trouble, had removed it as soon as he entered the premises. The author of this letter, "E.T. Nottingham", commented that helping himself to other people's ale was a favourite pastime of the old champion's which landed him in several tight corners. He wrote "It is regretted that a man who, when at his best, gained such a big reputation as a boxer, should in his later years have played the lowdown tricks of which he was undoubtedly guilty."[69]

As a boy, Ishmael Wilson was aware of Bendigo's fame. In 1922, long after the first publication of his pamphlet, which over the years had been re-printed several times, he wrote to the *Nottinghamshire Guardian*,

[68] ibid.
[69] *Nottinghamshire Guardian*, May 21st, 1921

stating that Bendigo was "one of the straightest men to his backers who ever lived – Mr Malpass of the Flying Horse, the Poultry, and Mr Ned Daniels, the Three Crowns, Parliament Street." Wilson could only have been repeating what he had heard, but he did have first-hand knowledge of the ex-champion:

> "From my earliest recollections, I remember Bendigo, who after his fighting days were over generally resided with his nephew, Ben Thompson, who kept a fish shop in St Ann's Street, next to the Forester's Arms. He became very unhappy after his fighting days were over, and took to drink. And what a handful of trouble it used to be to take him to the lock-up! I have seen it take eight policemen to get him there."

By his own admission, Bendigo was locked up a total of twenty-eight times in the Nottingham House of Correction for being drunk and disorderly. However, neither Police Court nor prison records have survived from the period and, while references to court appearances in contemporaneous newspapers have come to light, none of the cases mentioned resulted in imprisonment – perhaps surprisingly, in view of some of his performances in the dock.[70]

On 8th February, 1861, the *Nottingham Review* reporting under the sub-headline "Bendigo In The Police Court," described how on the previous Friday, "Thompson, the well known ex-pugilist, more often called by his *nom de guerre* of Bendigo", had appeared at the Police Court to answer to a complaint of assault preferred against him by a butcher, Charles Simkin. It stated that the Mayor had addressed both parties in the case, to see if the matter could be sorted out without the magistrates being called upon to adjudicate. The butcher said that Bendigo came to him in The Shambles and threatened to "knock his brains out", at the same time borrowing a stick from another butcher in order to thrash him.

When the Mayor asked Simkin, "But would you not be satisfied if Thompson was to beg your pardon and promise not to offend again?" Bendigo caused the court to burst into laughter, exclaiming "Me, beg *his* pardon? And he a dirty butcher!" The Mayor, who seems to have been extraordinarily patient, said the matter would be better settled out of court and Bendigo was asked if he would undertake not to annoy Mr Simkin

[70] I am grateful to Geoffrey Oldfield's article *Bendigo – a Local Hero?*, which was published in the Nottinghamshire Local Studies Research Series in 1990 as the source of these court appearances

again. His response did not augur well. "Will he undertake not to annoy me?" he asked, adding, "I don't want to speak to the man."

Simkin protested "I am not safe. My brother is just the same. Thompson has been pushing him about," at which Bendigo could not hold his disgust. " I wonder you dare look me in the face," he said.

The Nottingham House of Correction, St. John's Street

By now the Mayor was losing patience. He told the butcher: "You may take a summons."
Bendigo, to much laughter: "I'll have one too."
The Mayor: "So you shall, but are you in danger of your life?"
Bendigo, with a glance of contempt towards the complainant: "No sir. God forbid!"

As the courtroom rang with laughter, both parties left to obtain their summonses. Then, moments later they returned, Bendigo announcing that he'd "As lief shake hands as take out a summons." The pair promptly shook hands, the old fighter bowed to the butcher and they left the court together, seemingly the best of pals.

In December 1870 he appeared for having been drunk and disorderly in the Dog and Bear Inn on Bridlesmith Gate. When a constable removed him from the premises he became unruly, harassing a passer-by on the street, whereupon he was arrested. The passer-by did not appear in court but Bendigo admitted the offence and, after apologising, was fined one pound. On another occasion, charged with being drunk and disorderly and assaulting a policeman, he claimed the constable had approached from behind and tried to throttle him.

He blamed alcohol when he appeared for assaulting a female in the street in March 1871. It was alleged that he had "proceeded to use her very roughly, tearing her dress in several places." In court he was apologetic, saying he had visited a friend who had given him some whisky which had "taken hold" of him. He told the magistrates that he had been a teetotaller since Christmas and he hoped they would overlook his behaviour on this occasion. The complainant said she would be satisfied if he paid for the damage to her dress. He was fined £1, which he paid immediately.

Two later court appearances were not brought about by drunkenness, but his conduct in court on both occasions raises the question of brain damage from the effects of the head blows he had taken in the ring. On 6th January 1872 he was charged with trespassing on the Midland Railway at Lenton, while taking a short cut home. As the magistrates deliberated on how to deal with such a petty misdemeanour, he leaned over the rail of the dock and advised them "give me ten years". They declined, fining him a guinea instead.

The next year he was back again, this time charged with throwing a bucket of dirty water over one of his neighbour's furniture, which was outside her home. He vigorously denied the offence, gesticulating and expressing great surprise throughout the prosecution case. The neighbour, Emma Shelton, who lived close by to the cottage he rented at Wollaton Road, Beeston, said Bendigo had threatened to cut her eyes out if she took out a summons. He said he had two witnesses to prove he had not done the deed, but when asked to name them he said one was called "Tuffy Nanny". He was found guilty and fined two guineas.

He might not have recognised it at the time, but the court appearances revealed how far he had fallen. The athleticism, skill and courage which led to him never being beaten in the ring brought him the respect of thousands of people from all social classes. Now, in his sixties, the glory years well behind him, he was demeaned and humiliated by his own behaviour. Then, just as it seemed he had hit rock bottom and could not possibly regain his pride, he confounded his critics. Against all the odds and with little or no warning, Bendigo gave up drinking and being a public nuisance. He changed his ways in a manner no one could have anticipated. He turned to God.

12] Saved

The way Bendigo told it, the cold, grey, stone-walled House of Correction in St John's Street, Nottingham was where he found salvation. He was no stranger to its cells and the prison seems to have held some attraction for him, for he tended to go there even when he not taken by the police. Whether it was his curious sense of humour or just another example of drunken behaviour, he was said to frequently call at the prison at dead of night and ring the bell. When the hastily dressed, half-asleep turnkey came to the gate Bendigo would say "Goodnight, I don't want to come in," and wander off, laughing.[71]

But when he walked out of the prison on the twenty-eighth occasion, he never returned. His sentence, so he later told journalist James Greenwood, who interviewed him in 1874 was imposed for assault:

> "Well, this twenty-eighth time was for the old game. It was at one of the public houses where they were set against me, and wouldn't serve me with strong drink, even though I had the money to pay for it. So somebody got a pint of ale for me and just as I was going to drink it the landlord comes along and knocks the jug clean out of my hand. Well, no sooner was he knocked down himself than in comes the policeman and it was 'Bendigo in trouble once more.' And I had to make the best of it before the bench of magistrates. Of course, I knew 'em well enough and they knew me. There was one of 'em, a hearty, John Bull kind of man, that I took a likin' to, and I used always try and get round, and generally managed it, putting the matter to him in a man to man kind of way, d'ye see; but there was another, a vinegar-looking, narrow-jawed cove, who was always hard on me.
>
> Well, I made my story out pretty well, and made 'em laugh a bit, and, thought I, I shall get off this time; but I

[71] Recounted by Thomas Windle in *Bendigo, the Champion Prize Fighter of England*, a pamphlet published in 1904 by Morgan and Scott, London

didn't. Said my friend on the bench, 'Bendigo, when you're sober, you are one of the nicest men in Nottingham, but when you're drunk you ain't; therefore you will go to prison for two months and afterwards give bail to keep the peace for three months longer.'"[72]

Greenwood published several books about the seedier side of Victorian life, and included the chapter 'Bendigo's Conversion' in *Low-Life Deeps – an Account of the Strange Fish to be Found There*. While the interview shows signs of Bendigo's account having been edited, it also bears the hallmark of his odd terminology and gives a vivid impression of the route he took to religion. He began by speaking of the experiences in prison that influenced his thinking:

"Twice a day on Sunday we had to go to chapel to hear the parson. I didn't care much for listening to such things in general, but somehow this Sunday I did. When I say somehow, I mean to say I couldn't but do it. It was just in my line. It was about the set-to between David and Goliath. And when the parson began to talk about the big 'un – how tall he was, and how broad and strong - I was all the time picturing him as being a man after the style of the big 'un I had fought three times – Ben Caunt that was – and wondering how I should have got on in a stand-up with Goliath. Well, the parson went on and told us about the little `un – about David and about his pluck in facing the giant, though he only had a sling and a stone to tackle him with.

When he came to describe the fight, I listened with all my might, quite lost myself listening, and when it came to the wind-up, and David floored the giant and killed him, without thinking that I was in chapel and that it was against the rules to say a word, I bawls out 'Bravo! I'm glad the little 'un won!' It was very wrong and what made it worse for me was all the prisoners and warders burst out laughing. The parson he turned away, but I could tell by the movement of his shoulders that he was laughing too; which perhaps made it a little better. They thought it was a joke of mine, but it wasn't. I took it too serious for joking, and when I got to my cell and was quiet I kep' thinking about it, and about somebody must have helped little David, to lick the giant with his sword

[72] See James Greenwood, *Low Life Deeps.* Chatto & Windus 1876.

and armour, and about them old times when I used to ask that I might win the fight that I might keep my old mother out of the workhouse.

Well it was a sing'lar, as though it was done on purpose. The very next Sunday the parson preached another sermon which seemed hitting at me harder than the one the week before. It was all about the three men – Shadrach, Meshach and Bendigo – who was cast into the fiery furnace, and who was saved by the Lord from being burnt. Oh yes, I've heard about that since, it wasn't exactly Bendigo who was third man; but the name sounded like it to me and I took it as such, though I didn't say anything to anybody.

If one Bendigo can be saved, why not another? I said to myself; and I thought about it a great deal more than anybody there thought about it, I'll wager. If I'd have told 'em I might have thought that the sermons was got up for me. It really seemed so. Sunday after Sunday I looked out for something about me in the sermon, and there it always was.

After the one about the fiery furnace came one about the twelve fishermen. Now I'm a fisherman myself. Bless you! I should rather think I was; one of the best in England. I've won lots of prizes and I've a fishing-rod that Mr Walter of *The Times* give me. Well after that came another sermon about the seven hundred left-handed men in the Book of Judges; and I am a left-handed man. Of course I am. It was that what took in the knowing ones I have had to stand up against. Well, it was this always going on that made me make up my mind to change as soon as I got out."

He went on, to his release from the House of Correction:

"It was on a Thursday, and in the winter, and when I was let out at the gaol door there was my old friends kindly come to meet me. 'Come along Bendy, old boy,' they said. ' We've got something to eat for you all ready. Come along.' But I had made up my mind and wasn't to be shook; so I turned round and I ses 'Look here, I will never eat nor drink along with you or along with any man in a public house again as long as I live. I've done with it.' They looked at each other, I can tell you. They couldn't make it out. But there was one amongst 'em named Waters and he said 'Bendy, will you come with

> me. I'm going to Beeston.' And I knew if I went with him I should be all right; and I went. And there I met another friend who wished me well and said he, 'Bendy, what do you say to coming to the Hall tonight to hear Undaunted Dick?' 'Who's he?' says I. 'I never heard of him.' 'It's Dick Weaver,' says he, a collier chap who was once in a bad way but is now converted and turned preacher.' 'Ay,' said I, 'I'll go and hear him, he's one of my own sort;' and I went and I set on the platform, and there I could hear 'em: 'Why, how's this: there's Bendigo up there;' 'Look, look, there's old Bendy.' But I took no notice, only sat quiet and listened.
>
> Well, next night I was there again and heard what did me more good than ever. It was bad weather and snowing hard and I had to make my way home late at night across a park. When I was half way across I couldn't hold out any longer, so in the dark and with the snow coming down I went on my knees and prayed as well as I knowed how; and when I got up I felt a new man.
>
> I didn't quite go without ale; I had one half pint between then and Sunday and then I went to the chapel again and on to the platform and, in the face of everybody who was there, I knelt down and told 'em how I was changed, and that nothing should tempt me to go wrong again, and I've kept my word, and I mean to go on keeping it. Ever since that time not a drop of beer or spirits has passed my lips and I have never felt healthier or stronger or more lively than I do now. I've tried the right road for two years now but I ain't much of a hand at preaching as yet, because I can't read, but I'm learning as fast as I can and then I shall get on better."

Like other aspects of Bendigo's life, his conversion from drunkard to evangelist was dramatic - and hard to pin down to a date. He spoke of being "on the right road for two years now", which implies 1872, since the interview with Greenwood took place in December 1874, but Bendigo was not reliable on dates, years or the finer points of factual accuracy and a date later than 1872 is more likely. In the account Ishmael Wilson published he is quoted as saying he "fought and sinned for the Devil for nearly sixty-two years" – which places the turning point some time before November 1873. This is more feasible as it is ten months after he appeared in court for throwing water over a neighbour at Beeston – yet the interview gives the impression that he did not move to Beeston until after his last spell in prison.

Dick Weaver, whose meeting he attended, was a revivalist preacher who had himself risen from the mire of a wayward life. Popularly known as Undaunted Dick and sixteen years Bendigo's junior, as a Shropshire collier he had spent his youth drinking and fighting. In 1852 he got involved with the Evangelical movement which was gathering momentum across England but he soon slid back into his old ways. The real turnabout in his life came when he suffered a serious injury while working in the pit – his right hand was mangled by a truck wheel and the surgeon to whom he was taken decided the only option was to amputate. Weaver refused to allow it, believing that if he prayed hard enough his hand would be saved. A doctor dressed it daily and Weaver's prayers were answered, although he never recovered full use of his hand. The following year he married a woman of religious background and preached his first sermon soon afterwards at a village in Derbyshire. Still working in the coal mine, he held meetings in the evenings and moved to Liverpool where he lived by selling Bibles. Gradually his fame as 'the Converted Collier' spread as he undertook preaching missions all over the country until by the early 1860s he was travelling as far afield as Scotland and Ireland.

In Nottingham, Weaver's followers gathered at the Mechanics Hall and it was here that Bendigo's conversion took place. When Weaver saw him in the audience he invited him onto the platform and from that point on Bendigo, who had gone from being known as the Pride of Nottingham to the terror of the town was a new man. "I gave my heart to God," he later said. "I have fought and sinned for the devil for sixty-two years, but now I am determined by the grace of God to serve Him the best part of my days, and to win the crown in Heaven."[73]

It was a clever move on Undaunted Dick's part to invite Bendigo onto the platform. He immediately recognised the opportunities that association with the ex-champion would bring, especially by being known as the man who had played a key role in his conversion. He took his latest convert to his own home in Chester, had him measured for a suit and together they travelled to Liverpool to preach.

Bendigo's illiteracy and lack of experience at public speaking meant that he was never a preacher in the conventional sense. Besides this, he had lost most of his teeth and his speech was at times unintelligible to the ears of many of those who came to hear him. But when news spread that

---

[73] *Life, Battles, Conversion and Death of Bendigo, Champion of England.* Ishmael Wilson. 1889

he had renounced his old lifestyle to become an evangelist, crowds gathered to see and hear for themselves.

For years his championship belts and trophies had been in and out of various pawnbroker's shops in Nottingham. Now he redeemed them for the last time and when he appeared on platforms the mementoes of his glory days were displayed by his side. Meetings would proceed with Richard Weaver preaching a sermon and then introducing Bendigo. Weaver would encourage him to speak, suggesting anecdotes from his career in the prize ring. When the ex-champion had told his tale, Weaver drew some meaningful interpretation or lesson for the gathering to consider. Bendigo would exhort the audience to change along the lines of:

> "My Christian friends, I was never a coward in the devil's cause and I do not mean to be a coward in Christ's cause. All you that have been drunkards, fighters and used to a wicked course of life, I persuade you to shake yourselves from your evil ways and come to God. My friends, the Lord has saved me and he can save you."[74]

Many years later a correspondent to the *Notts. Guardian,*[75] Handly Cragg, told of seeing Bendigo at the Mechanics Hall in the company of another preacher, Jemmy Dupe. He recalled the old pugilist looking very demure "as Dupe waxed eloquent over 'Bendy' being snatched as a brand from the burning." Dupe called upon him to say a few words, whereupon Bendigo stood up and started to sing:

> "We are marching onward, singing as we go
> To a promised land where living waters flow."

Everybody joined in, but, said Cragg, "It was almost laughable to see the hard-bitten old veteran trying to beat time with his hand."

Jemmy Dupe took over from Dick Weaver as Bendigo's spiritual mentor. A local man and former pork butcher, he was more conveniently placed than Undaunted Dick to lead the celebrity convert along the path to righteousness. Dupe held large, open-air meetings in the Market Place and Bendigo joined him, amazing even the most doubtful sceptics with the transformation that he had achieved. Dupe's style of preaching involved a quiet start and as he built up his long grey beard began to wag and his appeals to his audience were communicated to all around by much

---

[74] ibid.

[75] Undated cutting in Nottingham Local Studies Library

gesticulation and waving of arms. Born in 1821 in Leicester, he too, like Weaver, was younger than Bendigo. His real name was James Dupee but he dropped the second 'e' in keeping with his plain and blunt manner.

Dupe is credited with finding Bendigo the cottage at Beeston, close to Nottingham but far enough away for him to avoid his old drinking friends. He joined the local Ebenezer Lodge of Good Templars, whose commitment to temperance and sobriety he was determined to follow and the Beeston cottage in Wollaton Road, which he rented for two shillings a week, would remain his home for the rest of his life. Under the influence of the Good Templars he changed his appearance; for some time he had favoured a short green 'jerry' coat with bright buttons, together with shortish trousers, gaiters and top boots. Now, when he stood with Jemmy Dupe, he wore a black frock coat, black velveteen waistcoat and white choker. His hair was damped down and unkind critics suggested he had a look of Stiggins, the hypocritical parson in Charles Dickens' *The Pickwick Papers*. [76]

With the charismatic Jemmy at his side, Bendigo travelled throughout the Midlands, encouraging audiences to follow his example and turn to God. Although Dupe, who was a natural public speaker, guided and prompted him, he did not find his new vocation easy. Usually he adopted a fighting stance, pointed to his trophies, saying "See them cups, see them belts? I used to fight for them but now I fight for Christ!" It was a simple and straightforward message, but he did not always pull it off. On one occasion he was so nervous that instead of pointing at the trophies he pointed at a pile of cabbages and fruit in a harvest festival display, saying "I used to fight for them . . ."

Such mistakes did not bother the hordes who came to witness the ex-champion and transformed boozer. His oddball delivery often made them laugh, as when he called upon God to turn all sinners away from their wicked paths. "Turn 'em round Lord," he prayed, "turn 'em right round." Then he paused and added "No, turn 'em half round – if they go right round they'll be where they was afore."

One trip to Wolverhampton, where Dupe and Bendigo regularly conducted their mission in a rented hall, coincided with an engagement in the town by the celebrated preacher Charles Haddon Spurgeon, up from London. Spurgeon's congregation was a cut above those who were drawn to Bendigo and Dupe – "crowds of the submerged tenth – prize-fighters, thieves, poachers, gamblers and harlots", as one report described them. At Spurgeon's Metropolitan Tabernacle, which seated six thousand people,

---

[76] *Bendigo- A Hundred Years On.* Pamphlet by R. Barker, 1980 in Nottingham Local Studies Library

he delivered powerful sermons to the more refined non-conformist. When he arrived in Wolverhampton, where he was booked to speak in a chapel, he inquired as to the state of spiritual work going on in the town. He was told that a small band of men from Nottingham had hired a small hall that was packed every night with all the ruffians of the slums. In his own service that night, Spurgeon digressed from his main theme to tell his followers of this inquiry. He had, he said, been informed that a certain hall was "filled with the rag, tag and bobtail class" and that the mission was a great success. He paused for a moment, holding his audience spellbound and then, with a flamboyant gesture, dramatically exclaimed "Go it rag! Go it tag! Go it bobtail!"

A preacher like Spurgeon was rarely subjected to barracking or troublesome opposition from an audience. His crowds came from the better parts of town. The motley crew who were drawn in to see Bendigo were not so polite, to them disorderliness was normal behaviour. Nor were they all easily convinced that the ex-pugilist's conversion was genuine. One meeting in Birmingham provided the inspiration for a poetic tribute to Bendigo by the great writer Sir Arthur Conan Doyle who published 'Bendigo's Sermon' in the April 1909 edition of *The Strand Magazine*.

In part of the nineteen verse poem Conan Doyle describes how on one notable occasion the ex-champion – "His hat was like a funeral, he'd got a waiter's coat/ With a hallelujah collar and a choker round his throat" could not resist the temptation to fall back on his old ways when the devil put temptation his way in the shape of hecklers:

"Now I'll tell you how it happened, he was preachin' down at Brum
He was billed just like a circus, you shoulda seen the people come;
The chapel it was crowded and in the foremost row
There was half a dozen bruisers who'd a grudge at Bendigo.

There was Tommy Platt of Bradford, Solly Jones of Perry Bar,
Long Connor from the Bull Ring, the same wot drew with Carr;
Jack Ball, the fightin' gunsmith, Joe Murphy from the Mews
And Ikey Moss, the bettin' boss, the Champion of the Jews

A very pretty handful, a-sittin' in a string,
Full of beer and impudence, ripe for anything;
Sitting in a string there, right under Bendy's nose,
If his message was for sinners, he could make a start on those.

Soon he heard the chaffin'; 'Hi, Bendy! Here's a go!'
'How much are you coppin' by the jump to Glory show?'
'Stow it Bendy! Left the ring! Mighty spry of you!

Didn't everybody know the ring was leavin' you?'

Bendy fairly sweated as he stood above and prayed,
'Look down, O Lord and grip me with a stranglehold!' He said.
'Fix me with a stranglehold! Put a stop on me!
I'm slippin', Lord, I'm slippin', and I'm clingin' hard to Thee.'

But the roughs they kept on chaffin' and the uproar it was such
That the preacher in the pulpit might be talkin' double Dutch.
Till a workin' man he shouted out, a jumpin' to his feet,
'Give us a lead, your reverence and heave 'em in the street.'

Then Bendy said 'Good Lord, since I first left my sinful ways,
Thou knowest that to Thee alone I've given up my days.
But now dear Lord!' – and here he laid his Bible on the shelf,
'I'll take with your permission just five minutes for myself.'

He vaulted from the pulpit like a tiger from a den,
They say it was a lovely sight to see him floor his men;
Right and left, and left and right, straight and true and hard.
Till the Ebenezer Chapel looked more like a knackers' yard.

Platt was standing on his head and looking at his toes,
Solly Jones of Perry Bar was feeling for his nose,
Connor of the Bull Ring had all that he could do,
Rakin' for his ivories that lay about the pew.

Jack Ball, the Fightin' Gunsmith was in a peaceful sleep.
Joe Murphy lay across him, all tied up in a heap.
Five of them were twisted in a tangle on the floor,
And Ikey Moss, the bettin' boss had sprinted for the door.

Five repentant fightin' men, sittin' in a row,
Listenin' to words of grace from Mister Bendigo,
Listenin' to his reverence, all as good as gold,
Pretty little baa-lambs, gathered to the fold.

For the creator of Sherlock Holmes it might have seemed a literary departure, but Conan Doyle had a serious interest in the prize ring, revealed in some of his other works.[77] The incident which he describes above is believed to have occurred at one of the many meetings Jemmy Dupe held at Carr's Lane Chapel, Birmingham, which were often attended by the prize fighting fraternity.

Whatever the origins of 'Bendigo's Sermon', there is no doubt that the ex-champion, despite abusing his health over many years through alcohol, still had remarkable strength and agility for a man of his advancing years.

---

[77] E.g. the play *The House of Temperley* and the novel *Rodney Stone*.

He remained keen to demonstrate it too - in 1872, just before he gave up the wanton lifestyle, he went along to watch a running match in Nottingham. Afterwards, for no other apparent reason than he felt like it, he put a sparring glove, threw a large stone into the air and hit it as it came down. The stone, which weighed ten or more pounds, flew between twenty and thirty yards without touching the ground.[78]

In late 1874, Bendigo and Jemmy Dupe arrived in London. Evangelicalism was in the ascendancy and nowhere had it caught on more than in the rougher parts of town. In the swarming, dirty, overcrowded rookeries, people who had little more to live on than their wits were vulnerable to the messages of hope and redemption brought to them by a new breed of preacher whose appeal was emotional rather than intellectual. A year earlier the celebrated American evangelists, Dwight L. Moody and Ira D. Sankey had made their first tour of Britain, attracting huge followings with their self-written hymns and old-fashioned gospel with its prophecies of a Second Coming. Moreover, old time heroes of the prize ring were always welcome in Cockney circles and the costermongers and street hawkers made haste to hear the reminiscences of Bold Bendigo, whose name and exploits had been told and re-told to the new generation.

At the People's Mission Hall in Whitechapel, a crowd estimated at 2,000 people turned up to witness Bendigo "fight for the Gospel" as he called it. The *Pall Mall Gazette* interpreted his conversion - achieved "to the great joy of the magistrates of Nottingham and the amazement of the Nottingham Lambs" – in profound terms.

> "The adaptability of the English race is held to be among the principal causes of the natural greatness, and it with much satisfaction that we note the admirable illustration of this capacity which is being afforded us by the members of a once popular profession. The gradual decline of pugilism is, it seems, directing the attention of its professors to other fields of industry."

Bendigo, "a stout, strong-built man of square face, with spectacles on nose," was said to have preached "with considerable zeal but without much oratorical finish," although the reporter believed that he would improve his style and delivery.

For nearly three months, on and off, Bendigo enchanted the Cockneys, recounting tales of his old fights alongside the account of his conversion.

[78] Cutting dated c. 1920 from *Notts Guardian* in Nottingham Local Studies Library

His popularity never wavered at all as he packed the 7,000 seats of the Standard Theatre and left thousands more standing outside. At the Agricultural Hall in Islington two thousand people attended and in St Giles, the heart of the Rookeries, the smell of alcohol in the hall was so powerful that Bendigo commented "they all must live on a pennorth o' gin". Charles Spurgeon, hearing that he was in town and recalling how their paths had almost crossed in Wolverhampton, invited him to appear at his Metropolitan Tabernacle, where the better class of congregation were so enamoured of his down-to-earth approach that he was asked back.

Bendigo and Dupe's headquarters in London was the Cabmen's Mission Hall at King's Cross, where Jemmy's brother John Dupee - he had kept the second 'e' in the surname - was Superintendent. Here, Bendigo was so popular that services had to be held in two shifts, he and the Dupe brothers speaking in the main hall and then going downstairs to address the 'overflow' waiting in a lower room. They held three services each Sunday and attracted great attention from the press, such was the impact of the former star of the prize ring. Not even the *Christian World* could ignore such an event:

> "On Saturday evening, Bendigo, no longer a prize-fighter, but a sincere Christian, spoke at the Cabmen's Mission Hall, King's Cross, of the Saviour he had found, to men ready to drink in every word – men to whom even an Archbishop might have appealed in vain. Bendigo is no scholar; he can't read the Bible. He is not much of an orator; but his honest, manly speech is calculated to be especially useful."

Even members of the established Church were impressed. The Reverend C. Maurice Davies, a Church of England minister, in his book *Unorthodox London, or phases of religious life in the Metropolis*, described Bendigo –

> "Old man though he was, erect as an arrow on the right hand side of the sleek parson, he was a slender, clean-limbed personage and I should never have suspected his former occupation from his appearance, but there was a considerable hardness about his wrinkled face and his eye was bright and clear as an eagle's . . . I saw that the third finger on his left hand had been broken." [79]

[79] Published in 1876

Davies commented that Bendigo's address was brief and uttered in a rapid, nervous manner which, along with his missing teeth, made it difficult to follow. He told how, when he began, his friends gave him a fortnight and said he would be locked up. When he did not get locked up they said "If God can save Bendy, he can save me." He compared himself to the dying thief in the Bible and said that he was happy now with his "little country seat" and £1 a week for the rest of his life.

Bendigo hinted that the seeds of his conversion could have been laid longer ago than was assumed, saying that even in his wild days he liked to hear preaching, but whenever he tried to go to church he was snubbed. "Now people say 'Bendy's making a good thing of it, Bendy's togs are better than they used to be'." He said he had first come to London thirty years earlier, to fight, and all through that time, "I was making plenty of money but I never had a penny to bless myself." He ended by saying "At sixty-three years of age and after fighting twenty-one prize fights, I feel like a boy. Champion of England is a big title, but it took a lot of trouble to get and it was no good when I got it. Now I'm struggling hard for another crown."

The Reverend Davies noted that the following Sunday Bendigo would receive the Lord's Supper, which his scruples as a teetotaller had caused him to decline previously, due to the wine. On this special occasion, the cup was to be "filled with unfermented juice of the grape" - little wonder that his old associates, more used to him taking other men's ale from under their noses, were both puzzled and sceptical at the turnabout in his behaviour.

Bendigo was of great value to the evangelists. Rev Davies, commenting on his statement that his conversion had brought him a better life than the one he had as champion of England, said "This single fact was worth a hundred theories". In promoting Bendigo, the Dupe brothers reaped enormous professional gain to their own ministries, becoming nationally known as a result, but the benefits were mutual because without Jemmy's guidance and support Bendigo might never have got out of Nottingham and enjoyed national acclaim for his remarkable conversion.

An account of his first appearance in London, from the *Weekly Budget* of 5th December 1874, gives full flavour of both the manner in which the Dupes ran their meetings, and Bendigo's contribution:

"BENDIGO IN A NEW LIGHT EXTRAORDINARY SCENES AT THE LONDON CABMEN'S MISSION HALL

On Sunday Bendigo, the once famous Champion of England, but of late better known in connection with the election business in his native town of Nottingham, made his first appearance in the pulpit in connection with a series of special services held at the London Cabmen's Mission Hall.

The evening service, crowded to overflowing, was opened with prayer by Mr John Dupee, superintendent of the mission, after which the congregation very vigorously joined in the singing of a hymn. A second hymn followed upon the reading of a psalm, and Mr Dupee proceeded to say a few words about 'their dear and saved brother, Bendigo'. With a frankness that in no wise disconcerted the veteran prize-fighter, Mr Dupee discussed and described the conditions in which he had lived up to about two years ago.

The speaker was, it appeared, a fellow townsman of Bendigo's, and his recollections of him went back for nearly 40 years, at which his state was so bad that Mr Dupee, then a lad, used to walk behind him through the streets of Nottingham praying that he might be forgiven. But now he was saved, and, quoting the handbill that had advertised the meeting, Mr Dupee hailed him as 'a miracle of mercy, the greatest miracle of the 19th Century', which view the congregation endorsed by fervent cries of 'Praise the Lord! Hallelujah'.

Whether Bendigo would stand steadfast in the new course he had begun to tread was a matter which, Mr Dupee did not hide it, was freely discussed in the circles where the ex-champion was best known. But Bendigo had now gone straight for two years and he, Mr Dupee, believed he would keep straight.

Before introducing Bendigo to the meeting, Mr Dupee said his own brother Jim would say a few words, his claim upon the attention of the congregation being that he was 'the next great miracle of the 19th Century'.

From particulars which Mr Dupee then proceeded to give in relation to the early history of his brother, it would be difficult to decide whether he or Bendigo had the fuller claim to the title of the 'wickedest man in Nottingham'. A single anecdote told to the discredit of his early life must suffice in indication of its general character. He was, it appeared, always getting tipsy and arriving home at untimely hours. 'One night,' said the preacher, 'he came home very late and was kicking up an awful row in the street just before he came in. I opened the window, and, looking out, said to him very gently, "Now Jim do come in without waking mother", and what do you think he said? Why, he said nothing, but just upped with a brick and heaved it at me. That was Jim in the old days' he continued, 'he always was a lively sinner, and he's just the same now he's on his way now to join the saints'.

Jim suddenly approached the pulpit desk with his hand stretched out, singing the 'Hallelujah Band'. In the course of an address with much animation and filled with startling phrases, it became clear that 'Jim' had been the immediate instrument of the conversion of Bendigo. He added considerably to the stock of information respecting the early life of that personage, and told in detail how better things began to dawn on him. At the outset Bendigo's enthusiasm was somewhat misdirected, as manifested at an infidel meeting he attended in company with his sponsor. 'Who's them fellows on the platform?' said Bendigo to Jim. 'Infidels,' said Jim. 'What's that?' queried Bendigo. 'Why, fellows that don't believe on God or the devil.' 'Then come along and we'll soon clear the platform,' said Bendigo, beginning to strip.

Mr Dupee then again appeared at the desk and said they would sing a verse of a hymn after which Bendigo would address them, and the plate would be handed round for a collection to cover the cost of the hall and of Bendigo's travelling expenses.

Bendigo, who had all this time been quietly seated on the platform, advanced, and began to speak in a simple, unaffected but wholly intelligent manner. He was decently dressed in a frock coat, with black, velveteen waistcoat, buttoned over his broad chest. He is still, despite his three score years, straight as a pole, and has a fresh, healthy-looking face, that belied the fearful stories told by his friends of his dissipation. Except a certain flattening of the bridge of the nose, a slight indentation on the forehead between the eyebrows, and the crooked

> finger on his left hand, he bore no traces of the many pitched battles of which he is the hero, and might in such an assembly have been easily taken for a mild mannered family coachman.
>
> 'I've been a fighting character,' he said, 'but now I'm a miracle. What could I do? I was the youngest born of 21 children and the first thing that was done to me was to put me in a workhouse. There I got among fellows who brought me out and I became a fighting character. Thirty years ago I came up to London to fight Ben Caunt and I licked him. I'm 63 now and I didn't think I should ever come up to London to fight for King Jesus. But here I am, and I wish I could read out of the blessed Book, and I could talk to you better. But I never learnt to read, though I'm hoping by listening to the conversation around me to pick up a deal of the Bible, and then I'll talk to you better.'
>
> This and much more to the same purport the old veteran said, and then Mr Dupee interposed with more "few words" and the plate was sent round."

It was during his stay in London that he was interviewed by the journalist, James Greenwood. The author of *Low-Life Deeps* found him to be good company, brimming with modesty and good nature by the parlour fire at the Cabmen's Mission Hall. Greenwood found the ex-champion holding a child's first spelling book and "doing his desperate utmost" to master the mysteries of the alphabet in order to help him achieve his ambition to be able to read the Bible.

Bendigo was depicted as a man in the best of health "Aged and used-up prize-fighters are not invariably pleasant objects to contemplate," wrote Greenwood, "But Bendigo is a shining example to the rule. He has the cheery aspect of an English country squire who has lived a life of unbroken serenity. His shoulders are immensely broad, and still as square as a plank. He is light on his feet, and as active with his arms as a schoolboy." Bendigo told the journalist how, from all his battles, he "never in my life had a hit on the nose hard enough to make it bleed, and in all my battles I never got a black eye." He showed him his broken thumb and finger and explained how part of his ear came to be missing – "Deaf Burke did that when I was six-and twenty." He said he also had a damaged big toe, inflicted by the spiked shoes of Ben Caunt but there was nothing else wrong with him that he knew of, "'cepting a broken kneecap which lamed me for seven years."

Greenwood was interested in how he had gone from being a boozer and brawler to a crowd-pulling evangelist, but Bendigo dismissed the dark days, saying "You won't care to hear of my queer ways from the time I turned up fighting until I found grace; besides I am going to get a kind friend to write my life and I mean to get it published shortly." Asked if in his young days he ever had religious thoughts, he replied that he did not, to speak of, although "when we little `uns were at home, mother used to make us say the Lord's Prayer and that." He told how, as a pugilist, although he knew nothing about religion, he used to go down on his knees the night before a fight and say 'Let me win this fight so that I may keep my old mother out of the workhouse." He said "It wasn't religion. I didn't know what religion was." He then went on to give his account of how he found redemption during his twenty-eighth time in the Nottingham House of Correction.

He told Greenwood, as he had told his audiences, that he had a pound a week income:

> "Yes, a pound a week – that's what I've got to live on. Did I save it up? Not I; I couldn't save. No, what I did when I was making a heap of money in the ring was to hand it over to my brother on condition that he always gives me a pound a week, and that's how it comes."

Once again, the story he gave was not quite accurate. He implied that his brother gave him the pound a week, but John Thompson, the only sibling that he ever publicly acknowledged, had died seventeen months earlier, in July 1873 – round about the time that Bendigo was converted.

John Thompson had led a life of respectability and honest business and is described in the National Probate Calendar as a "Gentleman". His wife, from whom he parted on their wedding day and never lived with afterwards, had died, he never re-married and had no children. Local newspapers reported that he left in total around £12,000, made provision for his housekeeper and left the remainder of his estate to Bendigo,[80] but his will tells a different story. He left several bequests, including one of £500 to the National Lifeboat Institution, and four sums of £100 each to Nottingham General Hospital, to the Dispensary, Eye Dispensary and Blind Institution.

[80] See *Nottingham & Midland Counties Daily Express*, 14 July 1873

Bendigo in old age.

The residue of his estate was to go to "my esteemed friend Maria Christian Cartwright", the wife of one of his executors and trustees, but he also instructed that £1200 was to be invested and the trustees were to pay the income from it "to my brother William Thompson during his life."

The wording of this bequest to Bendigo is puzzling. John instructed that his trustees were to "pay the income therefrom to my brother William Thompson during his life yet so nevertheless that if the said William Thompson shall assign charge or otherwise dispose of the said income or attempt to do so or suffer any act or thing whereby the said income if payable to him absolutely would become vested in any other person then and in such case the trust herein contained in favour of the said William Thompson shall absolutely cease as if he were dead."

The conditions attached to Bendigo receiving the money do not lend themselves to the interpretation that John was trying to influence his younger brother's lifestyle. He was unlikely to go bankrupt, had not been known to have any liaison with a woman – so a divorced spouse was unlikely to run off with his pound a week - and it is difficult to see what circumstances John had in mind when he placed the conditions on him receiving the money. Even if Bendigo had announced his conversion to God and teetotalism at the time his brother made the will - May 1873 – there was no reason to believe that it would be permanent, but the conditions do not appear to be any attempt to turn him from his long established lifestyle centred on public houses.

Bendigo told James Greenwood that John had held money for him from his fighting days, but if this were so, he must surely have exhausted it over the intervening twenty-four years. His employment had only ever been sporadic - training fighters and occasionally working as a waiter at Trent Bridge - and he had a raging thirst for alcohol. Without a doubt, the wording of the bequest is odd, suggesting that John Thompson thought his brother might give the money away. But who to?

Meanwhile, invitations flowed in from parishes all over London for him to speak at meetings. One involved dining with the clergyman at his vicarage beforehand. The vicar was six feet four inches tall and at the close of the meal asked Bendigo how he beat Ben Caunt. His reply was "Oh, I've stopped that game now," but the vicar persisted. He would not let the matter drop, saying there was no harm in talking about such things and he asked to be shown how the deed had been done. Bendigo told him to take off his coat and to hit him as hard as he could anywhere on his head. Taken aback, the vicar declined, saying he did not wish to hurt him but now Bendigo insisted, and as the man's hand came near his head he brought his own fist up sharply, halting a hair's breadth from the vicar's mouth, making him step swiftly back. "There," he said. "That's how I licked the Big `Un."

While in London he made no contact with those few old friends from the prize ring who were still around. There was a chance meeting on the street with Lord Longford, once a backer of Ben Caunt. Longford was surprised to see the old champion wearing a frock coat and choker and asked "Hello Bendy, what's your little game now?" Bendigo explained "I am fighting Satan and scripture sayeth that victory shall be mine, your Lordship." Amused, Longford replied "I hope so Bendy, but pray fight Beelzebub fairer than you did Ben Caunt, or I may change sides!"

After the excitement of London he returned to Nottingham, preaching in the small halls and outdoor missions around the town. He lived comfortably in his two shillings a week cottage on Wollaton Road, Beeston, cared for by a single woman, Hannah Chapman, who moved in as his housekeeper in 1875. Speculation arose that Jemmy Dupe had been offered £1,000 to take him on a preaching tour of America but nothing ever transpired.

He was a familiar sight in the town Market Place and at nearby Sneinton, his championship belts and trophies on display by his side as he gave away religious tracts and accosted possible converts. Even in his late sixties he remained sharp in his movements and quick on his feet. One day, spying an official of the Police Court, where a decade earlier he had been a regular in the dock, he turned swiftly round and feinted as if he was about to deliver a left-handed punch. As he did so he presented the startled passer-by with a tract from his right hand. It was a trick he pulled many times and he never ceased to enjoy the effect it had on people.

His life was on an even keel and the next few years passed without event. Contrary to the expectations of many Nottingham folk, especially his old associates, he maintained his sobriety and faith and never went back to the wild old ways. Always a proud man, in the bad times his dignity had seemed to desert him; now, in old age he could look back on his achievements with pride.

13] In Death like a Lamb

If he was not at his cottage in Beeston or in Nottingham Market Place, Bendigo could usually be found on the banks of the Trent. There he sat for hours at a time, fishing rod in his hand, his still sharp eyes focused on a bobbing float. All his life he had a passion for angling and if, as time went on, he became occasionally reluctant to recount his old victories in the prize ring – saying that his fight for the Lord was more important than championship belts - he never tired of telling of the prizes he had won at the York Great All-England fishing match.

He continued to enjoy good health, in spite of the privations of his childhood and the damage to his body from opponents' punches and two decades of drunken self-neglect. The constitution that had led him to become champion of the prize ring forty years earlier did not desert him now. He had a touch of gout but the only thing that really troubled him was his left knee, the one that had almost finished his fighting career when he fell while turning somersaults in 1840. Over the subsequent years the knee became increasingly painful and was prone to occasionally let him down.

One day in the early summer of 1880 he was fishing by Trent Bridge when his knee gave way and he fell, banging his head and tumbling into the river. Hauled out, he was taken home and put to bed, to be cared for by his housekeeper. The knee was slow to recover and for weeks he did not stray far from Beeston. But worse was to come. In the early hours of 1st August he was unexpectedly roused from his bed by a lodger who was staying at the cottage but had locked himself out. Bendigo rose to let him in but when he reached the top of the staircase his knee failed him and he tumbled down the steps to the bottom.

He complained to Hannah Chapman, his housekeeper, that his ribs hurt and a doctor was called. With a great deal of difficulty he managed to get back upstairs to bed but he was in severe pain. He did not realise it at the time but the fall had caused a rib to puncture his lung. Bronchitis set in and, although two doctors attended him, he showed no signs of improving. Visitors turned up to see him, among them Jemmy Dupe, his Ebenezer Lodge friends and his nephew Benjamin, but the most welcome caller was his fellow Nottingham Lamb and old pal from the prize ring, Harry

Paulson. In the years that had elapsed since 1856 when Bendigo trained Paulson for his fight with Tom Sayers, they had become great friends.

Late in the afternoon of Monday 23rd August, three weeks after his fall down the stairs, Paulson and Dupe were both at Bendigo's bedside when he murmured that he needed to say something to his old boxing friend. Paulson leaned forward to hear what he wished to say. With great effort he asked: "Harry, will you meet me in Heaven?"

Paulson was taken aback. "No," he said. "I'm too bad."

But Bendigo was not to be put off. "No," he persisted. "No. You're not. You've never been as bad as me and if the Lord could pardon and save me he could pardon and save you."

Bendigo had said what he wanted to say. As he sank back, whispering a prayer, Harry Paulson, ex-navvy, pugilist and as hard a man as ever stepped into a prize ring, leaned over and kissed his old pal. Bendigo tried to sing the words to his favourite hymn "For you must be a lover of the Lord, Or you won't go to Heaven when you die," but his voice faded away. He was seven weeks short of his sixty-ninth birthday.

An inquest was held two days later at the Commercial Inn, Beeston. Hannah Chapman, Bendigo's housekeeper, gave evidence of the fall downstairs three weeks earlier and his nephew Ben Thompson, the fishmonger, at whose home he had often lived before getting his own cottage, said that when he visited his uncle the week before his death, he told him of his fall. The Deputy Coroner who officiated said that Bendigo followed no occupation. He sometimes claimed to be an iron turner but earned his living by fighting in his earlier years. Latterly he lived on a sovereign a week coming in from money left him by his brother. Foul play was ruled out and the jury returned a verdict of accidental death.

Bendigo's funeral on Friday 27th August 1880 was a major public event in Nottingham, the like of which had never been seen. Thirty years earlier a big crowd had greeted him at the railway station when he returned victorious from seeing off the challenge of Tom Paddock. Now, on a bright summer's day, many thousands more gathered, lining the streets and following the coffin in a procession that stretched a mile long. The late champion was conveyed in a horse drawn hearse from Beeston to St Mary's Burial Ground on Bath Street in the centre of Nottingham.

Prior to the cortege setting off there had been a long delay. An argument arose between some mourners who claimed an interest in the late champion and wanted him to be interred at Beeston, and those who had made the arrangements for burial in Nottingham. A group of his old friends announced that any resting place in Beeston would only be temporary as they would return after nightfall and remove the body to a suitable place in the town. Eventually, Jemmy Dupe, who sided with the latter group, took possession of the coffin and got the procession on its way.

The journey took over two hours, as at several stages the route was blocked with people and vehicles, especially when the cortege stopped off for half an hour at the Sir Borlace Inn to take refreshments. Bendigo's nephew, Benjamin Thompson, and an old friend John Mallett were prominent, as were Jemmy Dupe and John Dupee, Richard Weaver, Harry Paulson and Bill Moulds, alias Winterflood, who Bendigo had fought and beaten in Bulwell Forest nearly fifty years earlier.

As the procession, led by Jemmy Dupe who walked in front of the hearse, wended its way through the streets of the town, many of those gathered on the pavements joined together to sing Moody and Sankey hymns, notably Bendigo's favourites, 'Welcome Home' and 'The Sweet Bye and Bye'. By the time the cemetery was reached, the grounds were packed with several thousand people, old bruisers and faces from the Fancy mingling with teetotallers and evangelists. The *Nottingham Journal* commented with lofty disdain that many of those present were of the lower classes, including a large number of women without hats or bonnets:

> "At the gates were stationed several constables, who appeared to be chiefly occupied in keeping out a number of roughs, who were anxious to gain admission. The scene was one to be remembered. On either side of the drive leading up to the chapel there was a thick belt of spectators composed of both sexes, old and young, and there were large numbers of people on the grass among the graves, which were ruthlessly trampled upon, and used without care or ceremony as coigns of vantage."

Such was the throng that the horse-drawn hearse had to force its way to the doors of the small chapel, where the police stood guard. The plain coffin, laden with wreaths of flowers, was carried inside by the bearers, followed by the mourners and as many of the gathering as could cram within the walls of the building.

Inside the chapel the service begun and outside it a man climbed up onto the front seat of one of the mourning coaches, parked by the doors, and began to address the crowd. He needed no introduction, most of the crowd recognised him as Richard Weaver, the man who had been largely responsible for Bendigo's conversion seven years before. As the Reverend

William Murray conducted Bendigo's official funeral, Undaunted Dick lived up to his name and led the huge crowd in another fervent rendition of 'Welcome Home'. Pointing into the chapel, he said what was in the coffin was only "the rags of old Bendy". He raised an arm to the sky: "They are only his rags, up yonder is the man". He went on to tell how Bendigo had come to his mission at the Mechanic's Hall and the part he himself had played in persuading him "to leave the devil's trickery". In an impassioned speech he said that Bendigo had been in an emaciated state when he first met him, but he, Weaver, had bought him a suit of clothes and restored him to a healthy condition at his home in Chester.

The outdoor crowd was roused to a fiery pitch when, without warning, the chapel doors were flung open and the congregation spilled out. Everyone was intent on following the coffin to its final resting place on the far side of the burial ground. There, flanked by Jemmy Dupe and Richard Weaver, the vicar concluded the official ceremony with an address on the life and character of Bendigo which he described as being "in every respect most remarkable". There had been, he said, no man who held up the repute of the country more honourably than he had done. But his victories in the ring had been "only animal victories" and he had done well to give up and make conquests of a different kind. Richard Weaver, wearing a handkerchief on his head to protect him from the sun, followed with an impassioned speech and Jemmy Dupe finished off the proceedings.

The odd goings-on that Bendigo was associated with for much of his life did not desert him at his funeral. Such was the crush and swaying to and fro that a number of people were fortunate they were not knocked into the grave to join him. While the final speeches were taking place a tall elderly man made a nuisance of himself by waving his umbrella and haranguing groups of mourners. He was dragged away by two police constables after knocking the handkerchief off Richard Weaver's head and then trying to knock it off again. Even when the grave was filled the crowd showed little inclination to disperse and it was some time before the burial ground was cleared of people.

Bell's Life in London, a paper that had often been critical of Bendigo during his fighting career, published a fulsome obituary:

"On Monday afternoon at a quarter to five William Thompson, better known as Bendigo, one of the most celebrated (though somewhat shifty) prize-fighters of his day expired at his home at Beeston near Nottingham. . .

His most memorable fights are with Ben Caunt, Deaf Burke and Tom Paddock. For many years after his fighting career in the ring had closed, he distinguished himself in the town of Nottingham and in the locality with his digits, a general readiness to appeal to arms under certain circumstances without the least justification often bringing him before the police magistrates where he had to suffer the penalty. Sometimes he would catch a tartar, but he had indomitable courage and many anecdotes could be told of his prowess against odds and his giant strength even when an old man. There is no doubt that the bold Bendy had a soft place in his head and, when too much refreshed, to him valour was the better part of discretion. At times his appearance was the cause of a general stampede to a place of general safety . . .

There was a good side to Bendigo's ungovernable, morose temper however. While finding himself one day by the side of the Trent he saved the life of a little girl who had fallen in the water and would take no reward, continuing his angling pursuits in his wet clothes. Having a little property we believe he was by no means deficient in helping the needy though his means were not great. Of late years Bendigo was induced to reform and he went body and soul over to the Revivalists, much to the relief of Nottingham society, generally. Since then he has endeavoured to make amends by doing all the good in his power and led a most temperate life." [81]

It was to be expected that the sporting press would mark the death of a man who had made such an impact in his lifetime, but a measure of Bendigo's fame beyond the Fancy came in *The Times*, whose obituaries were usually restricted to the great and the good of a more conventional leaning than old prize fighters. On the 24th August the paper announced:

"Death of 'Bendigo' – 'Bendigo', a once celebrated pugilist, and winner of eight prize-fights in the year, died yesterday evening at Beeston, Notts... aged 69. His death

[81] *Bell's Life in London*, 29 August 1880

> was occasioned by a fracture of the ribs, which penetrated the lungs. Of late years the deceased had been a preacher, and was well known as a leader of revivalist services."

For many years after Bendigo's death, his trophies and champion's belt were exhibited at the Forest Tavern on Mansfield Road, Nottingham. The landlord, John Ellis, acquired some of the late champion's property to add to a collection on permanent display in the pub, known locally as Ellis's Museum of Curiosities. Besides the belt presented to him by Jem Ward in 1839 after he defeated Deaf Burke, various items given to him during his career were also displayed. Among them was a fork "presented by the Fishermen of Boston", a knife from friends in Sheffield, a solid silver medallion presented to him by the St. Andrew's Society, a gold watch from Mr Malpass, one of his publican backers, and the colours he had worn when he fought Ben Caunt in 1845.

'Museum of Curiosities' was an apt description of John Ellis's collection. Bendigo's mementoes of the prize ring sat alongside such gems as a wax model of the murderer Mrs Maybrick, a "living" racoon, the largest owl in the world, a lamb with two bodies, two pigs with one head, a calf with two heads, old china, "common war implements from the land of the free", old paintings and pictures, stuffed fishes and reptiles and "freaks of nature galore from the top of the ceiling right down to the floor".[82]

When Ellis died in 1913 the collection was broken up. Bendigo's belt and other items were later reported to have been purchased by the Marquis of Queensberry and then taken to America by Nat Fleischer, founder of *Ring Magazine.*[83] During the research for this biography efforts were made to trace them, without success.

Although his funeral had been such a spectacle, Bendigo was laid to rest in an unmarked grave. At the time, it was reported that he had been interred alongside his parents in the burial ground at St Mary's, but both Benjamin and Mary Thompson were buried not at St Mary's but over half a mile away in the General Cemetery. Bendigo left no will and is believed to have had no savings. His funeral must have been paid for either by his nephew Ben, the fishmonger, with whom he had often stayed in Old Street but who had since moved to Newark, or by his evangelical friends. Whoever paid, they did not mark his final resting place with a headstone.

---

[82] *Nottingham Evening Post,* 1st October, 1890
[83] *Nottingham Evening News,* 1st August 1957

Eleven years later, a subscription among local evangelists, old pugilists and local publicans raised 50 guineas to erect a monument on the site of his grave. On the afternoon of 2nd June 1891 a colourful crowd, including a man named Piggy Wolf, one of the pall-bearers at Bendigo's funeral, gathered to see Jemmy Dupe unveil an imposing statue of a large lion reclining on a plinth.

The lion's right paw holds a scroll which bears the inscription:

IN MEMORY OF
WILLIAM THOMPSON
"BENDIGO"
OF NOTTINGHAM
WHO DIED AUGUST 23rd 1880
AGED 69 YEARS

On the plinth are the words:

IN LIFE ALWAYS BRAVE, FIGHTING LIKE A LION.
IN DEATH LIKE A LAMB, TRANQUIL IN ZION.

Of Bendigo's contemporaries in the prize ring, few survived him. Harry Paulson, his protégé and friend, lived another ten years, dying at the age of seventy-one. Paulson's last years were marked by poverty and when John L. Sullivan visited Nottingham on a sparring tour the ex-navvy was particularly grateful for the £10 note given to him by the American Champion.

The illegal nature of prize fighting and attention it received from the expanding police force meant that respectable members of the Fancy like Joseph Whitaker, the Duke of Limbs, were rarely if ever mentioned in press reports of ring matters. Bendigo was always grateful for the support Whitaker had given him in his youth and when he retired from the ring in 1850 he presented his old backer with an impressive penknife and a gold pencil case inscribed "Presented to Joseph Whitaker Esq. of Ramsdale by Bold Bendigo". Whitaker was a heavy drinker and when age restricted his exercise his weight rose to twenty stones. He died at the age of seventy-six in 1874.

Another of Bendigo's sterling supporters was Sam Turner who, as well as being his early mentor had seconded or trained almost every Midlands fighter of his time. He outlived his pupil, dying in 1887 at the age of eighty-five.

Jem Ward had passed away three years earlier in the Licensed Victuallers' Asylum on the Old Kent Road, London. The sherry-drinking, pipe smoking Black Diamond moved down from Liverpool in the 1850s to keep London pubs but his business sense deserted him and he became bankrupt. Besides his prowess as a fighter and trainer, Ward was a noted artist and accomplished musician and he encouraged his only daughter to a successful career as a classical pianist.

Bill Atkinson and Patsy Clay, both favourites of the Nottingham Lambs, died within months of each other. Atkinson, the Nottingham Pet, lived until 1866 by his trade as a tailor, while still keeping the company of ruffians; Clay, ended his life sleeping rough. He was found dead in March 1867.

John Leechman, better known as Brassey, and beaten by Bendigo in 1836, went on to suffer heavy losses to Ben Caunt and Tass Parker. He died at the age of thirty in the Coach and Horses, Todd Street, Manchester and was buried in the Baptist graveyard in his hometown of, Bradford.

Sad endings were not uncommon for old prize fighters. Bill Looney, beaten by Bendigo in ninety-nine brutal rounds in 1837, never entered the ring again. For a short while he kept a tap in Liverpool where in 1838 he was convicted of felony and transported to Botany Bay for fourteen years. He never returned, dying there of a fever in 1843.

Consumption brought about the demise of Young Molyneux at the age of forty-three. In his prime a fearsome fighter and an oft-mentioned opponent for Bendigo, he acted as his second in championship fights against Caunt and Tom Paddock. His last years were marked by dire poverty.

Tom Paddock, in 1850 Bendigo's last opponent, had several subsequent fights in spite of poor health. He discharged himself from hospital to fight Tom Sayers, who beat him, and in his last bout, against the six foot three inch Stalybridge Infant, he suffered a broken rib that protruded through the skin. He died of heart disease in 1863 at the age of thirty-nine.

Deaf Burke, after fighting his way from the bottom to the top, was deserted by his swell friends and forced to beg for a bare subsistence in the streets. His fighting days ended in 1843 and from then on he was to be found outside the West End sporting houses, ill-clad and half starved, uttering his pathetic but familiar "Don't forget the old Deaf `Un sirs", as he touched the brim of his battered hat. Burke had been ruined after he was taken up by a set of fast-living Corinthians and he paid the penalty. Said the editor of *Pugilistica*, Henry Downs Miles: "His qualities were his own, his vices the grafting of his so-called 'betters' in society." He died of consumption, aged thirty-four, on 8 January, 1845 at a house in Francis Street, Waterloo, nursed to the end by his old trainer Tommy Roundhead. Bendigo contributed generously to an appeal in *Bell's Life* on behalf of his widow

The Big `Un – Ben Caunt – for so many years Bendigo's bitter rival but later his friend, did not live to old age. His retirement from the ring was spent in his pub, the Coach and Horses on St Martin's Lane where the London Fancy could always be assured of a warm welcome. His musical evenings were renowned for their jollity, and his glory days kept to the forefront of customers' memory by the sculptured bust of him clad in a toga on display behind the bar.

Caunt enjoyed a good living and was proud of his achievements in life. But tragedy loomed. In 1851, while he was away in the country, following his sporting interests, a fire occurred in the upstairs room of the pub and two of`his children died. He remained in the pub and died there in September 1861 after catching pneumonia while shooting pigeons. The last time he was seen out and about, a few weeks earlier at a sale in London, he bought the belt given to the American fighter Tom Heenan the previous year, following his loss to Tom Sayers. Of Caunt, *Sporting Life* said:

> "Death has added another victim to his long account, one who a short week ago appeared in all the vigour of manhood and a veritable 'mountain of flesh'. Ben Caunt is no more."[84]

He was buried in the village churchyard at Hucknall Torkard. The *Nottingham Journal* reported that Bendigo, who was present, "seemed much affected".[85]

Away from the ring, the two men who had been Bendigo's guiding lights during and after his conversion both lived on for many years. Richard Weaver – Undaunted Dick – at whose meeting the ex-champion had realised his wish for a new life, died at his home in Alderley Edge, Cheshire, in 1896. The pork butcher-turned preacher Jemmy Dupe lived on to 1902; a very wealthy man for the times, he left an estate of £2530.

By the close of the 19th Century, the Bendigo legend was gathering momentum. The fame he had earned in the ring fifty years before had endured, not least through his revival in public life during the 1870s as an evangelist. James Greenwood's interview, published first in the *Daily Telegraph* and then in *Low Life Deeps*, laid down for posterity certain 'facts' about Bendigo's early life that in the future would be repeated times over without ever being examined.

Greenwood, a London journalist, would have had no reason to question or doubt what he was told. It is difficult to tell whether Ishmael Wilson, the York Street, Nottingham printer who published a short biographical booklet in 1889, was elaborating on information given to him directly by Bendigo, or merely collating that gained by other means. Wilson, as a young man, did claim to have known the elderly Bendigo, as he explained in letters to local papers in his own old age. His booklet, priced at one penny when first published, sold well and was re-printed many times.

There would be numerous short accounts like Wilson's; in 1904 a London publisher brought out Thomas Windle's *Bendigo – Champion Prize Fighter*, a forty-eight page offering that brimmed with inaccuracies but nonetheless served to fuel the legend. Five years after that came a short but heavyweight contribution, worthy of the subject himself, when Sir Arthur Conan Doyle published his poetic tribute in *The Strand Magazine* of April 1909. The creator of Sherlock Holmes had a great

---

[84] Sporting Life 11th Sept 1861
[85] Nottingham Journal 20th Sep 1861

interest in boxing and wrote 'Bendigo's Sermon' to commemorate the forthcoming anniversary of the ex-champion's birth.

Thus the name of Bendigo was kept alive in print; not that the sporting fraternity were inclined to let it die. In 1883 a racehorse named Bendigo won the Cambridgeshire Stakes at 50-1. Born in the same year that the ex-champion died, it also won the Kempton Jubilee, Lincolnshire Handicap, the Hardwicke stakes at Ascot and the Champion Stakes at Newmarket – the latter victory coming only two days after running second in the Cesarewitch, giving the winner 29lb. The horse won a total of £20,100 in stakes and much later Bendigo Handicaps were run at Kempton Park and Nottingham racecourses.

The 1920s saw a wave of reminiscences published in the Nottingham papers by people who had known Bendigo in his lifetime, or who were simply repeating tales of his escapades as passed down from their elders. Some were true, some apocryphal, some downright nonsense - but the effect was to keep his name alive: the stuff of folklore, of modern legend. Most fitting to the reputation he enjoyed before his conversion, the locally based Home Brewery Company introduced Bendigo Ale, advertised of course as a "strong ale", and in 1957 a newly built pub was named after him in the Sneinton district of Nottingham, close to where he once preached on market days.

Whatever the truth of his life out of the ring, Bendigo's achievements within it are indisputable. He was never beaten, his only set-back coming by way of a disqualification in the second Caunt fight. In an age of toe-to-toe slugging, where brute strength and capacity to sustain punishment were the normal modes of combat, he introduced speed and technique. He was the first champion to fight southpaw and his tricky skills were a harbinger of what was to become modern boxing. In 1955 he received the posthumous accolade of election to the Boxing Hall of Fame, when, along with five former world champions, including Gene Tunney, he was chosen by over a hundred writers and broadcasters from around the world.

Another, perhaps indirect, tribute to him is the city of Bendigo in Australia. A hundred miles north west of Melbourne in the state of the Victoria, and originally a small settlement known as Bendigo Creek, it is said to have been named after a local shepherd and fighting man who adopted the name of the then reigning champion back in his homeland. In 1848 a contingent of emigrating Nottingham lacemakers landed at Adelaide and some are believed to have found their way to the region.

Three years later gold was discovered at Bendigo Creek and the small settlement developed over the years into a thriving city.[86]

The Nottingham where Bendigo was born and lived for most of his life is unrecognisable today. The narrow streets and alleys where he scuffled as a boy have been transformed into a modern shopping centre. The inns and tap rooms of Long Row and Chapel Bar where he and the Lambs drank, argued and caused mayhem have long disappeared, along with the Workhouse, the House of Correction and the Mechanics Hall where he found redemption among the evangelists. His birthplace in New Yard, re-named Trinity Walk, was demolished in 1974; the site is marked by a plaque. Only his grave in St Mary's Rest Garden remains as a monument to an extraordinary life. There, guarded by the reclining lion, its mane weather-worn by the years, lies William Thompson, admired in his time and way beyond by rich and poor throughout the land as Bold Bendigo, Champion of England.

[86] *Notts. Guardian* 5th September 1925 and cutting from *Notts. Guardian* August 1927, citing R.R. Haverfield, former editor of the *Bendigo Advertiser*

Bendigo's Record in the Prize Ring

1832	Joe Healey (won, 16 rounds)
	Bill Faulkner (won, 11)
1833	Ned Smith (won, 5)
	Charlie Martin (won, 2)
	Lew Jackson (won, 3)
	Tom Cox (won, 9)
	Charles Skelton (won, 3)
	Bob Burton (won, 9)
	Bill Mason (won, 3)
	Bill Moulds, alias Winterflood (won, 1)
	Bill Keyworth (won, 11)
1834	'Bingham Champion' (won, round not recorded)
1835	Ben Caunt (won, 22)
1836	John Leechman, alias Brassey (won, 52)
1837	Young Langan (won, 32)
	Bill Looney (won, 99)
1838	Ben Caunt (lost - disqualification, 75)
1839	Deaf Burke (won, 10)
1845	Ben Caunt (won, 93)
1850	Tom Paddock (won, 49)

BIBLIOGRAPHY

Bailey, William, *The Angler's Instructor*, 3rd edition, Longmans, 1879.

Beardsmore, J.H., *The History of Hucknall Torkard*, Linney, 1909

Bell's Life in London. 1833 to 1880.

Bonnell, C., *Lions of Lambkinville*, Pub. Nottingham Daily Express, 1904.

Brailsford, Denis, *Bareknuckles – A Social History of Prize Fighting*, Lutterworth Press, 1988.

Bryson, E., *Portrait of Nottingham*, Robert Hale, 1983.

Chesney, Kellow, *The Victorian Underworld*, Temple Smith, 1970.

Cleveland, Harry E., *Fisticuffs*, Sampson Low, 1927.

Cuming, E.D. (ed), *Squire Osbaldeston: His Autobiography*, Lane, 1926.

Cutting, David, *The Nottingham Parliamentary Election of 1865*, Unpublished M.Phil dissertation 1972, University of Nottingham Regional History Library.

Daft, Richard, *Kings of Cricket*, Tillotson & Son, 1893.

Daft, Richard, *A Cricketer's Yarns*, Chapman & Hall, 1926.

Ditchfield, P.H., *The Old English Country Squire*, Methuen, 1912.

Dowling, Vincent George, *Fistiana*, 1841.

Egan, Pearce, *Boxiana; or Sketches of Ancient & Modern Pugilism*, Smeeton 1812.

Felkin, William, *History of the Machine-Wrought Hosiery and Lace Manufactures*, David & Charles, 1967.

Golding, Louis, *The Bare Knuckle Breed*, Hutchinson, 1952.

Gorn, Elliot J., *The Manly Art- The Lives and Times of the Great Bare-Knuckle Champions*, Robson, 1986.

Greenwood, James, *Low Life Deeps*, Chatto & Windus, 1881.

Henning, Fred, *Fights for the Championship- the Men and their Times, Volume2*, - reprinted from the *Licenced Victuallers' Gazette*, 1901.
Johnson, Dick, *Bare Fist Fighters of the 18th &19th Century - 1704-1861*, Book Guild, 1987.
Johnson, Dick, *The Bare-Knucklers*, Self-published, 1999.
Lloyd, Alan, *The Great Prize Fight*, Cassell, 1977.
Low, Donald A., *Thieves' Kitchen*, Alan Sutton, 1987.
Miles, Henry Downes, *Pugilistica*, Grant, 1906.
Mortimer, R., *The History of the Derby Stakes*, Cassell, 1962.
Mortimer,,R., Onslow,R. & Willett,P., *Biographical Encyclopedia of British Flat Racing*, Macdonald & Jane's, 1978.
Nottingham Date Book 1750- 1879, pub. H.Field, 1880.
Rae, Simon, *W.G. Grace*, Faber & Faber, 1998.
Stephen, Sir L. & Lee, Sir S., *Dictionary of National Biography*, Oxford University Press, 1993.
Thompson, F.B., *Biographical Sketches of Modern Pugilists*, Dipple, 1850.
Transactions of the Thoroton Society of Notts.Vol XLVII (Samuel Collinson's Diary), 1943.
Ward, Andrew, *Cricket's Strangest Matches*, Robson, 1990.
Windle, Thomas, *Bendigo –the Champion Prize Fighter*, Morgan & Scott, 1904.

INDEX